COVENANTAL THEONOMY

COVENANTAL THEONOMY

A Response to
T. David Gordon and Klinean Covenantalism

Kenneth L. Gentry, Jr., Th.D.

VICTORIOUS HOPE
PUBLISHING
Fountain Inn, South Carolina

"Proclaiming the kingdom of God and teaching those things which concern
the Lord Jesus Christ, with all confidence."
(Acts 28:31)

Covenantal Theonomy:
A Response to T. David Gordon and Klinean Covenantalism
© 2005 by Gentry Family Trust udt April 2, 1999
VICTORIOUS HOPE PUBLISHING publication date: 2012

Published by Victorious Hope Publishing
P.O. Box 1874
Fountain Inn, South Carolina 29644

Website: www.VictoriousHope.com
E-mail: KennethGentry@cs.com

PRINTED IN THE UNITED STATES OF AMERICA

ISBN 978-0-9826206-4-9

VICTORIOUS HOPE PUBLISHING is committed to producing Christian educational materials for promoting the whole Bible for the whole of life. We are conservative, evangelical, and Reformed and are committed to the doctrinal formulation found in the Westminster Standards.

For information on Dr. Gentry's non-profit ministry:
    GoodBirth Ministries
    P.O. Box 1874
    Fountain Inn, SC 29644
    www.GoodBirthMinistries.com

For more books and other materials by Dr. Gentry:
    www.KennethGentry.com

Cover design by Brian Godawa of Godawa Creative (www.Godawa.com)

Table of Contents

Analytical Outline

I. Introduction

A. The Theonomic Debate

B. The Meredith Kline Angle

C. Gordon's Methodological Approach
1. Gordon's Taxonomic Procedure
2. Gordon's Hermeneutic Focus
3. Gordon's Tri-dimensional Critique
4. Gordon's Primary Source

D. My Initial Disappointments
1. Gordon's Taxonomic Failure
2. Gordon's Varying-arguments Confusion
3. Gordon's Bahnsen-focus Failure

E. Gordon's Bold Position
1. Gordon's Argumentative Distortion
2. Gordon's Historical Error
3. Gordon's Practical Implications

II. The Argument from Necessity

A. Dialectical Tension in Gordon's Presentation

B. General Problems in Gordon's Presentation
1. Gordon's Mischaracterization of the Theonomic Concern
2. Gordon's Confusion of the Fields of Concern
   a. Gordon confounds moral and scientific issues
   b. Gordon fumbles the Christian worldview
   c. Gordon overlooks the facts of the matter
3. Gordon Forgets a Distinctive of the Biblical Worldview
4. Gordon's Self-contradiction in his Presentation

C. Specific Deficiencies in Gordon's Position

D. Gordon's Rhetorical Challenge

Abbreviations

BTS Greg L. Bahnsen. *By This Standard: The Authority of God's Law Today.* Tyler, Tex.: Institute for Christian Economics, 1985. CT T. David Gordon. "Critique of Theonomy: A Taxonomy." *Westminster Theological Journal,* 56 (1994): 23-43.

IS T. David Gordon. "The Insufficiency of Scripture." *Modern Reformation* (Jan-Feb, 2002): 18-23.

LC *The Larger Catechism* of the *Westminster Standards.*

NOS Greg L. Bahnsen. *No Other Standard: Theonomy and Its Critics.* Tyler, Tex.: Institute for Christian Economics, 1991.

SC *The Shorter Catechism* of the *Westminster Standards.*

TCE or *Theonomy* Greg L. Bahnsen. *Theonomy in Christian Ethics* (3d. ed.: Nacogdoches, Tex.: CMP, 2002).

WCF *The Westminster Confession of Faith.*

Chapter 1
INTRODUCTION

The Theonomic Debate

Theonomic ethics, especially as articulated and defended by Greg L. Bahnsen, has been the subject of enormous scrutiny by a number of evangelical and Reformed theologians.[1] Bahnsen himself noted in surprise regarding his book *Theonomy in Christian Ethics* (hereinafter either TCE or *Theonomy*)[2]:

> The book was met with far greater enthusiasm than I ever reasonably expected — and a handful of very strong reviews. I never anticipated it to be a piece of literature which appealed to a wide reading audience. The subject matter had an academic cast (exegetical and theological reasoning about the normative standard of conduct), the text was long and detailed (justifying the occasional charge of overkill), and the prose was sometimes ponderous and other times polemical. Still, for all those genuine drawbacks, it obviously touched — and continues to touch — on matters of vital moral concern to others like myself. It also occasioned 'spirited' opposition (to put it politely).[3]

---

[1] For further details, see my chapter "Theonomy and Confession" in Steve M. Schlissel, ed., *The Standard Bearer: A Festschrift for Greg L. Bahnsen* (Nacogdoches, Tex.: CMF, 2002), 161-63.

[2] Throughout this study all references to *Theonomy in Christian Ethics* will be to the most recent edition published in 2002.

[3] Greg L. Bahnsen, *No Other Standard: Theonomy and Its Critics* (Tyler, Tex.: Institute for Christian Economics, 1991), 4.

In the present work I will be responding to the critique of Theonomy by T. David Gordon (Ph.D., Union Theological Seminary). Gordon is currently Associate Professor of Religion at Grove City College (since 1999) in Grove City, Pennsylvania, but has also served on the faculty of Gordon-Conwell Theological Seminary (1984-97). He is an ordained minister of the Presbyterian Church in America.

My response will focus primarily on his article: "Critique of Theonomy: A Taxonomy" (hereinafter: CT) which appeared in the 1994 edition of the *Westminster Theological Journal*, and is widely posted on the Internet and frequently cited in anti-theonomic literature. Unfortunately, it was not actually released until around the time of the 1995 death of Dr. Greg L. Bahnsen whose work forms its major focus. I will also interact somewhat with his more recent article "The Insufficiency of Scripture" (hereinafter: IS). This article was published in *Modern Reformation* magazine in January/February 2002. It is useful for illustrating certain deficiencies in Gordon's core convictions and theological methodology.

The Meredith Kline Angle

One of the more remarkable aspects of the academic debate over Theonomic Ethics is the oftentimes vehement and even vitriolic responses it generates. Bahnsen was "heartbroken" over such derogatory assaults against him and his views.[4] And some of the more caustic attacks derive from Old Testament theologian Meredith G. Kline and some of his disciples. It appears that some of those following the innovative theological constructs of Kline not only endorse his theological method and conclusions but even follow his acerbic approach to the debate.[5]

Though publishing in the venerable *Westminster Theological Journal*, Kline stooped to personal ridicule, quite demeaningly denouncing Bahnsen's work. He even opens his "review" of *Theonomy* complaining

---

[4] Greg L. Bahnsen, "Foreword" in Gary DeMar, *The Debate Over Christian Reconstruction* (Atlanta: American Vision, 1988), xiv.

[5] Gordon admits the widespread concern about Kline when he laments that "the most celebrated example" of concern regarding theological slippery slopes "has been the tendency to perceive Meredith G. Kline's views as unusual or novel" (CT, 36). See discussion below.

about "the over-heated typewriter of Greg Bahnsen."[6] In the same opening paragraph he immediately laments "the tragedy of Chalcedon [an intellectual center for promoting theonomic studies] is that of high potential wasted — worse than wasted" due to its "delusive and grotesque perversion of the teaching of Scripture" which is being promoted by "cult-like fanaticism."[7] Bahnsen expressed dismay at the tone of Kline's ridicule as he offered his response under the title: "M. G. Kline on Theonomic Politics: An Evaluation of His Reply."[8]

Sadly, Gordon follows in the steps of his mentor[9] in using sarcasm and denunciatory language regarding Theonomic Ethics — though not in an *ad hominem* fashion against Bahnsen himself, but at Theonomy as a Reformed ethical perspective. The scorching opprobrium with which he torches Theonomy is surely surprising in reputable theological journals, but such is the hatred of Theonomic Ethics in some circles. Gordon writes in his *Modern Reformation* article:

> Theonomy is not merely an error, though it has manifestly been regarded as erroneous by the Reformed tradition. It is the error du jour, the characteristic error of an unwise generation. It is the error of a generation that has abandoned the

---

[6] Bahnsen was disappointed in that "in a real sense, Dr. Kline has not offered a 'review' of my book," in that "the reader is not told the purpose and thrust of the book, not told how the book progresses, not told the main line(s) of argumentation, not told its theological significance, etc. . . . Instead, Dr. Kline narrowly attends only to section VII of the book (with passing remarks concerning Appendix 2). Greg L. Bahnsen, "M. G. Kline on Theonomic Politics: An Evaluation of his Reply," *Journal of Christian Reconstruction*, 6:2 (Winter, 1979-80): 196. And even then he does not review this one section of the treatise, but directly launches a frontal attack upon it." Meredith G. Kline, "Comments on an Old-New Error: A Review Article," *Westminster Theological Journal* 41:1 (Fall, 1978): 194.

[7] Kline, "Comments on an Old-New Error," 172.

[8] Bahnsen, "M. G. Kline on Theonomic Politics: 195-221.

[9] Note Gordon's immense appreciation for and strong reliance upon Kline: Kline is one of the scholars to whom Gordon is "profoundly indebted" (CT, 25). He seems to adopt Kline's full theological position as is evident in his notice that "all of Kline's writings are implicitly germane" (25). Since Kline writes on a wide range of topics, this appears to mean that Gordon adopts Kline's overarching theological construct, since "all" of his writings "are implicitly germane." Gordon's positions on other issues also betray a strong reliance upon Kline (see below).

biblically mandated quest for wisdom on the assumption that the Bible *itself* contains all that we need to know about life's various enterprises. It is the proof-textual, Bible-thumping, literalist, error par excellence. It is not merely the view of the unwise, but the view of the never-to-be-wise, because it is the view of those who wrongly believe that the Scripture sufficiently governs this arena, and who, for this reason will never discover in the natural constitution of the human nature or the particular circumstances of given peoples what must be discovered to govern well and wisely. (IS, 22)

Despite the condescending mockery of Theonomy by Gordon, his calling as a Reformed minister and theological professor, and the wide endorsement of his response, his critique merits a thoughtful — even if belated — response. The need for a response is heightened in that he believes he has written an irrefutable critique of Theonomy. At one point he writes: "I have never received an answer to this line of questioning from any of the Theonomists with whom I have conversed. I do not think it likely that I will" (CT, 27). At another point he muses regarding one angle of his analysis: "One of the most profound ironies has been the failure of covenant theologians (with some exceptions) to critique Theonomy on this point" (CT, 40).

Interestingly, Gordon follows Kline in another matter of great interest to Presbyterian Theonomists: he also admits *the theonomic tendencies of the Westminster Standards.*[10] Two decades ago Kline had lamented that because of the Confession's theonomic affinities "ecclesiastical courts operating under the Westminster Confession of Faith are going to have their problems, therefore, if they should be of a mind to bring the Chalcedon [i.e., theonomic] aberration under their judicial scrutiny."[11] He notes further:

If, providentially, anything good is to come of the Chalcedon disturbance, perhaps, paradoxically, it will come from the very embarrassment given to churches committed to the

---

[10] See my confessional defense of Theonomic Ethics: Gentry, "Theonomy and Confession," in Schlissel, *The Standard Bearer*, 161-212.

[11] Kline, "Comments on an Old-New Error," 173.

4

Westminster standards by the relationship that can be traced, as noted above, between the Chalcedon position and certain ideas expressed in the Westminster Confession. Perhaps the shock of seeing where those ideas lead in Chalcedon's vigorous development of them may make the church face up to the problem posed by the relevant formulations and reconsider the Confessions position on these points.[12]

More recently Klinean theologian Mark Karlberg has admitted: "Certain elements in the *Confession* indicate an orientation toward 'theonomic politics.'"[13]

Gordon agrees with Kline's confession (pun intended) when he writes: "Theonomists are not the first to abstract legislation from the Sinai covenant. The Westminster Assembly appears to have done it beforehand" (CT, 40).

Despite these qualifications, it must be admitted that the work of the assembly established the precedent of abstracting covenantal duties from the covenant in which they were given. This precedent, combined with the reactionary response to the errors of dispensationalism, created soil in the twentieth century which virtually guaranteed that Theonomy, or something like it, would take root. Theonomy follows the a-covenantal hermeneutic of the Westminster Assembly. (CT, 42)

Theonomy did not appear 'out of the blue,' as some may think. Individuals in our tradition who consider Theonomy to be an outrageous or extreme viewpoint are only partially correct. It is true that Theonomy denies *WCF* 19:4,[14] and it is true that Theonomy is even more extreme than Dabney or Murray in the resistance to recognizing the distinctive traits of the Sinai covenant. Theonomy would indeed establish the extreme end of the covenant theology spectrum. However, Theonomy genuinely shares some of the distinctives embraced

---

[12] Kline, "Comments on an Old-New Error," 189.

[13] Karlberg, *Covenant Theology in Reformed Perspective*, 67.

[14] This is patently false: Theonomy does not "deny" WCF 19:4. See: Chapter 5 below.

by others within that tradition. It shares the assembly's abstracting of the decalogue from the Sinai covenant, and then goes further. (CT, 42)

Elsewhere Gordon expresses disappointment with the Assembly's wording of WCF 1:6, which reads in part: "The whole counsel of God concerning all things necessary for His own glory, man's salvation, faith and life, is either expressly set down in Scripture, or by good and necessary consequence may be deduced from Scripture." He complains:

> I clarify, however, that 'faith and life' must be taken in its religious sense. I also clarify that the entire matter would have been better expressed had the divines articulated a more manifestly covenantal statement, indicating that the Scriptures are a sufficient guide to the various covenants God has made with various covenant people through the centuries, and that the entire canon, taken in its entirety, is sufficient, therefore, to govern the members of the new covenant made in Christ. By 'faith and life' the divines intended what one is to believe and do as a member of the new covenant community. (*IS*, 18)

The wording of the Confession certainly does not fit his Klinean approach to ethics and worldview thinking.

Many non-theonomic scholars recognize the respectable roots of Theonomy in the Westminster tradition, including professors from notable Reformed seminaries: D. Claire Davis, Sinclair Ferguson, and R. Laird Harris, to name but a few.[15] Though disappointed in the acerbic nature of Gordon's and Kline's responses, Theonomists have generally been undeterred by the innovative theological constructs of Meredith Kline and his disciples and of their dismissive attitude toward our Confession of Faith.

Gordon's Methodological Approach

The primary article upon which I will be focusing is Gordon's "Critique of Theonomy: A Taxonomy." By way of introducing his critique, I will list his leading stated objectives and then will follow these

---

[15] See my discussion in Gentry, "Theonomy and Confession," 167-73.

with brief comments demonstrating his failure to meet his own objectives. Some of his failures are not destructive of his critique, but they do demonstrate the way anti-theonomic discourse can wander off course — especially when generated out of emotion-laden reflexes.

Gordon's Taxonomic Procedure

As the title of his article suggests, Gordon is gathering and organizing the arguments of others against Theonomic Ethics. Indeed, he clearly informs his reader that:

> I would like to make clear that what follows is profoundly indebted to insights first raised by others. It is not my intention to advance exclusively new arguments against Theonomy, but rather, to gather in one place a brief taxonomy of the major arguments. I have been profoundly helped by others, and much of what follows was already expressed or at least germinal in the writings of others. Especially to be acknowledged, in no particular order, are Meredith G. Kline, Vern S. Poythress, Paul D. Fowler, and Richard B. Gaffin, Jr.[16] (CT, 25)

Gordon's Hermeneutic Focus

His fundamental concern regards the interpretive methodology employed in the theonomic program. He wants to evaluate that which governs the Theonomic Ethic.

> It is also not my purpose to examine in detail the particular recommendations for legislation, nor the particular exegetical conclusions of the various Theonomists. Those varying particulars are worthy of separate analysis and discussion, but my purpose is much more limited: to examine the hermeneu-

---

[16] Oddly, Gordon's taxonomic critique fails to reckon with Bahnsen's published responses to Kline, Poythress, Fowler, and Gaffin. He appears unaware that Bahnsen has already answered their objections. If he is aware, I would think he should have mentioned it, at least in a footnote — as he does Bahnsen's own exegesis of Matt. 5:17ff (see: CT, 28 n7). I will deal with this deficiency more under Gordon's second response to Bahnsen.

tic governing the entire process. I am evaluating the engine, not the entire train (CT, 24).

Individual Theonomists are not intended to be the point of an examination such as this; rather, what is evaluated is the viewpoint that distinguishes Theonomy from other approaches to biblical ethics (CT, 3).

Gordon's Tri-dimensional Critique

Gordon recognizes the sophisticated and complex nature of the theonomic ethical program. Thus he offers a three-pronged front in attacking it rather than simply focusing on one key component. Under the heading "Dividing the Question" he comments:

> It will also be my purpose to critique Theonomy in several ways, in terms of the varying arguments by which it is promoted. Theonomy does not stand on a single leg, but on several . . . I will not attempt here a refutation of that particular leg of Theonomy known as postmillennialism. Many others have very ably discussed that matter, and the reader is encouraged to read Geerhardus Vos, Richard B. Gaffin, Jr., Herman Ridderbos, O. Palmer Robertson, Meredith G. Kline, and others who have written in this area. (CT, 24)
>
> The following 'legs' of the Theonomic stool will be discussed here: the argument from necessity; the Theonomic dependence upon and understanding of Matt 5:17–21; the Theonomic understanding of covenant theology. (CT, 25)

Effectively his three arguments are philosophical (the argument from necessity), exegetical (Matthew 5:17-21), and theological (the covenant).

By declaring his commendable intent to engage "the varying arguments by which it is promoted," Gordon agrees with Bahnsen's desire: "Critics of theonomy ought to focus on the generic school of thought (its essential tenets), selecting those presentations or particular applications which are representative of its key published proponents and which show the school of thought at its best" (*No Other Standard*, 25; hereinafter, NOS).[17]

---

[17] Greg L. Bahnsen, *No Other Standard: Theonomy and Its Critics* (Tyler, Tex.: Institute for Christian Economics, 1991).

Gordon's Primary Source

Gordon is well aware that theological movements have a large number of advocates — involving some greater and some lesser lights. Oftentimes those proponents disagree over various issues. Consequently, he has (wisely) determined to limit himself to evaluating the argument of Theonomy's leading apologist, Christian philosopher Greg L. Bahnsen (Ph.D., Philosophy, University of Southern California). He mentions Bahnsen by name twenty times in his short article and expressly declares:

> Despite the variety on particulars, however, there can be little doubt that the clearest, most deliberate attempt to describe and defend Theonomy is contained in Gregory L. Bahnsen's *Theonomy in Christian Ethics*. It is my purpose to employ this volume as the most reliable indicator of what Theonomy is. Those who embrace a particular variation differing from Bahnsen's are thus free of the critique here developed, at least potentially. (CT, 24)

My Initial Disappointments

Gordon's stated objectives are quite worthy in a debate such as this. Regrettably though, he fails to meet his own intentions in several respects. Before engaging his actual critique of Theonomy, I believe it important to note up-front his failure in securing his own objectives. These may help explain his overall inability to damage Theonomy.

Gordon's Taxonomic Failure

Gordon's taxonomic approach is a helpful idea for distilling key issues in the debate. It certainly far excels Kline's alleged "review" of TCE which failed miserably in its attempt.[18]

But Gordon does not accurately express himself in his endeavor. He states that he will be presenting arguments "first raised by others" and that he will avoid "exclusively new arguments" (CT, 25). Yet on page 27 he writes: "I have never received an answer to this line of

---

[18] See previous mention of Bahnsen's disappointment regarding Kline's effort in Footnote 6 above.

questioning from any of the Theonomists with whom I have conversed."
By his own statement this appears to be his own argument (and not
"first raised by others") and as an unpublished argument it is effectively
a "new argument" to the public debate. Of course, this does not directly hinder his public critique, but it does expose his tendency to
carelessness, even causing him to fail at his own stated intentions. This
is a recurring problem throughout his critique, as I will show.

Gordon's Varying-arguments Confusion

Gordon wisely determines to deal with "varying arguments" for
Theonomy in an attempt to avoid a strawman approach (CT, 24). And
when he actually gets to his critique, he does focus on important issues.
Yet in his introduction he immediately evidences confusion regarding
Theonomy when he states "I will not attempt here a refutation of that
particular leg of Theonomy known as postmillennialism" (CT, 24).

Simply put: postmillennialism is not a "leg of Theonomy."
Postmillennialism deals with eschatology, not ethics; it deals with what
will be, not what *ought* to be. Theonomists can — and *do* — hold to
various evangelical eschatologies. In introducing this comment, Gordon began to "distinguish" Theonomy and Christian Reconstructionism in his second paragraph: "2. Distinguishing Theonomy from Christian Reconstruction." Oddly though, he really has the matter reversed:
Postmillennialism and Theonomy are actually legs of Christian Reconstructionism. In 1989 Bahnsen noted this in *House Divided* : "Such be-
liefs and practices are at the heart of what is labeled 'Reconstructionism' today. Its ethical perspective is termed "theonomic,' and its
eschatological outlook is called 'postmillennial."[19] In *No Other Standard*
(hereinafter: NOS) Bahnsen wrote: "'Reconstructionism' popularly
names a theological combination of positions which usually includes
presuppositional apologetics, a postmillennial view of eschatology, and
a theonomic view of ethics" (NOS, 7 n12).

Even non-theonomists recognize this. Bruce Barron writes: "The
Reconstructionists' intricate, complex program weaves together three
levels of ideology. . . . Next come their three key theoretical foundations:

---

[19] Greg L. Bahnsen and Kenneth L. Gentry, Jr., *House Divided: The Break-up of
Dispensational Theology* (2d. ed.: Tyler, Tex.: Institute for Christian Economics, 1997), 3.

biblical law, postmillennial eschatology, and presuppositional philosophy."[20] Ron Nash expresses concern about the "confusion" resulting from "a sloppy use" of terms. He then answers the question "What Is Christian Reconstructionism?" by sorting out subsidiary issues such as Theonomy and postmillennialism.[21] The *Christian Dictionary of Theology in America* defines the Christian Reconstructionist "agenda": "Three foundational ideas underlie the Reconstructionist agenda: (1) a presuppositional apologetic; (2) a belief that Old Testament law applies today, in 'exhaustive' and 'minutial' detail; and (3) postmillennialism."[22]

In the text of TCE itself Bahnsen declared that it is "illogical, and inexcusable propaganda for some theonomic critics to dismiss it as allegedly . . . demanding postmillennial eschatology."[23] He clearly noted that "the thesis of theonomic ethics is not logically tied to any particular school of millennial eschatology."[24] He even deems as a *faux pas* Richard B. Gaffin's linking postmillennialism and Theonomy (NOS, 52). In *By This Standard* he reiterated this: "What these studies present is a position in Christian (normative) ethics. They do not logically commit those who agree with them to any particular school of *eschatological* interpretation" (BTS, 8).

Why does Gordon seize this issue only to fumble it? And especially since he is responding to Bahnsen, and Bahnsen himself specifically, clearly, frequently, publicly, and dogmatically denies any necessary connection between Theonomy and postmillennialism? And strangely, Gordon raises this issue immediately after distinguishing Christian Reconstructionism (which *does* entail postmillennialism) from

---

[20] Bruce Barron, *Heaven on Earth? The Social & Political Agendas of Dominion Theology* (Grand Rapids: Zondervan, 1992), 23.

[21] Ronald H. *Nash, Great Divides: Understanding the Controversies That Come Between Christians* (Colorado Springs, Col.: NavPress, 1993), 155. See Ch. 8.

[22] Daniel G. Reid, Robert D. Linder, et. al, eds., *Concise Dictionary of Christianity in America* (Downers Grove, Ill: InterVarsity, 1995), 285.

[23] Greg L. Bahnsen, *Theonomy in Christian Ethics* (2d. ed.: Nutley, N.J.: Craig, 1982), xxx.

[24] NOS, 51-52. I suspect that Gaffin's chapter is the source of Gordon's mistake, since he mentions some dependence on Gaffin and he tends to pick up on the mistakes of his secondary sources (as with Fowler also).

Theonomy.[25] These sorts of missteps will plague his formal analysis later, as well.

And compounding his failure in offering a supposedly unanswerable critique, I am disappointed that some of Bahnsen's major arguments are overlooked. Now obviously in an article-length project Gordon could not deal with all the arguments for Theonomy. But I would think his declared objective to deal with Bahnsen's *key* issues should focus on *Bahnsen's* key issues. This is especially problematic when I note in the next point below that one of the key arguments Gordon employs against Bahnsen is one that he himself admits cannot be found in Bahnsen!

This failure is made all the more remarkable in that Bahnsen even helps his critics by listing in summary fashion the basics of his argument for Theonomic Ethics. In both his 1983 second edition of *Theonomy* (p. xxvi) and his 1991 *No Other Standard* (p. 12), which is his detailed response to his critics, he states key components of his system.[26] In *Theonomy* he introduces his seriatim presentation with these words: "The following analysis draws together, clarifies, and states in distilled form the vital teachings elaborated in the full text of *Theonomy in Christian Ethics*." Why does Gordon not consider these summarily-stated matters which Bahnsen himself tosses out in slow-pitch fashion to his critics when they step up to the plate?

---

[25] On p. 24 of CT Gordon urges his reader to consider refutations of postmillennialism in the writings of Gaffin and other Vosian scholars. I have rebutted their arguments in several places: Gentry, "Whose Victory in History," in Gary North, ed., *Theonomy: An Informed Response* (Tyler, Tex.: Institute for Christian Economics, 1991), 207-230. Gentry, "A Postmillennial Response to Robert B. Strimple," in Darrell L. Bock, ed., *Three Views on the Millennium and Beyond* (Grand Rapids: Zondervan, 1999), 130-142. Gentry, "Agony, Irony, and the Postmillennialist" and "Victory Belongs to the Lord" in, Kenneth L. Gentry, Jr., ed., *Thine Is the Kingdom: Studies in the Postmillennial Hope* (Vallecito, Calif.: Chalcedon, 2003), 83-176.

[26] It seems that Gordon was unaware of Bahnsen's NOS even though it was published at least three years before Gordon wrote his article. Gordon never refers to it, even though it would have been an invaluable resource for his article. In NOS (p. 15) Bahnsen states his purpose: "The focus of this volume will be on the hermeneutical, exegetical, theological, and political matters which have been raised by the critics of theonomic ethics." Bahnsen also comments: "The opening portion of this short summary of theonomic principles is taken from the first part of my position paper in *God and Politics: Four Views on the Reformation of Civil Government*, pp. 21-25.

Note two key components of the theonomic argument *as summarily listed by Bahnsen* in *No Other Standard* (p. 12) and which were omitted by Gordon:

5. We should presume that Old Testament standing laws continue to be morally binding in the New Testament, unless they are rescinded or modified by later revelation. . . .[27]

7. God's revealed standing laws are a reflection of His immutable moral character and, as such, are absolute in the sense of being non-arbitrary, objective, universal, and established in advance of particular circumstances (thus applicable to general types of moral situations).[28]

Bahnsen's fifth point highlights a general principle of special revelation which declares that revelatory obligations laid down in Scripture may only be repealed by God himself through later inscripturated revelation. Poythress recognized this as an important — and even helpful

---

The summary has appeared in a few places, sometimes in shorter, sometimes in longer, form. Cf. *By This Standard: The Authority of God's Law Today* (Tyler, Texas: Institute for Christian Economies, 1985), pp. 345-348; 'Ten Theses of Theonomy' in *Journey*, vol. 1, no. 6 (Nov.-Dec., 1986), p. 8; 'Christ and the Role of Civil Government' in *Transformation*, vol. 5, no. 2 (April-June, 1988), pp. 24ff. The annotation upon the enumerated principles is taken from chapter 31 in *By This Standard* (NOS, 9 n 22).

[27] Attacks on this principle come from "many critics," according to Bahnsen in NOS, 25. Two samples will suffice: "David Neilands, "Theonomy and Its Unqualified Language," a paper presented to the Presbytery of Northern California in the Orthodox Presbyterian Church in 1982. John Frame, "The One, the Many, and Theonomy," in Barker and Godfrey, *Theonomy: A Reformed Critique*, 89.

[28] This principle is a common subject of critique by various scholars. See for example: Frame, "The One, the Many, and Theonomy," 90. H. Wayne House and Thomas D. Ice, *Dominion Theology: Blessing or Curse?* (Portland, Ore.: Multnomah, 1988), ch. 5. Doug Chismar in Douglas E. Chismar and David A. Rausch, "Concerning Theonomy: An Essay of Concern," *Journal of the Evangelical Theological Society* 27:3 (Sept., 1986): 315-23. See Bahnsen's response to Chismar in "Should We Uphold Unchangeable Moral Absolutes?," *Journal of the Evangelical Theological Society*, 28:3 (September, 1985): 309-315. Consider Bahnsen's statement: "The presumption of continuing and universal validity for the moral provisions (underlying demands, not specific cultural details) of God's law does indeed 'follow' from their reflection of His

— principle of Theonomic Ethics: "Bahnsen's advocacy of a presumption of continuity is understandable in a Christian atmosphere given to ignoring the Old Testament in general and its penology in particular. He is summoning the troops to awake from their slumber and their compromises with the evil world around and to recognize the wisdom of the Old Testament."[29]

Bahnsen's seventh point roots ethics in the unchanging character of God (avoiding the twin horns of an ethical dilemma: voluntarism and relativism). In *Theonomy in Christian Ethics* Bahnsen wrote: "Since God's law reflects His immutable character it was impossible that the law should be abrogated; to speak of the law's abrogation, said the Puritans, was to dishonor God himself" (TCE, 526). Bahnsen even wrote an article in *Journal of the Evangelical Theological Society* responding to an earlier criticism of him on this very point.[30] Bahnsen noted that: "since God himself is ever the same (immutable in character), the moral principles expressive of his nature are universal in validity, applying to all men in all places at all times."[31] Even from within his own unique perspective Kline accepts this principle of immutability. Of laws five through ten of the Decalogue, Kline notes: "They are also founded on the nature of God. For they simply apply to specific cases the grand principle that man must reflect the moral glory of God on a finite scale. This principle is immutable because it concerns the relationship of man to God."[32]

Jones well recognizes the significance of these two principles in Bahnsen's argument: "Theonomists characteristically argue from the immutability of God's holiness to the immutability of God's law." And:

---

essential and unchangeable character. They may be 'expressed' in different ways, but God's moral requirements (e. g., self-giving love to one's neighbor) are the same everywhere" (*House Divided*, 89).

[29] See Bahnsen's citation of Poythress, NOS, 29. This is taken from Poythress' chapter in Will S. Barker and W. Robert Godfrey, *Theonomy: A Reformed Critique* (Grand Rapids: Zondervan, 1990), 123. See also his statement on p. 106 in the same book.

[30] Chismar and Rausch, "Regarding Theonomy: An Essay Of Concern," 315-325.

[31] Bahnsen, "Should We Uphold Unchanging Moral Absolutes?," 310-315.

[32] Kline, *Structure of Biblical Authority*, 159. In the next sentence, however, his Intrusion Ethic in his left hand takes away the immutability principle of the right: "On the other hand, the relations governed by this immutable principle are themselves mutable."

"Greg Bahnsen, who is the movement's chief apologist, argues for the presumptive continuity of the Mosaic laws on the principle that laws continue in force until revoked. Discontinuity must assume the burden of proof."[33] Why does Gordon overlook these well-known features of Bahnsen's hermeneutic? He never mentions either of these two important theonomic methodological principles.[34]

Gordon's Bahnsen-focus Failure

Gordon well chooses his sample Theonomist when he determines to focus on Greg Bahnsen; no reputable Theonomist could fault him for employing Bahnsen's works in his critique. In fact, theonomic critic Bruce K. Waltke writes: "It is generally conceded that Bahnsen's book *Theonomy in Christian Ethics* lays the theory's cornerstone."[35] Will Barker agrees.[36] Peter Jones calls Bahnsen "the movement's chief apologist."[37] However, for some inexplicable reason Gordon even forgets this noble objective when he finally gets into his critique. Under the heading: "II. Specific Arguments" he finally engages the actual debate (CT, 25). We find his *first* argument under his sub-heading: "1. The Argument from Necessity." But what are the first three sentences in Gordon's opening salvo, which begins *four* paragraphs after stating his focus on Bahnsen? He writes:

> To my knowledge, Bahnsen's *Theonomy in Christian Ethics* does
> not depend in any particular measure on this argument. Yet, it
> is my observation from conversations with Theonomists that

---

[33] David Clyde Jones, *Biblical Christian Ethics* (Grand Rapids: Baker, 1994), 113.

[34] I must confess my uneasy feeling in reading Gordon's critique: I might be mistaken, but I really wonder if he has actually read all of *Theonomy*. I wonder because he overlooks some key points and he expressly states he is offering a taxonomy of the critics of theonomic ethics. For instance, he follows Gaffin's mistake in equating postmillennialism and Theonomy, even though Bahnsen specifically disassociates theonomic ethics and postmillennial eschatology. Bahnsen himself expresses frustrations with some reviewers in this regard, noting that "sometimes . . . the book has simply not been read, or read completely" (TCE, xxiii).

[35] Bruce K. Waltke in Will S. Barker and W. Robert Godfrey, *Theonomy: A Reformed Critique* (Grand Rapids: Zondervan, 1990), 74.

[36] Barker and Godfrey, *Theonomy*, 227.

[37] David Clyde Jones, *Biblical Christian Ethics* (Grand Rapids: Baker, 1994), 113.

many others rely heavily on this argument. Indeed, many individuals seem to embrace Theonomy because of their conviction that Theonomy, or something like it, is necessary. (CT, 25).

Well what was the point of Gordon's introductory preparation and statement of objectives? He categorically declared: "It is my purpose to employ this volume [TCE] as the most reliable indicator of what Theonomy is. Those who embrace a particular variation differing from Bahnsen's are thus free of the critique here developed, at least potentially." If Bahnsen's TCE is "the most reliable indicator of what Theonomy is" why is Gordon's *first* critique dealing with a matter that he admits is *not* found in the book? And if "those who embrace a particular variation differing from Bahnsen's are thus free of the critique here developed" why is not Bahnsen himself free of Gordon's critique which is not found in his book? Consequently, one-third of his three-step critique is rendered null and void in the very first sentence of his actual critique.

Gordon's Bold Position

Gordon's Klinean commitments lead him to make rather bold claims that I hope most Reformed Christians would not only disavow but deem troublesome. His claim serves as the title to his other anti-theonomic article: "The Insufficiency of Scripture" (*IS*). This article draws a clear line of distinction in ethical discourse between the theonomic emphasis upon special revelation and the Klinean emphasis on general revelation. In fact, Gordon lists three ethical issues that led him to adopt his current position on the insufficiency of Scripture:

Where the big change has occurred in my own thinking has been to the disastrous consequences that follow the common misunderstanding of the sufficiency of Scripture. . . . If anything has changed, then, it is that I would now argue with equal zeal for the insufficiency of Scripture in other than religious or covenantal areas. . . . This change has occurred as a result of three considerations: two theological and one practical. IS, 22.

One of the two theological issues was the arising of "Theonomy" in Reformed ethical discourse (IS, 22).

In both the article on "insufficiency" (IS) and the earlier one on Theonomy (CT) he associates this principle directly to the theonomic debate:

> Many Theonomists appear to have developed a novel, and erroneous, understanding of the sufficiency of Scripture. They imply that Scripture is a sufficient guide for the various departments of life, in all their specificity. In fact, the Reformational doctrine of the sufficiency of Scripture is a highly nuanced and sophisticated doctrine.
>
> The Reformational doctrine of the sufficiency of Scripture does not mean that the Scriptures are sufficient to answer all of our questions. Rather, the doctrine means that the Scriptures are a sufficient guide to our communion with God, a guide to faith and life in the religious sense. (CT, 27)

In that I want to focus on Gordon's direct opposition to theonomic principles, I will not deal at length with his view of the "insufficiency of Scripture" (although I will return to one important implication of this theme below when Gordon specifically challenges all biblical directives for political authority under the heading: "The Argument from Necessity"). I would, however, like to make three quick observations regarding this surprising position, which I deem a "Gordonian knot" for evangelicals accepting Gordon's lead.

First, Gordon's Argumentative Distortion. Gordon's summary of theonomic practice terribly overstates the theonomic position. He writes that its approach to the sufficiency of Scripture entails biblical directives to "the various departments of life, *in all their specificity*" and that it answers "*all* of our questions" (emphases mine). So put, Gordon's charge attacks a straw man, for not even Bahnsen — the archetypical Theonomist and the focus of Gordon's critique — holds such an exaggerated view. You might say that Gordon has written a right strawy dismissal. Careless overstatements of this nature confuse the reader, hinder dialog, misdirect the debate, and undermine Gordon's argument.

Actually Theonomists argue that God's special revelation forms the *foundation* of the Christian's worldview, and that it does contain *much*

— not *total* — direct revelation on socio-political specifics. As Bahnsen states: "The Old Testament revelation of God's moral will took into account *numerous* details of socio-political behavior, while the New Testament does not repeat the same emphasis. There is *much* more to be found in the Old Testament about the larger concerns of civil society than in the New" (emphasis mine).[38] Note that Bahnsen does *not* write: "The Old Testament revelation of God's moral will took into account socio-political behavior 'in all of its specificity' so that it answers 'all of our questions.'"

Bahnsen even warns against such a misreading of the theonomic program:

> Of course, nothing which has been said above means that the work of Christian ethics is a pat and easy job. Even though the details of God's law are available to us as moral absolutes; they still need to be properly interpreted and applied to the modern world. It should constantly be borne in mind that no school of thought, least of all the theonomist outlook, 'has all the answers.' Nobody should get the impression that clear, simple, or incontestable 'solutions' to the moral problems of our day can be just lifted from the face of Scripture's laws. A tremendous amount of homework remains to be done, whether in textual exegesis, cultural analysis, or moral reasoning— with plenty of room for error and correction. None of it is plain and simple. It must not be carried on thoughtlessly or without sanctified mental effort.[39]

In his Preface to the second edition of *Theonomy* he writes: "*Theonomy* does not make the determination of our moral obligations or the elucidation of God's commands a cut-and-dried, easy, obvious, or simplistic task. It rather advocates a basic approach to ethical questions which still requires (even if it does not always get) skilled exegesis and sensitive application. It does not automatically remove all difficulties in

---

[38] Bahnsen in *House Divided*, 20.

[39] Bahnsen in *House Divided*, 42. Also repeated in Bahnsen, "The Theonomic Position," in Smith, *God and Politics*, 41

ethical reasoning, and theonomists certainly do not 'have all the answers'! I have made such observations before." (TCE, xxix)

Bahnsen does, however, emphatically disagree with Gordon's approach to worldview issues, wherein special revelation is limited to issues solely regarding religion: "The Christian's political standards and agenda are not set by unregenerate pundits who wish to quarantine religious values (and thus the influence of Jesus Christ, speaking in the Scripture) from the decision-making process of those who set public policy."[40]

Second, Gordon's Historical Error. Gordon's complaint against a theonomic conviction is mistaken historically. He states that Theonomists have a "novel" view of the sufficiency of Scripture wherein they apply it to areas beyond issues of "faith and life in the *religious sense*" (emphasis mine). A few quick observations ought to expose his factual error.

Hoeffecker reminds us that 450 years ago Calvin "attempted to reform not simply doctrine and church organization, as Luther did, but also the social-political order according to the Word of God."[41] This certainly speaks to issues beyond "faith and life in the religious sense." After all, did not Calvin write in his Prefatory Address to King Francis I of France: "He is deceived who looks for enduring prosperity in his kingdom when it is not ruled by God's scepter, that is, his Holy Word"?[42] McNeill notes: "Calvin declares that it is 'true royalty' in a king to acknowledge himself 'the minster of God,' and that it is his duty to rule according to God's Holy Word."[43] In Sermon Five on the Ten Commandments Calvin states that "if we take the law of God [i.e., the Ten Commandments] in itself, we shall have a perpetual norm of justice."[44]

---

[40] Bahnsen in *House Divided*, 42-43.

[41] Hoeffecker, *Building a Christian Worldview*, 127.

[42] John Calvin, *The Institutes of the Christian Religion*, ed. by John T. McNeill, trans. by Ford Lewis Battles (Philadelphia: Westminster, 1960), 1:12.

[43] *Institutes*, lxv. It is true, though, that Calvin denounced the Anabaptist radicals who opposed governments that were not erected on biblical principles (*Inst.* 20:4:14). Calvin was not an anarchist.

[44] Published in Benjamin W. Farley, *John Calvin's Sermons on the Ten Commandments* (Grand Rapids: Baker, 1980), 102. In these sermons Calvin repeatedly speaks of the continuing authority of the Ten Commandments, 25, 48, 49, 238, 249. In fact, this is

Calvin's editor notes that "this is in harmony with Calvin's threefold use of the law; see the *Institutes* 2.7.6-12."[45] In fact, he even writes: "Absurd is the cleverness which some persons but little versed in Scripture pretend to, who assert that . . . the obligations under which Moses laid his countrymen are now dissolved" (commentary at Lev. 28:6). Calvin certainly did not forbid the Scripture's application to issues beyond the "religious sense" — indeed, he encouraged it.

Even anti-theonomist R. Laird Harris admits that the theonomic "view is not really new; it is just new in our time. It was the usual view through the Middle Ages, was not thrown over by the Reformers and was espoused by the Scottish Covenanters who asked the Long Parliament to make Presbyterianism the religion of the three realms — England, Scotland and Ireland."[46] In my "Theonomy and Confession" study I cite numerous illustrations of the application of God's law outside the realm of "faith and life in the religious sense."[47] Furthermore, does not the Massachusetts Civil Bay Code provide clear historical evidence of the *direct* application of the Mosaic judicial law to modern civil jurisprudence outside the realm of "faith and life in the religious sense"?[48]

Third, Gordon's Practical Implications. Gordon's position leads to alarming implications for Klinean ethics (i.e., "Intrusion Ethics"[49]). This problem has recently been exposed in dramatic fashion within conservative Presbyterian circles. An Orthodox Presbyterian Church minister argued that same-sex marriage rights can be affirmed on a Klinean principle;

---

why God inscribed the Ten Commandments on tables of *stone*, to project its permanence, 249, 250. In his classic study *Moral Law*, Kevan declares: "The Law, then, is the Christian's rule of life, and the believer finds that he delights in the Law of God after the inward man (Rom. 7:22) . . . . The Law of Moses is none other than the Law of Christ." Ernest F. Kevan, *Moral Law* (Phillipsburg, N.J.: P & R, 1991), 1.

[45] Farley, *John Calvin's Sermons on the Ten Commandments*, 102 n 34.

[46] R. Laird Harris, "Theonomy in Christian Ethics: A Review of Greg L. Bahnsen's Book," in *Presbuterion: Covenant Seminary Review*, 5:1 (Spring, 1979): 1.

[47] See Gentry in Booth, *The Standard Bearer*, 174-182. See also Martin A. Foulner, *Theonomy and the Westminster Confession* (Edinburgh: Marpet, 1997).

[48] See Bahnsen, *Theonomy in Christian Ethics*, App. 3: "A Historical Specimen of Theonomic Politics."

[49] Meredith G. Kline, *The Structure of Biblical Authority* (Grand Rapids: Eerdmans, 1972), Part II, Sec. 3: "The Intrusion and the Decalogue," 154-171. See Bahnsen's response in TCE, App. 4, and my discussion in Chapter 5 below.

this is directly related to Gordon's view of the "insufficiency of Scripture." The original ecclesiastical charges filed on June 1, 2002 against Lee Irons (a Kline-enthusiast who hosts a website extolling Kline's theology) opened: "The Presbytery of Southern California of The Orthodox Presbyterian Church charges you, the Rev. C. Lee Irons, with publicly promoting and encouraging the practice of homosexuality, in violation of the seventh commandment." The charges went on to declare: "The advocacy of 'same-sex marriage' as a 'civil right' has brought scandal to the OPC and other Bible-believing Christians."[50]

In a public letter dated July 19, 2002 Irons related the issue of concern directly to his opposition to Theonomy and to his affirmation of "common grace" (i.e., general revelation) as a sufficient source for political ethics:

> I have decided to write this paper in order to answer questions about my views on homosexuality. My wife Misty Irons has argued that conservative Christians should change their political strategy by adopting a civil libertarian position on same-sex civil unions. She articulated this in a paper titled "A Conservative Christian Case for Civil Same-Sex Marriage." On January 4, 2002, I posted this opinion piece on my www.upper-register.com website as an illustration of how *a non-theonomic, common grace approach to civil government might be applied in one particular area.* (Emphasis mine)[51]

---

[50] The documentation regarding issues surrounding the trial may be found on Rev. Irons' "Upper Register" (a Kline phrase) website at www.upper-register.com/Irons_trial.html.

[51] The paper that generated this trial was written by Irons' wife and its position was defended by him. In her paper "A Conservative Christian Case for Civil Same-Sex Marriage" she wrote in the second paragraph: "let me be absolutely clear: Conservative Christians should support civil same-sex marriage. Why? Because the question of whether to allow civil same-sex marriage is a civil liberties question, and maintaining a respect for people's civil liberties in this country is always to the church's advantage. In fact, it is absolutely essential for the survival of our religious freedom in a pluralistic society."

Before the matter came to trial, the homosexual-rights charge was dropped.[52] Instead, the underlying hermeneutic focused upon by the judicatory was the issue of whether the Decalogue binds Christians today. Irons argues that it does *not*, and this was a major factor in his "non-theonomic, common grace approach to civil government" in "one particular area," i. e., "same-sex marriage." Gordon formally represented and defended Irons in his ecclesiastical trial.

Conclusion

These three observations should correct some errors in Gordon's critique of Theonomy. Despite his stumblings, however, Gordon is generally correct in noting that Theonomists tend where possible to employ the Scriptures as a foundational source for dealing with moral, cultural, social, and political issues. As Bahnsen puts it: "Christian involvement in politics calls for recognition of God's transcendent, absolute, revealed law as a standard by which to judge all social codes" (NOS, 12). This practice distinguishes the theonomic from his Klinean ethic which tends to limit Scriptural directives and application to the realm of "faith and life in the religious sense" and to affirm that "natural revelation is a sufficient guide in each of these areas. In the field of natural revelation, the tools for understanding our duty are different than in the field of special revelation" (CT, 26). (I will have more to say about this in Ch. 5 below.)

Now then, we are ready to engage Gordon's fundamental arguments against Theonomy. In his *Westminster Theological Journal* article he summarizes those as: "the argument from necessity; the Theonomic dependence upon and understanding of Matt 5:17–21; the Theonomic understanding of covenant theology" (CT, 25).

---

[52] According to a "Chronology of Events" the presbytery withdrew this charge "without prejudice in light of new and better evidence, which was now available (meaning that the same or similar charge may be introduced in the future if deemed appropriate)."

Chapter 2
The Argument from Necessity

Gordon's first argument against Theonomy involves the argument from necessity, which he summarily presents and vigorously rebuts. He defines the theonomic argument from necessity as follows:

> The argument from necessity is essentially this: we need to know how to function in the civil arena, and therefore the Word of God must provide us with such instruction. This leads quickly to embracing the Mosaic legislation for such guidance, since all parties agree that the only place where statecraft of any sort is comprehensively recorded in the Scriptures is in the Sinai legislation. (CT 25-26)

Dialectical Tension in Gordon's Presentation

Before I engage this argument, I must point out its irrelevance to Gordon's own presentation:

First, as I noted in Chapter 1 above, Gordon promises to focus on *Bahnsen's* views (CT, 24). Yet he admits that this — his *first* point which he presents as "unanswered" by Theonomists (CT, 25) — is not even presented by nor in any way derived from Bahnsen: "To my knowledge, Bahnsen's *Theonomy in Christian Ethics* does not depend in any particular measure on this argument. Yet, it is my observation from conversations with Theonomists that many others rely heavily on this argument." (CT, 25). Which being interpreted means: "Despite Bahnsen's meticulously detailed, philosophically rigorous, academically intense, foundationally important 600 page presentation of Theonomy (and all of his other books on Theonomic Ethics with their hundreds of pages of additional detail), I was not able to find this at all in his writings, but I will use it against his views, nevertheless."

Bahnsen was often exasperated by misguided criticisms:

> Often enough critics of the theonomic position have unfairly attributed to it claims which are quite contrary to what it teaches or which do not logically follow from the ten propositions outlined above. Such inaccurate representations may make criticism easier, but simultaneously make it irrelevant since it misses the intended target (TCE, xxix).

Second, Gordon himself promises to "gather in one place a brief taxonomy of the *major* arguments" (CT, 25; emphasis mine). If this is a "major argument" against Theonomy, and if, according to Gordon, Bahnsen provides the "clearest, most deliberate attempt to describe and defend Theonomy," "the most reliable indicator of what Theonomy is" (CT, 24) *why* is the argument absent from Bahnsen? This is especially odd in that Bahnsen presents numerous other arguments for Theonomy not even mentioned by Gordon in his "taxonomy" while totally overlooking this one. How can Gordon include this unmentioned argument as a "major" one? This does not make sense.

Third, what is worse, Gordon admits that this argument is not even found in theonomic *literature* produced by any of its published advocates. He has to derive it from informal discussions with Theonomists (college students? members of his congregation? people standing in line at the bank?): "it is my observation from conversations with Theonomists that many others rely heavily on this argument" (CT, 25). And even though he does not produce one *written* document arguing in this way, he complains: "Theonomists often argue that it is 'necessary for...man's...life' that humans have revealed directives for statecraft" (CT, 27). Had Gordon's article appeared before Bahnsen passed away, I am sure he would have included it in a future revision of *No Other Standard* in its third chapter titled: "Spurious Targets and Misguided Arrows" (NOS, 37). This is a most unusual approach in an academic paper of this sort.

Fourth, as I have already noted, this is all the more confusing when Gordon declares: "It is not my intention to advance exclusively new arguments against Theonomy, but rather, to gather in one place a brief taxonomy of the major arguments" (CT, 25). Yet, this argument is one that he himself discerns, for he provides no documentation of it being presented elsewhere by theonomic critics. Thus, it does appear to be a *new* argument (in the world of theological discussion). And, again, it certainly cannot be deemed a "major" argument for Theonomy. Why does he drop his stated intention of approaching the matter taxonomically?

Consequently, despite Gordon's prefatory comments, we are left with an argument that (1) does not derive from Bahnsen, (2) is not a "major" argument, (3) has never been published by any adherent to Theonomy, and (4) is a apparently a concern unique to Gordon. Why does he waste these three pages of his twenty-three page argument? And why has he chosen to lead off with such a "misguided arrow" (as Bahnsen would deem it)? And especially since he deems his response so devastating to Theonomy: "I have never received an answer to this line of questioning from any of the Theonomists with whom I have conversed. I do not think it likely that I will. Yet I think the line of questioning not only deserves an answer, I also think it reveals something about Theonomy's agenda" (CT, 25).

Despite all of this dialectical tension within Gordon's presentation, I nevertheless must interact with it. If I am to rebut his article, it would be difficult to leave out one of his three major points — even though it should not have appeared there in the first place. And especially since he is so pleased with his argument. If Gordon can publicly rebut theonomic arguments that *do not exist*, I am sure I will be held accountable if I do not respond to his anti-theonomic complaint that *does* exist. As I will demonstrate below, Gordon would have been wise to avoid this point on several counts, for not only is it contrary to his own stated plan of approach, but it represents the most poorly crafted argument in his whole paper, despite his grand hopes for it.

General Problems in Gordon's Presentation

Three general problems defuse Gordon's explosive argument against Theonomy: his mischaracterization of the theonomic position; his confusion of the fields of concern; and his self-contradiction in his presentation. I will briefly explain these general encumbrances, then back up and engage a focused critique of his "rebuttal." These failures on his part are significant in that the whole point of his argument is to demonstrate the *methodological* failure of Theonomy. Ironically, the methodology he employs in critiquing Bahnsen's methodology is flawed.

Gordon's Mischaracterization of the Theonomic Concern

Gordon misconstrues the theonomic concern by claiming it is built upon an "argument from necessity" which demands that "we need to know how to function in the civil arena, and therefore the Word of God must provide us with such instruction" (CT, 25). Theonomy does not at all argue on the basis of a philosophical argument from necessity. Gordon inadvertently admits this when he confesses that he could not find such an argument in Bahnsen's foundational treatise and in his failing to cite documentary evidence for his complaint. Consequently, his charge against Theonomy as entailing an "argument from necessity" is a "spurious target" (to employ Bahnsen's handy phrase).

Actually, Gordon places his concern over Theonomy in the wrong intellectual category. Rather than being a philosophical argument from necessity, it is a theological argument for a Christian worldview. And the Christian worldview must be rooted in Scripture — for Christianity is a revealed religion. Bahnsen writes in *Theonomy*: "This summary highlights the fact that theonomic ethics, proceeding in terms of salvation by grace alone, (1) is committed to developing an overall Christian world-and-life view (2) according to the regulating principle of sola Scriptura (3) and to the hermeneutic of covenant theology" (TCE, xxvii).

The Dutch Reformed theologian Albert M. Wolters presents a widely-held Reformed approach to worldview thinking. This summary statement is acceptable to Theonomists, but seems contrary to Gordon's Klinean approach:

> Our worldview must be shaped and tested by Scripture. It can legitimately guide our lives only if it is scriptural. . . . A good part of the purpose of this book is to offer help in the process of reforming our worldview to conform more closely to the teaching of Scripture. . . . There is considerable pressure on Christians to restrict their recognition of the authority of Scripture to the area of the church, theology, and private

morality — an area that has become basically irrelevant to the direction of culture and society as a whole. That pressure, though, is itself the fruit of a secular worldview, and must be resisted by Christians with all the resources at their disposal. The fundamental resources are the Scriptures themselves.[1]

Wolters continues:

> Scripture speaks centrally to *everything* in our life and world, including technology and economics and science. . . . In a certain sense the plea being made here for a biblical worldview is simply an appeal to the believer to take the Bible and its teaching seriously for the totality of our civilization *right now* and not to relegate it to some optional area called "religion."[2]

> What makes the light of Scripture so helpful and indispensable is that it spells out in clear human language what God's law is. Even without Scripture we have some notion of the requirements of justice, but Moses and the prophets, Jesus and the apostles put it into clear, unmistakable imperatives.[3]

I would not argue that Wolters is a Theonomist. But I would suggest that Theonomy is an acceptable application of this sort of Reformed worldview argument, and that Gordon's "argument from necessity" allegation is erroneously framed. His concerns would better be subsumed under the notion of a Christian worldview. This is especially so in that Gordon specifically declares that he is critiquing not so much our *conclusions*, as our *method*: "It is also not my purpose to examine in detail the particular recommendations for legislation, nor the particular exegetical conclusions of the various Theonomists. Those varying particulars are worthy of separate analysis and discussion, but my purpose is much more limited: to examine the hermeneutic governing the entire process. I am evaluating the engine, not the entire train" (CT, 24).

---

[1] Albert M. Wolters, *Creation Regained: Biblical Basics for a Reformation Worldview* (Grand Rapids: Eerdmans, 1985), 6.

[2] Wolters, *Creation Regained*, 7-8.

[3] Wolters, *Creation Regained*, 33.

Interestingly, Gordon mentions his being "profoundly helped" by Poythress (CT, 25) and specifically mentions his work on Theonomy's employment of Matthew 5 (CT, 30). But Poythress' book, which Gordon references, writes of Theonomy: "this emphasis on evaluating politics, economics, business, and social action by the Bible is sorely needed in our day."[4]

Gordon specifically recognizes that we are "obliged . . . to serve him in all aspects of life" (CT, 26), which certainly sounds worldviewish. And *biblical* worldview thinking has a glorious history within Reformed theological reflection. Gordon may not accept our *specific application* of the biblical worldview in this area, but may we not attempt to develop it in the civil sphere — *as a worldview implication*? As an attempt to flesh out *how* we are "obliged . . . to serve him in all aspects of life"?

A worldview — by the very nature of its being a *world* view — necessarily involves civil and jurisprudence issues. The Bible frames in a Christian worldview and we should, therefore, search the Scriptures to see what sort of directives for the civil realm it might offer. This is not an argument from necessity, but an application of worldview thinking. Three classic models of the Christian approach to culture and politics exist. The Pietist Model is retreatist, discouraging participation in political and cultural matters as "worldly" concerns. The Accomodationist Model is malleable, in encouraging adoption of the prevailing norms in political and cultural matters in that we are a part of our society. The Transformationalist Model is critical, encouraging the transforming of political and cultural matters as we challenge the fallen world with a Christian perspective.

The theonomic argument is an application of a Transformationalist Christian worldview in the realm of jurisprudence. Gordon has woefully mischaracterized it.

Gordon's Confusion of the Fields of Concern

In rebutting the (alleged) "necessitarian" methodology of Theonomic Ethics as it relates to matters of jurisprudence, Gordon attempts a *reductio ad absurdum* by parallel examples:

---

[4] Vern Poythress, *The Shadow of Christ in the Law of Moses* (Brentwood, Tenn.: Wolgemuth and Hyatt, 1991), 314.

Where does the Bible address other matters, such as state-craft, science, or medicine? Does the Bible contain a cure for cancer? Does it contain a solution to the long-standing debate between engineers and mathematicians regarding the stability of suspension bridges? And if it does not, why is state-craft different from these areas? . . . why do we expect biblical directives here and not elsewhere?... If the Theonomic plea from necessity is valid in the field of statecraft, then someone should indicate either that it is also valid in other fields, or that statecraft is a different field of human endeavor, subject to special considerations. (CT, 26)

That is, if we argue that our needs regarding statecraft must be met by *direct* scriptural revelation, we could just as easily argue by parity of reasoning that our other needs — such as in medicine or engineering must be so met. And yet no one argues thus, hence the *reductio*.

Gordon is so taken by his necessity argument rebuttal that he spends two full pages of his critique on it and confidently concludes:

I have never received an answer to this line of questioning from any of the Theonomists with whom I have conversed. I do not think it likely that I will. Yet I think the line of questioning not only deserves an answer, I also think it reveals something about Theonomy's agenda. (CT, 27)

I am not sure why he thinks this line of critique should incapacitate Theonomy. Or even why he believes Theonomists are compelled to deal with it. As I noted above, Gordon himself admits he cannot even find the argument in *Theonomy in Christian Ethics*. This is a notorious example of a strawman argument. However, since he deems it so valuable, I must respond.

(1) Gordon confounds moral and scientific issues. In statecraft and jurisprudence we are dealing with extraordinarily important *moral* issues: We are justifying some men (government authorities) putting other men (criminals) to death (capital punishment), enslaving them (imprisonment), and taking their property from them (fines). These are fundamentally moral concerns. Gordon, of course, knows this; he even

29

comments in his article: "Roman civil authority, at least in a general way, was indeed fulfilling the divine mandate to punish the wicked (Romans 13)" (CT, 27). To "punish" men accused of being "wicked" involves *moral* considerations. We must distinguish capital punishment from murder, imprisonment from kidnaping, and fines from theft. And we must do so on the basis of some universal, invariant, publicly-accessible moral principle — which the Theonomist argues is revealed by God in his law.

Issues of criminal penology are moral issues, whereas engineering and disease treatment are technological matters. Justice involves a few men controlling other people's lives and fortunes, which must be governed by moral considerations. I am astounded that Gordon asks "why is statecraft different from these areas?" (CT, 26). Why can he not see that "statecraft is a different field of human endeavor, subject to special considerations" (CT, 26)? As a Theonomist I am not at all impressed with his attempted *reductio*.

(2) Gordon fumbles the Christian worldview. Although Gordon is no materialist, he inadvertently argues as if he were:

> In the field of medicine, for instance, we develop instruments which assist us in our ability to observe: more powerful microscopes, CAT-scan machines, etc. When we are able to observe accurately the physical realities, we then propose theories for dealing with them, and we test those theories by trial-and-error. It is not different in the field of statecraft. We observe human nature, and especially human nature in society (sociology, anthropology, political science, psychology and social psychology, history). (CT, 26)

How can he speak of observations and measurements of "physical realities" in medical treatments, then declare that this is "not different" from our approach to "the field of statecraft" where "we observe human nature"? Surely measuring the fracture lines of broken ribs, observing the presence of bacteria, and detecting the swelling of the brain are not the same as observing "human nature." The soft sciences of sociology, anthropology, psychology and so forth are not "sciences" at all. And that is because they are dealing with human personalities operating as free moral agents. What instrument allows us to see "human nature"? Or to discern moral directives?

(3) Gordon overlooks the facts of the matter. As a matter of objective revelatory fact, Scripture *does* deal directly and at length with issues of statecraft, particularly in the area of jurisprudence (which is the leading concern over Theonomy from among anti-theonomists). It does issue mandates in this field, whereas it does not do so in engineering and medical technology. I say Gordon "overlooks" it, not that he is "ignorant" of it. He admits that "statecraft" is "comprehensively recorded in the Scriptures" in "the Sinai legislation" (CT, 26).

If, as Gordon admits, Scripture speaks "comprehensively" of "statecraft," why should we not bow to its authority? Of course, later he will give his covenantal reasons for denying the continuing relevance of the Mosaic legislation. But he has not done that at this stage of his argument. So at present, the Theonomist has the upper hand: God has spoken, and he has spoken "comprehensively" (according to Gordon's own admission). This is what Theonomy is all about. So Theonomy, rooted in "comprehensive" Scriptural revelation, cannot be ruled out by Christians in advance.

Gordon forgets a distinctive of the biblical worldview

In Romans the civil magistrate is specifically appointed by God (Rom. 13:1) as a "minister of God" (Rom. 13:4). Nowhere are doctors or engineers called such. The civil magistrate is established in the Bible as one possessing a distinct and high calling that classifies him as a "minister." How can they "minister" for God if they do not have some revelation from God to minister? What are they to "minister"? Especially since the very context of Romans 13 points to their ministry in terms of the "sword" being brought to bear against "evil" (Rom. 13:4).

In Romans the flow of Paul's argument and the correspondence of terms employed vitally connects chapters 12 and 13 as Paul speaks to the problem of evil in society: "Repay no one evil [κακόν] for evil [κακοῦ]" (Rom. 12:17). He directs us: "Beloved, do not avenge [ἐκδικοῦντε] yourselves, but rather give place to wrath [ὀργή]" (Rom. 12:19a). Why does he command this? "For it is written, 'Vengeance [ἐκδίκησις] is Mine, I will repay,' says the Lord" (Rom. 12:19). Thus, he urges us not to take the law into our own hands: "Be not overcome of evil [κακόν]" (Rom. 12:21).[5] He then engages a discussion of the God-ordained role of the civil magistrate as God's avenger.

---

[5] Which, with the whole context as I am presenting it, is compatible with Jesus' instruction in Matthew 5:38ff and is very much contrary to Waltke's remarkable

In Romans 13 the matter of the civil magistrate is approached prescriptively, rather than descriptively.[6] As such, he has been "ordained of God" (Rom. 13:1), so that "he does not bear the sword in vain." He is, in fact, "God's minister, an avenger [ἔκδικος] to execute wrath [ὀργήν] on him who practices evil [κακόν]" (Rom. 13:4). Clearly, then, the magistrate is to avenge the wrath of *God* against those who practice evil (Rom. 13:4, 6).

As he continues Paul refers to the law of God, citing four of the Ten Commandments (Rom. 13:9a) and a summary case law from Leviticus 19:18 (Rom. 13:9b). Finally, he concludes the thought regarding personal vengeance, which he began in Romans 12:17-19: "Love does no harm [κακόν, "evil"] to a neighbor; therefore love is the fulfillment of the law" (Rom. 13:10).

His reference to God's law[7] in this context is important. Ultimately, God's eternal vengeance is meted out according to his holy law (cf. Rom. 2:3, 5-6, 12-15), which is objectively revealed (and therefore publically accessible) in the Mosaic law. But proximately and mediatorially, God's temporal "minister," the civil magistrate, must mete out the "just reward" (Heb. 2:2; cf. Rom. 7:12; 1 Tim. 1:8) to those against whom the penalties of the law are directed: evil-doers. Paul specifies this even more particularly in 1 Timothy 1:9-10: "The Law is not made for a righteous person, but for the lawless and insubordinate, for the ungodly and for sinners, for the unholy and profane, for murderers of fathers and murderers of mothers, for manslayers, for fornicators, for sodomites, for kidnappers, for liars, for perjurers, and

---

statement: "Bahnsen will not concede the obvious point that in Matthew 5:38-42 Christ abrogates the principle of immediate justice; Christ will bring justice in the *parousia*"! (Will S. Barker and W. Robert Godfrey, *Theonomy: A Reformed Critique* [Grand Rapids: Zondervan, 1990], 82.) Shall we await the Lord's Return before we seek criminal justice?

[6] How could Paul be *describing* Roman imperial authority as an avenger of God's wrath, when Christ had earlier warned against the idolatrous assertions of Rome (Matt. 22:15-21) and was shortly thereafter illegally crucified by Rome (John 19:4, 6, 16)? See William Hendriksen, *The Gospel of Matthew* (Grand Rapids: Baker, 1973), 802-4. See also Kenneth L. Gentry, Jr., *Before Jerusalem Fell: The Dating of the Book of Revelation* (Tyler, Tex.: Institute for Christian Economics, 1989), ch. 16.

[7] Earlier he deemed this law "established" (Rom. 3:31) and called it "holy, just, and good" (Rom. 7:12).

if there is any other thing that is contrary to sound doctrine."[8] And all of this was "according to the glorious gospel of the blessed God which was committed to my trust" (1 Tim. 1:11) – not according to a passé example.

Gordon's Self-contradiction in his Presentation

In one place at a focal point of the debate, Gordon "denies himself" — but not in the spiritually commendable sense. Oddly enough, he even makes the contradictory statements on the same page. In the second line on page 26 he writes: "all parties agree that the only place where statecraft of any sort is comprehensively recorded in the Scriptures is in the Sinai legislation." But then just five sentences later he asks: "Where does the Bible address other matters, such as statecraft, science, or medicine?" (CT, 26). I would point him back to his preceding statement: "all parties agree that the only place where statecraft of any sort is comprehensively recorded in the Scriptures is in the Sinai legislation."

In that same context, while he is rebutting Theonomy's alleged argument from necessity, Gordon makes a self-contradictory admission when he reminds us of "the nature of the curse on the human race subsequent to the Fall" (CT, 26). It is certainly true that we must remember the "nature of the curse"; and this is especially important in any *Christian* analysis of world and life issues. But by this statement he undercuts a major point of his own method — and *theological method* is important to Gordon. Let me explain the contradiction.

A key component of his critique of Theonomy is his favoring natural revelation over special revelation on issues outside the narrow confines of religion: "In fact, it is my judgment that natural revelation is a sufficient guide in each of these areas. In the field of natural revelation, the tools for understanding our duty are different than in the field of special revelation." But how does this create tension in his system?

---

[8] A case may be made for Paul's generally following the order of the Ten Commandments, H. D. M. Spence, "I and II Timothy" in Charles John Ellicott, ed., *Ellicott's Commentary on the Whole Bible*, 8 vols., (Grand Rapids: Zondervan, rep. n.d.), 7:180. At the very least it may be said that "the apostle now gives a summary of the law of the Ten Commandments." William Hendriksen, *I and II Timothy and Titus* (Grand Rapids: Baker, 1967), 67.

Since Gordon has reminded us of "the nature of the curse on the human race" (CT, 26), we are inescapably led to expect that fallen nature would actually lead to a *blurring* of "natural revelation." Bahnsen commented frequently on the problem of preferring natural revelation over special revelation. He noted that natural revelation is (1) necessarily sin-obscured (Eph. 4:17-19), (2) intentionally suppressed in unrighteousness (Rom. 1:18, 21), (3) inherently less detailed and clear (Rom. 3:1-2), and, in the final analysis, (4) wrongly deemed contrary to special revelation (Rom. 2:14-15).[9]

Specific Deficiencies in Gordon's Position

Now I will engage a running response to his anti-theonomic argument in "Critique of Theonomy," drawing in some supplementary material from his later "The Insufficiency of Scripture" article in *Modern Reformation.*

Gordon's Rhetorical Challenge

Gordon confronts the Theonomist in terms of Theonomy's alleged argument from necessity:

> Where does the Bible address other matters, such as statecraft, science, or medicine? Does the Bible contain a cure for cancer? Does it contain a solution to the long-standing debate between engineers and mathematicians regarding the stability of suspension bridges? And if it does not, why is statecraft different from these areas? Is a well-run state more necessary than efficient agriculture? Is a well-run state more necessary than good medicine? If not, why do we expect biblical directives here and not elsewhere? (CT, 26)

---

[9] Bahnsen points out that "the moral obligations communicated through both means of divine communication are identical (Rom. 1:18-21, 25, 32; 2:14-15; 3:9, 19-20, 23). Scripture never suggests that God has two sets of ethical standards or two moral codes, the one (for Gentiles) being an abridgement of the other (for Jews). Rather, He has one set of commandments which are communicated to men in two ways: through Scripture and through nature (Ps. 19, cf. w. 2-3 with 8-9)" (NOS, 206-07). See also: TCE, 386-87; NOS, 9n23, 155; Greg L. Bahnsen and Kenneth L. Gentry, Jr., *House Divided: The Break-up of Dispensational Theology* (2d. ed.: Tyler, Tex.: Institute for Christian Economics, 1997), 93ff.

The Theonomist gladly takes up the challenge of this series of rhetorical questions: "Where does the Bible address other matters, such as statecraft"? Answer: In the Sinai legislation. "Where does the Bible address other matters, such as . . . science"? Answer: Nowhere. "Where does the Bible address other matters, such as . . . medicine"? Answer: Nowhere.

We must remember that Gordon himself noted that "statecraft . . . is comprehensively recorded . . . in the Sinai legislation" (CT, 26). You will not find either him or Theonomists averring that science and medicine are "comprehensively recorded" anywhere in Scripture. The Theonomist argues that the Bible *does in fact* speak frequently and forcefully to issues of statecraft. In fact, our complaint against other systems of ethical thought is that they suppress this very large, most relevant, and quite obvious portion of God's direct revelation.

A little later in his fleshing out this "problem" for Theonomy he queries:

> Theonomists often argue that it is 'necessary for . . . man's . . . life' that humans have revealed directives for statecraft. If this argument were valid, however, why would it not be equally (or more) valid to argue that it is 'necessary for . . . man's . . . life' that humans have revealed directives for medicine? Is it not the case when our loved ones die that the Scriptures have not been, in their medicinal instructions, sufficient in providing what is "necessary for . . . man's . . . life'? Is it not the case, when a suspension bridge collapses due to no construction failure, that the Scriptures have evidently not provided adequate instruction in the field of design? (CT, 27)

Frankly these questions could easily be left to Mark Twain who once responded to a questioner: "I was gratified to be able to answer quickly. I said, 'I don't know.'" You see, even if we do not know why God has not revealed more to us in Scripture, the fact remains that he *did* reveal much in the field of statecraft. After all, does not Scripture teach us: "The secret things belong to the Lord our God, but the things revealed belong to us" (Deut. 29:29a). This fact has to be dealt with, and theonomy does so.

Gordon's Inconsistency Charge

After his rhetorical challenge, Gordon confronts the Theonomist: "If the Theonomic plea from necessity is valid in the field of statecraft, then someone should indicate either that it is also valid in other fields, or that statecraft is a different field of human endeavor, subject to special considerations" (CT, 26). Once again, we deny that Theonomy involves the argument from necessity. Nevertheless, his challenge deserves a response. He is failing to conceive the issues rightly. The Theonomist does hold that statecraft (I prefer, "jurisprudence" over Gordon's "statecraft"[10]) "is a different field of human endeavor, subject to special considerations," i.e., differing from agriculture, engineering, and medicine.

To orient our thinking, we should remember that at the beginning of time Adam was placed in Eden *under a moral test*, not a technological test (Gen. 2:16-17). God examined him in the foundational matters of moral authority and personal obligation. Adam's test was whether or not he would allow God to be the sovereign, determining good and evil (Gen. 3:5). Of course, we know that Adam determined that he himself would be the moral legislator: he took the forbidden fruit in defiance of God's directive, thereby failing his divine test (Gen. 3:1-19; Rom. 5:14). Furthermore, at the end of time on Judgment Day God will not judge man on the basis of his technological prowess, but his moral conduct (Matt. 11:24; 12:36; John 5:29; Rom. 2:14-15; 14:10-12; 2 Cor. 5:10; Rev. 20:12). After the fall, Cain killed Able then feared a "judicial" response involving capital punishment (Gen. 4:14); he did not mention a technological obligation to create a cure for polio. *Jurisprudence is inherently a moral issue*, rather than a technological one, for the reasons stated previously regarding the imposition of law upon free moral agents.

In fact, Gordon woefully stumbles when he writes: "In the field of natural revelation, the tools for understanding our *duty* are different than in the field of special revelation. In studying special revelation, we learn Hebrew and Greek, ancient history and culture, etc. In studying natural revelation, we learn to weigh, measure, test, etc. Put most plainly, natural revelation is studied by observation, and by trial-and-error" (CT,

---

[10] Bahnsen puts the matter thus: "the law continues to offer us an inspired and reliable model for civil justice or socio-political morality (a guide for public reform in our own day, even in the area of crime and punishment)" NOS, 4.

26, emphasis mine). How is our "duty," our *moral obligation*, discerned by our learning "to weigh, measure, test"? Does it come to us "by observation" of the natural world? Is morality established by "trial and error"? To what kind of morality is Gordon committed?

Gordon's Methodological Deficiency

A key factor in Gordon's vehement anti-theonomic method, as noted above, is his preferring natural revelation over special revelation regarding non-religious issues. This problem flows directly from his Klinean convictions. I have already pointed out Bahnsen's response to the strategic error in this, but Gordon's difficulty here is even deeper than first appears.

Gordon clearly states that "it is my judgment that natural revelation is a sufficient guide in each of these areas" of worldview concerns (CT, 26). He is so committed to the sufficiency of natural revelation that he charges the Westminster divines with imprecision in framing WCF 1:6, which reads: "The whole counsel of God concerning all things necessary for His own glory, man's salvation, faith and life, is either expressly set down in Scripture, or by good and necessary consequence may be deduced from Scripture." Gordon explains their deficient statement:

> I clarify, however, that 'faith and life' must be taken in its religious sense. I also clarify that the entire matter would have been better expressed had the divines articulated a more manifestly covenantal statement, indicating that the Scriptures are a sufficient guide to the various covenants God has made with various covenant people through the centuries, and that the entire canon, taken in its entirety, is sufficient, therefore, to govern the members of the new covenant made in Christ. By 'faith and life' the divines intended what one is to believe and do as a member of the new covenant community. (IS, 18)

He rather surprisingly declares:

> If anything has changed [in my position], then, it is that I would now argue with equal zeal for the *in*sufficiency of

Scripture in other than religious or covenantal areas. As such, Scripture is *not* a sufficient guide to many aspects of life, other than in the sense of providing religious direction and motivation to all of life. (IS, 18)

And all of this is relevant to his critique of Theonomy, for

> Many Theonomists appear to have developed a novel, and erroneous, understanding of the sufficiency of Scripture. They imply that Scripture is a sufficient guide for the various departments of life, in all their specificity. In fact, the Reformational doctrine of the sufficiency of Scripture is a highly nuanced and sophisticated doctrine.
>
> The Reformational doctrine of the sufficiency of Scripture does not mean that the Scriptures are sufficient to answer all of our questions. Rather, the doctrine means that the Scriptures are a sufficient guide to our communion with God, a guide to faith and life in the religious sense. (CT, 27)

I will respond by pointing out that I believe he is mistaken in his reading of the Westminster divines; consequently his attempt to "clarify" their statement actually appears to serve as a rebuttal to it. The divines appear to employ "faith and life" globally rather than just religiously. For instance, consider the answer to Larger Catechism question 99 regarding the rules for understanding the Ten Commandments. Two of the rules expose Gordon's error:

> 7. That what is forbidden or commanded to ourselves, we are bound, *according to our places*, to endeavor that it may be avoided or performed by others, *according to the duty of their places*.

> 8. That in what is commanded to others, we are bound, *according to our places and callings*, to be helpful to them; and to take heed of partaking with others in what is forbidden them.

The Ten Commandments are most certainly portions of Scripture, which is special revelation. Yet they are applied by the divines

38

"according to our places and callings," not just in our religious activities, and certainly not just for Israel (as per Gordon's Klinean covenantalism). For instance, the Second Commandment (according to the divines) obligates us "according to each one's place and calling" to engage in "removing . . . all monuments of idolatry" (LC 108). This means that we are to engage our callings by applying Scripture "whether in family, church, or commonwealth" (LC 124 on the Fifth Commandment). Hence, the civil magistrate is to apply the Second Commandment in his calling as civil magistrate.

Contrary to Gordon, contemporary Reformed theologian Albert Wolters states: "In a certain sense the plea being made here for a biblical worldview is simply an appeal to the believer to take the Bible and its teaching seriously for the *totality of our civilization* right now and *not to relegate it to some optional area called 'religion.'*"[11] In this application of Scripture to worldview issues Wolters follows Calvin, for "Calvin developed a scriptural world-and-life view that transformed medieval society. More strongly than Luther, Calvin sought to reorder all of life — school, marketplace, home, state, society, and the arts — *according to Scripture.*"[12] Or as C. Gregg Singer put it: Calvin "with full assurance assert[ed] that the Scriptures are the final authority *in all areas of human life.*"[13] Even more particularly, Philip Schaff wrote: "Calvin's plea for the right and duty of the Christian magistrate to punish heresy by death stands or falls with his theocratic theory and the binding authority of the Mosaic code."[14] Calvin is followed in this conviction by later Reformed scholars, such as Abraham Kuyper who demonstrated "that his beloved Calvinism was more than just a church polity or doctrinaire religion but an all-encompassing *Weltanschauung.*"[15]

Surely Gordon's declaration "I clarify, however, that 'faith and life' must be taken in its religious sense," is not *the* Reformed understanding of the Confession's statement. I would not declare that each of the

[11] Wolters, *Creation Regained*, 7-8. Emphasis mine.

[12] Hoffecker, *Building a Christian World View*, 2:234. Emphasis mine.

[13] C. Gregg Singer, *John Calvin: His Roots and Fruits* (Greenville, S.C.: A Press, 1989), 10. Emphasis mine.

[14] Philip Schaff, *History of the Christian Church* (Grand Rapids: Eerdmans, rep. n.d. [1910]), 8:792.

[15] David K. Naugle, *Worldview: The History of a Concept* (Grand Rapids: Eerdmans, 2002), 17.

men just cited was a "Theonomist." I would, however, point out that they believed in the application of Scripture in non-religious areas of life, just as does Theonomy and as over against Gordon.

And how shall we respond to Gordon's complaint: "If we could not develop and refine statecraft by this method [trial and error], then how can we account for the fact that many governments have proceeded, with varying degrees of success, by this method?" (CT, 27) Several responses come quickly to mind.

Gordon's question is absolutely irrelevant. It is akin to asking of Mormonism: "if we could not develop and refine religion by this method, then how can we account for the fact that many cults have proceeded, with varying degrees of success, by this method?" He is assuming that historical success (for a period of time) is evidence of moral legitimacy. And on the historical plane, Mormonism appears quite successful.

Furthermore, Theonomy does not argue that every aspect of government is written in Scripture. Theonomy allows for and even expects the ongoing refinement of governmental organization. It lays out the foundational principles and a variety of illustrative precepts (case laws) directing the civil magistrate — without fleshing out all of the details for framing in a full, bureaucratic governmental structure (just as it does not provide a *detailed* exposition of the government of Christ's church).[16]

Besides, the Theonomist wonders, how is Gordon evaluating "varying degrees of success"? By measuring economic prosperity? Historical longevity? Internal peace? Stable transfer of political power? Global expansion? Multi-cultural representation? Or, as the Theonomist would, by biblical standards of righteousness and truth? After all, Reformed theology acknowledges that God's common grace allows apparent success — even for those ultimately cursed by God.

Gordon's Theonomist Misunderstanding

Gordon makes a common mistake in assuming that because Theonomists write so much on civil governmental issues, they thereby elevate those issues above all others:

---

[16] I believe in *jure divino* church government, but recognize that not every detail of church government is outlined in Scripture. God has not revealed a *Book of Church Order*.

For Theonomists, statecraft is simply more important than medicine, science, engineering, etc. Possibly due to their postmillennialism, possibly due to their (understandable) heart-break over the decline of the West, and possibly due to other, less tangible factors, they have simply placed statecraft higher on their agenda than it is on other people's agenda. Yet they have not demonstrated why the solution to statecraft is more pressing than the solution to these other matters. (CT, 27)

Why does Gordon claim this? Why does he declare statecraft is "higher on their agenda than it is on other people's agenda"? I do not know, because he does not say. He does not quote any Theonomist who argues statecraft issues are "more important" than other cultural matters. In fact, by supposing that it might be due to the "postmillennialism" held by many Theonomists, he undercuts his own case. For postmillennialism certainly does not focus solely on the civil governmental outcome of kingdom victory in history. Rather, it expects the *full-orbed, culture-wide* influence of the Christian faith as a consequence of the widespread and long term gospel success promoted by preaching, evangelism, missions, mercy ministries, and Christian education.[17]

Gordon appears to be committing a hasty generalization: Theonomists write about civil government, therefore they are only interested in civil government. Actually, Theonomy only seems to elevate statecraft issues because that is where an important debate is. By parity of reasoning we could just as well argue that Gordon deems denying Theonomy more important than affirming Christ's resurrection simply because he has written more on it.[18]

---

[17] See my definition of "postmillennialism" in Darrell L. Bock, ed., *Three Views on the Millennium and Beyond* (Grand Rapids: Zondervan, 1999), 13-14. See also the following works by theonomic postmillennialists: Greg L. Bahnsen, *Victory in Jesus: The Bright Hope of Postmillennialism* (Texarkana, Ark.: CMF, 1999). R. J. Rushdoony, *God's Plan for Victory: The Meaning of Postmillennialism* (Fairfax, Vir.: Thoburn). Gary North, *Millennialism and Social Theory* (Tyler, Tex.: Institute for Christian Economics, 1990).

[18] He has focused on Theonomy in a number of articles, including "Critique of Theonomy: A Taxonomy" in the *Westminster Theological Journal*; "The Insufficiency of Scripture" in *Reformation Today*; and "Van Til and Theonomic Ethics," in Howard Griffith and John R. Meuther, eds., *Creator, Redeemer, Consummator: A Festschrift for Meredith G. Kline* (Greenville, S.C.: Reformed Academic Press, 2000).

Conclusion

Gordon's critique of Bahnsen's theonomic argument from necessity fails on numerous grounds. The most important being: Bahnsen does not employ the argument. He makes this mistake not only despite his own stated determination to deal with Bahnsen, but after declaring that "individuals should be evaluated individually, and those who do not embrace the hermeneutic that I here describe are free of the critique" (CT, 23). If he is critiquing *Bahnsen*, and if "individuals should be evaluated individually" so that those not embracing an issue may be "free of critique," then ironically Bahnsen is free of this critique of Bahnsen!

What is more, he opened his article drawing some careful distinctions. He distinguished between "Theonomy" and "Theonomists," and between "Theonomy" and "Christian Reconstruction" (CT, 21). Then he distinguished the "details from the basic program" (CT, 24), and engaged in "dividing the question" (CT, 24). After opening so carefully, I stand amazed that he would commit so egregious an error, but given the influence of his article, it is important that we challenge him on this matter.

Chapter 3
The Argument from Matthew 5

Fortunately, after badly misfiring his opening salvo in his "unan-swered" challenge, Gordon's second volley is much more strategic. This section is titled: "The Role of Matt 5:17-21 in the Theonomic Hermeneutic." Here he critiques a well-known, widely-debated issue of some significance for Bahnsen: his exegesis of Jesus' comments on the law of God in the Sermon on the Mount. Strategically, it is always better to rebut what someone actually believes than what you feel he should have believed. Gordon's critique now engages a four step argu-ment by which he attempts to demonstrate fatal flaws in Bahnsen's exegesis.

Unfortunately, our delight with the new material quickly fades. Our *coup d'oeil* discovers that Gordon's rebuttal of Bahnsen's Matthew 5 ex-egesis is woefully deficient — and once again for an absolutely unnec-essary reason. He seems unaware of Bahnsen's several detailed defenses of *Theonomy* in general and of his exegesis of Matthew 5 in particular. In those responses he answered many of Gordon's specific and most-pointed objections — and he did so several years *before* Gordon pub-lished them. Therefore, Gordon's unsuspecting reader comes away from reading his rebuttal armed, but not dangerous.

Most incredibly, Gordon never mentions Bahnsen's well-known 325 page book *No Other Standard: Theonomy and Its Critics* (1991). This book provides meticulously detailed responses to all of his major pub-lished critics — including many of the very ones quoted by Gordon, such as Kline, Poythress and Fowler. *No Other Standard* is recognized as an invaluable apologetic for Theonomic Ethics — and it deals exten-sively with Matthew 5 (NOS, App. A).

Gordon never mentions Bahnsen's even earlier 110 page defense of Theonomy published in *House Divided: The Break-up of Dispensational*

Theology, though it was published in 1989. In that work he answered dispensational critics (who happen to hold some discontinuity positions very similar to the followers of Kline). Chapter 3 particularly deals with complaints about his Matthew 5 exegesis.

Gordon never mentions Bahnsen's chapter "The Theonomic Position," in *God and Politics: Four Views on the Reformation of Civil Government*, ed. Gary Scott Smith (1989). He never cites Bahnsen's defensive Preface in his second edition of *Theonomy in Christian Ethics*, though it too was published in 1989. He never mentions Bahnsen's much earlier article "The Authority of God's Law" published in *The Presbyterian Journal* (Dec. 6, 1978). This article represents his first major published response to Reformed criticisms by editor G. Aiken Taylor which appeared earlier in several issues of that journal. Nor does Gordon ever mention Bahnsen's extensive, sessionally-published, widely-distributed 1979 paper "The Theonomic Thesis in Confessional and Historical Perspective."[1] Nor Bahnsen's thirty-nine page paper "The Theonomic Antithesis to Other Law Attitudes" (1982). Gordon appears totally unaware of their existence.

Whereas the first of Gordon's three major arguments against Bahnsen fails to score because it misses the target, this second one goes astray because it is guided by dated research. Nevertheless, I must respond since his article is published in the widely-respected *Westminster Theological Journal* and is deemed a major coup by many Reformed anti-theonomists.

Gordon's Overstated Case

"Critique of Theonomy: A Taxonomy" opens with a few comments on polemics, noting potential areas of difficulty (CT, 23). He recognizes (as we all should) that our polemics can be undercut by "whatever is untrue, unclear, or unhelpful" (CT, 25). Unfortunately, by overstating his case he inadvertently succumbs to that which is "untrue, unclear, or unhelpful."

Bahnsen's "Only" Argument

Gordon's first point in this section of his critique is blunted by his exaggerated claims regarding Bahnsen's dependence on Matthew 5. He

---

[1] This was the expanded, eighty-six page edition of the *Presbyterian Journal* article. It was distributed by the Session of St. Paul Presbyterian Church, Jackson, Mississippi, in 1979.

writes: "Paul Fowler correctly observed that Bahnsen's entire case for his approach to the 'abiding validity of the law in exhaustive detail' was based upon his understanding of Matt 5:17–21. . . . If Bahnsen cannot make his case from this text, his case is not made" (CT, 28). One supporting evidence for Fowler's statement affirmed by Gordon is: "Fowler pointed out how frequently this passage is cited in *Theonomy in Christian Ethics* as proof of the observation" (CT, 28).

Because Gordon did not make the effort to check whether Bahnsen might have responded somewhere along the way to his critics on this supposed problem, he is not aware of how Bahnsen counters such objections. This is all the more remarkable because of the enormous volume of critiques of Bahnsen — and because *Theonomy* itself confronts it. As Gordon surely knows, resistance to Theonomic Ethics has spawned widespread and prolonged rebuttals in presbytery debates,[2] public symposia,[3] lengthy articles,[4] and whole books.[5] We know that Gordon is aware of this immense backlash against Theonomy, after all,

---

[2] See for example, the following minutes of the Presbyterian Church in America General Assembly: M7GA (1979), 195ff; M9GA (1981), 196ff.; M10GA (1982), 107ff.; M11GA (1983), 87ff.; M20GA (1992), 235. Paul R. Gilchrist, *PCA Digest Position Papers 1973-1993* (Decatur, Geo.: Presbyterian Church in America, 1993). See sympathetic analyses by G. Brent Bradley, "The 20th General Assembly: What Did and Did Not Happen," *Presbyterian Witness* 6:2 (Sept., 1992), 9ff. Byron Snapp, "The Live Oak Case," *Presbyterian Witness* 6:2 (Sept., 1992), 19ff.

[3] J. Ligon Duncan, "Moses' Law for Modern Government: The Intellectual and Sociological Origins of the Christian Reconstructionist Movement" presented October 15, 1994 to the Social Science History Association, Atlanta, Georgia. Dennis M. Swanson, "'Theonomic Postmillennialism': A Continuation of the Princeton Tradition?" presented on April 22, 1994 to the Far-West Region of the Evangelical Theological Society annual meeting.

[4] Meredith G. Kline, "Comments on an Old-New Error: A Review Article," in *Westminster Theological Journal* 41:1 (Fall, 1978) 173. Douglas E. Chismar and David A. Rausch, "Regarding Theonomy: An Essay of Concern," *Journal of the Evangelical Theological Society*, 26:4 (Dec., 1983), 315_323. T. David Gordon, "A Critique of Theonomy: A Taxonomy," *Westminster Theological Journal*, 56:1 (Spring, 1994): 23-43.

[5] Will S. Barker and W. Robert Godfrey, *Theonomy: A Reformed Critique* (Grand Rapids: Zondervan, 1990). Walter Chantry, *God's Righteous Kingdom: The Law's Connection with the Gospel* (Edinburgh: Banner of Truth, 1980). H. Wayne House and Thomas D. Ice, *Dominion Theology: Blessing or Curse?* (Portland, Ore.: Multnomah, 1988). Lewis Neilson, *God's Law in Christian Ethics: A Reply to Bahnsen and Rushdoony* (Cherry Hill, N.J.: Mack, 1979).

he took the time to jump into the fray and cites several of the objectors in offering his "taxonomy" on the matter.

In *No Other Standard* Bahnsen alludes to *various* foundational texts, when he responds to a particular critic. He complains that the critic rebuts the theonomic argument "*only after* the main supporting texts for the theonomic view (viz., Matthew 5:17-19 and Romans 13:1-7) have been *removed* from consideration" (NOS, 163). Notice that Bahnsen himself declares that there are "main supporting texts" (plural), and even cites one of them in addition to Matthew 5: Romans 13.

In another place, Bahnsen parallels 2 Timothy 3:16-17 with Matthew 5:17 as a key text: "Jesus warned against dismissing even the least Old Testament commandment (Matt. 5:19), and Paul taught that every Old Testament scripture instructs us in righteousness (2 Tim. 3:16-17)" (NOS, 99). In fact, 2 Timothy 3:16-17 is a favorite text for Bahnsen, which he often cited along with Matthew 5. For example: "Nor is it clear how this restriction can be harmonized with the New Testament endorsement of every scripture (2 Tim. 3:16), every command (James 2:10), even the least command (Matt. 5:19), every word (Matt. 4:4) and every letter (Matt. 5:18) of the Old Testament" (NOS, 125). Obviously, Bahnsen focuses on a variety of foundational biblical texts — though Matthew 5 remains the key one among them.

Why does Gordon not suppose that somewhere along the way Bahnsen would provide counter-evidence on the objection that his whole argument rests solely on one text? Was not Bahnsen a philosophically-trained debater (he earned a Ph.D. in philosophy from the University of Southern California and has several public debates on tape)? Did he not possess an "over-heated typewriter" (Kline's derogatory statement regarding Bahnsen's prodigious output)? Was he not subjected to relentless criticisms regarding his Theonomic Ethics? According to Gordon himself, did not Theonomy generate "an intellectual movement" (CT, 43)? Why would he not think it likely that the movement had dealt with such a complaint? This is especially problematic in that Gordon was offering a rigorous, academic response to Bahnsen and in a respected Reformed theological journal.

In point of fact, Bahnsen does respond to this very objection in Strickland's *The Law, the Gospel, and the Modern Christian*. Bahnsen answers Strickland thus:

He makes a weak effort in this under his discussion of "The Mosaic Law and the Christian," starting off with a misbegotten attempt to reduce how much effort would be needed for the task. First, Strickland tries to reduce the theonomic position to Matthew 5:17-19 (calling it "the major justification for theonomy"). . . . Ah, would that it were so easy! The fundamental operating premises of Theonomic Ethics could be — indeed, in my books, are — readily proven from any number of New Testament passages, only one of which is Matthew 5:17-19. . . . The theonomic thesis could be demonstrated without any reference to this text at all.[6]

Gordon fumbles here by employing Fowler's older study, released in 1979, and then again in 1980 (after changing it radically due to Bahnsen's devastating response[7]).

Interestingly, in his "Conclusion" to *Theonomy* Bahnsen only mentions Matthew 5 in one place, and that only as a closing motto (TCE, 476). In fact, he declares in his six page conclusion: "The theonomic ethic is substantiated in multiple ways throughout the pages of the New Testament" (TCE, 474).

In his later Preface to the *second* edition of *Theonomy* (1983) Bahnsen provides a ten point statement "that draws together, clarifies, and states in distilled form the vital teachings elaborated in the full text of *Theonomy in Christian Ethics*" (TCE, xxv). Not one of these ten points either alludes to Matthew 5, references it, or quotes words or phrases from it. This is contrary to Gordon's assertion that "if Bahnsen cannot make his case from this text, his case is not made" (CT, 28).

Elsewhere Bahnsen expressly denies that Theonomic Ethics rests solely on Matthew 5. In responding to Reformed theologian Paul G. Schrotenboer, he comments on the role of πληρῶσαι ("fulfill") in Matthew 5:17 for his argument. He not only states that this important aspect of Jesus' declaration is not "in any way essential to its [*Theonomy's*] argumentation," but he believes "the debate over how to translate or

---

[6] Bahnsen, in Wayne, G. Strickland, ed., *The Law, the Gospel, and the Modern Christian: Five Views* (Grand Rapids: Zondervan, 1993), 297-98.

[7] See Bahnsen on Fowler in NOS, 275-282.

interpret that Greek word is really irrelevant."[8] This does not sound like a statement from someone whose case "cannot be made" apart from this passage.

In *No Other Standard* Bahnsen states:

> Did Jesus assume basic continuity or basic discontinuity between His ethic and that of Moses? In asking whether we should presume that the old covenant law is binding or abrogated today, *one relevant and important passage* which cannot be avoided is Matthew 5:17-19. Thus it was given detailed attention in my book *Theonomy in Christian Ethics, even though it is not the only text which could be used to substantiate the theonomic operating premise*." (NOS, 273, emphasis mine)

Thus, even though Gordon complains: "If Bahnsen cannot make his case from this text, his case is not made" (CT, 28), Bahnsen himself writes: the "theonomic operating premise" is *not* "substantiate[d]" on this one "text" (NOS, 273).

In fact, the evidence for Gordon's statement is based on Fowler's research: "Fowler pointed out how frequently this passage is cited in *Theonomy in Christian Ethics* as proof of the observation" (CT, 28). If Fowler's research method is followed consistently, though, we could actually reach the *opposite* conclusion, for *Theonomy*'s Scripture index contains thirteen pages of three column references to the New Testament (TCE, 597-610), of which less than a page of them index Matthew 5.

Contrary to Gordon, then, Matthew 5 is Bahnsen's *locus classicus*, not his *sine qua non*.

Yet theonomists gladly affirm that Bahnsen does emphasize Matthew 5:17-21 as a key passage in establishing the *presumption* of continuity between the Old and New Testament ethical standards. So then, despite his tendency to overstatement, if Gordon could demonstrate that Matthew 5 was woefully mishandled in *Theonomy*, he would have significantly impaired Bahnsen's argument — at least *as it is presented in*

---

[8] Gary Scott Smith, ed., *God and Politics: Four Views on the Reformation of Civil Government* (Phillipsburg, N.J.: Presbyterian and Reformed, 1989), 242.

Theonomy in Christian Ethics. But he would not have destroyed the entire foundation to the theonomic system. To be sure, Bahnsen certainly never backed off of his emphasis on the passage; thus, his exegesis is fair game for criticism (unlike with Gordon's first criticism).

Bahnsen's New Testament "Failure"

Gordon claims Theonomy cannot be established elsewhere in the New Testament. He writes:

> We might go further and suggest that Bahnsen not only found in this passage a convenient defense of his hermeneutic, but that he could have found such a defense only here. The rest of the NT is so entirely silent on the issue, that it was necessary to *Theonomy's* case to establish itself on the basis of this text. Other NT passages provide counter-evidence. (CT, 28).

So then, he initially charged Bahnsen himself with establishing his whole case on Matthew 5. Now he determines to "go further and suggest" that Bahnsen had to do this because he *cannot* establish it elsewhere. This is as mistaken — and obviously so — as the first aspect of the charge.

Again his unsuspecting reader will receive a mistaken impression of Bahnsen's work. And the alert reader should be somewhat taken aback by this charge. Certainly Gordon may disagree with Bahnsen's exegesis and application of the New Testament elsewhere, but that is not the same as the New Testament being "so entirely silent on the issue that it was necessary to *Theonomy's* case to establish itself on the basis of this text" (CT, 28).

After all, was not *Theonomy* well over 500 pages long? And did it not deal at length with New Testament evidence beyond Matthew 5? As noted previously, the Scripture index contains thirteen pages of three column references to the New Testament. A simple, cursory survey of just the chapter titles should alert the reader to Gordon's over statement:

• Ch. 10. "The Alleged Negative Passages" (which analyzes many of the ones Gordon will focus on)

- Ch. 12. "New Testament Substantiation of the Thesis"
- Ch. 19. "The Civil Magistrate in the New Testament"
- App. 1. "An Exegetical Study of Galatians 3:15-18"

Thus, from entire chapters of *Theonomy* we see that Bahnsen had already dealt with Gordon's charge which was presented over fifteen years later. Bahnsen's argument from the wider New Testament is not hidden away in a footnote. Consequently, if an alert reader of Gordon would simply peruse *Theonomy'* s "Table of Contents" his suspicions should be raised.

In Chapter 12, "New Testament Substantiation of the Thesis," Bahnsen's very first sentence reads: "The thesis of this treatise finds confirmation throughout the pages of the New Testament" (TCE, 249). This sort of comment appears time and again in this chapter:

- "The thesis will now be shown to be substantiated as a recurring theme throughout the New Testament. Not only does the Bible teach that the believer should obey God's law, it continually assumes and applies this point" (TCE, 250).
- "We must contend, then, that the New Testament does not turn back the Older Testamental law of God in the slightest; rather, the New Testament substantiates the abiding validity of God's law. The law is not deprived of sanctity in the New Testament; it is intensified" (TCE, 261).
- Bahnsen concludes this chapter: "Based on all the foregoing lines of argument the conclusion is inescapably driven home that the New Testament *consistently* supports the Christian's obligation to God's law as expressed in the stipulations of the Older Testament, both inside and outside the Decalogue. Christ affirmed that He did not come to abrogate the law; the writers of the New Testament follow His example. Throughout the New Testament the validity of God's law is stated, assumed, appealed to, and acted upon." (TCE, 261-62)

Gordon's Faulty Evidence

Not only does Gordon overstate the alleged problem with Bahnsen's dependence on Matthew 5, but in one sentence (admittedly a lengthy complex-compound sentence) he tries to set aside Bahnsen's conclusions by alluding in a rapid-fire manner to several New Testament passages and themes.[9] After stating that "the rest of the NT is so entirely silent on the issue, that it was necessary to Theonomy's case to establish itself on the basis of this text," he declares that "other NT passages provide counter-evidence":

> The sweeping statement (covenantally conditioned) in Heb 7:12 that where the priesthood changes, necessarily the law must change; Paul's general statement that believers are "not under the law"; Paul's discussing the matter of civil obedience without any reference to the Sinai legislation (Romans 13); and the evident suspending of the ceremonial legislation by the Jerusalem Council, Paul, and the author of Hebrews are matters which point compellingly away from Bahnsen's suggestion that the Sinai legislation is abidingly valid in exhaustive detail. (CT, 28)[10]

This global assertion is absolutely incredible in that Bahnsen explains these supposedly counter-evidentiary texts in his original version of *Theonomy*, which is the basis of Gordon's critique! In fact, he provides his understanding of these passages in a chapter titled: "Alleged Negative Passages" (ch. 10). I will consider just briefly Bahnsen's direct references to these passages of Gordon. Since Gordon's compound charge is made in one sentence and is not elaborated upon, I will not engage detailed analysis of each element.

Regarding Hebrews 7:12, Bahnsen writes: "A shallow reading of Hebrews 7:11ff. might seem to contradict this, for it mentions a necessary 'change of law' (NAS). The context makes it clear that this phrase

---

[9] Ironically, his quick spraying out of texts makes one concerned with the very "proof-textual, Bible-thumping" approach that he himself decries (IS, 22).

[10] Gordon footnotes the phrase from Rom. 6:14, "not under the law," with a statement from Moo's study of the law in Paul. Interestingly, Gordon includes in Moo's citation the following: "As we have seen, the Reformers, as most theologians today, use 'law' to mean anything that demands something of us. . . . What is crucial to recognize is that this is *not* the way in which Paul usually uses the term *nomos*." CT 28 n6. How frequently Gordon has to discount the Reformed view!

does not have reference to a new moral code under the New Covenant" (TCE, 224; cp. BTS, 310-11; NOS, 244ff).[11] Gordon's shot-gun approach to these alleged problems leaves the unwary reader in the dark regarding Bahnsen's position.

Regarding Romans 6:14 Bahnsen writes: "Here we come across the most 'sloganized' verse in the dispensationalist's polemic. The antinomian must wrench the statement 'you are not under law, but under grace' out of its textual and theological context in order to justify belief that one is no longer responsible to God's holy law" (TCE, 219). And, of course, he provides a counter, Reformed analysis to this verse, not only in *Theonomy* but also in *No Other Standard* (81ff).[12]

Regarding Romans 13, Bahnsen provides an entire chapter on the matter: "The Civil Magistrate in the New Testament" (TCE, ch. 19). Ironically, this is one of Bahnsen's leading *proof-texts* for Theonomy. Remember the quote already given wherein Bahnsen complains that a critic rebuts Theonomy "*only after* the main supporting texts for the theonomic view (viz., Matthew 5:17-19 and Romans 13:1-7) have been *removed* from consideration" (NOS, 163).[13] Bahnsen also heavily employs this important text in Smith, *God and Politics* (ch. 1) and in Bahnsen and Gentry, *House Divided* (Part I).

Regarding the ceremonial law, Bahnsen has a full chapter discussing the issues: "The Ceremonial (Restorative) Law" (TCE, ch. 9). He deals with this in another chapter in *No Other Standard*: "Categories of Old Testament Law" (NOS, ch. 6). Regarding the Jerusalem Council, *Theonomy* focuses on the matter in "Alleged Negative Passages" (ch. 10).

On and on I could go with examples. I simply do not understand how Gordon could hope to cripple Theonomy by such a sweeping statement. The widespread use of Gordon's article is an illustration of

---

[11] I would also note that I focus in depth on it and several other issues flowing out of the Epistle to the Hebrews in my 1991 defense of Theonomy titled: "Church Sanctions in the Epistle to the Hebrews." Gentry in Gary North, ed., *Theonomy: An Informed Response* (Tyler, Tex.: Institute for Christian Economics, 1991), 164-193.

[12] Interestingly, Reformed critiques of Theonomic Ethics generally do not mention Rom. 6:14, which is a favorite text of dispensationalists. See the Scripture index in Smith, *God and Politics*. The one entry in Barker's, *Theonomy: A Reformed Critique*, refers to the dispensational usage of the text.

[13] I also have a lengthy section of Romans 13 in my 1991 defense in North, *Theonomy: An Informed Response*: "Civil Sanctions in the New Testament" (ch. 6).

the disappointing level of the theonomic opposition. After all, Bahnsen himself states:

> Theonomy teaches that we should presume continuity with the Old Testament law *unless Scripture elsewhere* gives warrant for modification of it or laying it aside. For example, in Acts 10 and Hebrews 9-10 we see the use of ceremonial features of the law altered, and in texts such as Matthew 21:43; Galatians 3:7, 29; Ephesians 1:3-14; and I Peter 1:3-5 we see changes relevant to the identity of God's people today and to the land of Israel's inheritance. When a Christian offers *scriptural* exegesis as the basis for not applying an Old Testament command today, he is behaving like a theonomist. (NOS, 274)

He points out that we "must deal honestly with the absolutistic character of Christ's words in Matthew 5:17-19. Theonomists see Him using a common teaching device of laying down the general principle, but allowing for qualifications and refinements to be brought in later" (NOS, 274n). We must recognize this sort of "problem" in Scripture interpretation. Does not Mark 10:11 appear to forbid *any* and *all* divorce, whereas Matthew 19:9 clearly allows divorce on certain grounds?

Gordon's Matthew 5 Rebuttal

We come now to the heart of Gordon's rebuttal, under the heading: "(2) The Theonomic Understanding of Matt 5:17-21." Here he provides "four specific ways" in which "Bahnsen's treatment of Matt 5:17ff. is deficient." I will provide a running, seriatim response.[14]

Gordon's "Law and the Prophets" Argument [15]

Gordon accuses Bahnsen of washing out "the prophetic half of the 'law and the prophets,' effectively leaving only the 'law' under consideration" (CT 28-29). He argues that the addition of "and the prophets" casts doubt on Bahnsen's teaching that Jesus is focusing on

---

[14] The reader should keep in mind that I will be quoting from a newer printing of *Theonomy in Christian Ethics* with re-set type. My pagination of *Theonomy* will not match with Gordon's. The text is the same, though.

[15] Both Bahnsen and Gordon recognize that "law *and* prophets" is effectively identical to "law *or* prophets" (as per Matt. 5:17). We see this by Gordon's not even mentioning the slight grammatical difference and by Bahnsen's actual notation in that direction (TCE, 52).

ethical issues. Therefore, this foundational passage cannot support the theonomic contention. I would respond with the following:

Gordon's argument is tenuous. He begins by considering the phrase "the law and the prophets." In his very first sentence regarding the phrase he confesses: "'Law and prophets' is a somewhat difficult expression in the Scriptures, and we do not intend to suggest that its precise meaning is self-evident" (CT, 29). Then he follows this with a rather feeble surmise: "it is *very unlikely* that 'law and prophets' can be taken as a reference exclusively, or even primarily, to the '*ethical stipulations* contained in the canon of the entire Older Testament'" (CT, 29, first emphasis mine). Thus, Bahnsen's view is merely "very unlikely."

Gordon's problem is worse than that. His use of the phrase shifts in meaning, causing his argument to change from being frustratingly nebulous to aggravatingly fluid. That is, not only is he unable to demonstrate precisely what it means in Matthew 5, but it becomes a chameleon in his argument, changing meaning according to the different argumentative environments. Early on he states: "If we take the 'law and prophets' together as a reference to the Sinai covenant, or the era in which God's people are governed thereby . . ." (CT, 30). So it can be *either* the "Sinai covenant" *or* the "era" of the Sinai covenant. But later he argues on the basis of it meaning the "revelation" of God "within the Sinai administration": "Had the 'law and prophets' been correctly understood [by Bahnsen] as a reference to the entire revelation within the Sinai administration. . . ." (CT, 31). This supposedly is how the phrase should be "*correctly* understood," but this differs from his previous definition.

Theonomists are unlikely to change their understanding of the text on Gordon's hesitant analysis. After all, he complains that it involves a "difficult expression" (which does not appear difficult to theonomists: the phrase is common and the words are clear), that he cannot "suggest the precise meaning" (his argument boils down to: "I don't know what it means exactly, but I know you are wrong"), and that he can only charge that Bahnsen's position is "unlikely" (how can his admissions of personal difficulty and imprecision convince anyone?). I cannot help but wonder why Gordon would open with such a flimsy observation. Yet, despite his sputtering trumpet emitting an "uncertain sound," he believes he has effectively rallied the troops to charge on against Bahnsen and the theonomic exegesis.

Gordon's argument is confused. Bahnsen is not "washing out" the prophets; he recognizes that the phrase "law and prophets" represents the *whole* Old Testament revelation: "Jesus phrases His teaching in such a way as to embrace the entire canon of the Older Testament" (TCE, 52). In doing this, he is following widespread scholarly practice.[16] In fact, he observes that on his view "'law or prophets' in Matthew 5:17 functions just as 'law and prophets' elsewhere in Scripture" (TCE, 53). But he then points out why Jesus refers to the Old Testament: it is the source of ethical directives for God's people: "While 'law or prophets' broadly denotes the Older Testament Scriptures, Jesus' stress is upon the ethical content, the commandments, of the Older Testament" (TCE, 53).

But Gordon's confusion is even deeper, for his partial, out-of-context citation of Bahnsen misconstrues Bahnsen's actual position. Gordon complains: "But it is very unlikely that 'law and prophets' can be taken as a reference exclusively, or even primarily, to the '*ethical stipulations* contained in the canon of the entire Older Testament'" (CT, 29). Bahnsen, however, does *not* argue that "law and prophets" is a reference "exclusively, or even primarily" to the "ethical stipulations" of Scripture. Rather he states very clearly: "Being placed next to τόν νόμον in Matthew 5:17, προφήτας" most likely indicates the contents of those books other than the Pentateuch (cf. Matt. 7:12; 22:40). *Jesus phrases His teaching in such a way as to embrace the entire canon of the Older Testament,* none of the existing Scriptures are abrogated by His advent or redemptive work" (TCE, 52, emphasis mine).

Later Bahnsen shows the Lord's *point* in speaking of the Old Testament revelation: "There is reason to hold that the phrase 'law or prophets' is best taken as focusing on the ethical stipulations contained in the canon of the entire Older Testament" (TCE, 53). Thus, Bahnsen recognizes *grammatically* that the phrase refers to the whole Old Testament; but then he points out *contextually* Jesus is *highlighting* the ethical directives of the Old Testament revelation.

---

[16] For instance, Leon Morris writes: "The combination is a way of referring to the whole of Old Testament Scripture (cf. 7:12; 22:40)." *The Gospel According to Matthew* (Pillar) (Grand Rapids: Eerdmans, 1992), 107. Carson concurs: "For that is what 'Law or the Prophets' here means: the Scriptures." D. A. Carson "Matthew," in Frank E. Gaebelein, ed., *The Expositor's Bible Commentary*, 12 vols. (Grand Rapids: Zondervan, 1984), 8:142.

Gordon's argument is only one of several plausible interpretations. Gordon focuses on the phrase "law and prophets" which is common enough in the New Testament (Matt. 5:17; 7:12; 11:13; 22:40; Luke 16:16; Rom. 3:21) and in Jewish literature (e.g., 2 Macc. 15:9; 4 Macc. 18:10). And despite denying Bahnsen's approach to this familiar phrase, Gordon himself admits (as do virtually all commentators) that it can legitimately be interpreted in several ways, three of which he mentions: "There are places where it could be a reference to the OT Scriptures"; "The expression could refer to an entire revelatory era"; "The expression might even be a reference to the written constitutional document of the Sinai covenant" (CT, 29).

Gordon's argument allows Bahnsen's emphasis. Oddly, Gordon admits there are places "where the expression appears to focus on the *ethical requirements* of that [Sinaitic] administration" (CT, 29, emphasis mine). This further weakens his tenuous rebuttal and makes one wonder why he chose to attack Bahnsen at this point while providing Bahnsen this ammunition. Note though, that Bahnsen is not imposing the Sinai "administration" upon the New Covenant people. Rather, he is continuing the "ethical requirements" which are also found in the Sinai "administration." See further argumentation below regarding the distinction we must make between temporal administration and ethical obligation.

Gordon's argument discounts the position of many commentators. The *Word Biblical Commentary*, for instance, largely agrees with Bahnsen's ethical focus in Matthew 5:17-21:

> This passage is placed here for a very important reason. The *ethical teaching* of Jesus that follows in this sermon, as well as later in the Gospel, has such a radical character and goes so much against what was the commonly accepted understanding of the *commands of the Torah* that it is necessary at the outset to indicate Jesus' full and unswerving loyalty to the law. Only when this is set before the listeners or readers will they be in a position to understand correctly Jesus' teaching about the *righteousness* of the kingdom.[17]

---

[17] Donald A. Hagner, *Matthew 1-13* (Word Biblical Commentary) (Dallas: Word, 1993), 103. Emphasis mine.

The commentary goes on to observe that "prophets" is added "in the first instance [to] refer to the further stipulation of the *requirements of righteousness*, i.e., of the will of God."[18]

- Hendrikson concurs when he introduces Matthew 5:17ff: "The high standard of life demanded by the King is now set forth. First we are shown that *This Righteousness Is in Full Accord with the Moral Principles Enunciated in the Old Testament*."[19]
- Keener provides a compatible heading for this section in his commentary: "Disciples Must *Obey* God's Law (5:17-20)."[20]
- France notes that Matthew 5:17-20 "is a general statement of Jesus' attitude to the Old Testament, *especially . . . in its legal provisions*, designed to introduce the detailed examples of Jesus' *ethical* teaching in relation to the Old Testament law in vv. 21-48.[21]

Gordon's argument is contra-contextual. Writing in *Theonomy* long before Gordon's critique, Bahnsen had already provided ample contextual argumentation which demonstrated the phrase's function in emphasizing ethical considerations. Not only is Bahnsen's argument much fuller than Gordon's rather weak and seriously truncated counter-interpretation (TCE, 51-55), but Gordon fails even to cite and rebut Bahnsen's argument.

In *Theonomy* Bahnsen argues: "The entire passage is concerned primarily with Christ's *doctrine*, not His life. . . . The concern of Matthew 5:17 is Christ's doctrine as it bears upon theonomy (God's law). While 'law or prophets' broadly denotes the Older Testament Scriptures, Jesus' stress is upon the ethical content, the commandments, of the Older Testament" (TCE, 53). Consider the wealth of contextual evidence available which supports the *ethical* function of this phrase:

---

[18] Hagner, *Matthew 1-13*, 105. Emphasis mine.

[19] William Hendrikson, *The Gospel of Matthew* (Grand Rapids: Baker, 1973), 287.

[20] Craig S. Keener, *A Commentary on the Gospel of Matthew* (Grand Rapids: Eerdmans, 1999), 175. Emphasis mine.

[21] R. T. France, *The Gospel According to Matthew* (Tyndale New Testament Commentary) (Grand Rapids: Eerdmans, 1987), 113. Emphasis mine.

1. Christ opens the Sermon on the Mount with the Beatitudes, which encourage *righteous* conduct despite its difficulty and even in the face of opposition (Matt. 5:1-12). Note particularly verses 6 and 10: "Blessed are those who hunger and thirst for *righteousness*, for they shall be satisfied." "Blessed are those who have been persecuted for the sake of *righteousness*, for theirs is the kingdom of heaven." How apropos that Jesus would shortly thereafter mention "the law and the prophets" with an ethical focus.

2. The Beatitudes are immediately followed by a call to be the "salt" and "light" of the world. That is, the Lord calls his disciples to show by their "good works" the glory of the Father (Matt. 5:13-16). "Good works" certainly are an ethical concern.

3. After mentioning "the law or the prophets," he reiterates his concern. But this time he speaks simply of "the law" without "the prophets": "Do not think that I came to abolish *the Law or the Prophets*; I did not come to abolish, but to fulfill. For truly I say to you, until heaven and earth pass away, not the smallest letter or stroke shall pass away from *the Law*, until all is accomplished" (Matt. 5:17-18). In fact, in the context he never mentions or alludes to anything formally "prophetic." He clearly is emphasizing the moral component of the Old Testament revelation.

4. Upon declaring that he has not come to "destroy the law or the prophets," he immediately warns his disciples against annulling one of the "least of the commandments" and urging their teaching them to others and their personally keeping them themselves (Matt. 5:19). Commands to teach-and-keep are ethical directives, not prophetic predictions. This careful concern for God's righteous law appears often in Matthew's gospel (e.g., Matt. 15:6; 22:34-40; 23:2-3, 23).

5. He then calls his disciples to vigorous ethical conduct: "Unless your righteousness surpasses that of the scribes and Pharisees, you shall not enter the kingdom of heaven" (Matt. 5:20). Much of his ministry was spent countering the Pharisees and their mis-application of the ethical requirements of the law. For example, he teaches: "The scribes and the Pharisees have seated themselves in the chair of Moses; therefore all that they tell you, do and observe, but do not do according to their deeds; for they say things, and do not do them" (Matt. 23:2-3).

6. Immediately upon declaring Matthew 5:17-20, he counters the tradition of the elders regarding the ethical requirements of the law. He even expressly mentions several of the Ten Commandments particularly (Matt. 5:21-47). Nothing in this section points to prophetic fulfillment; all points to ethical obligation.

7. He concludes this section of the Sermon by calling his followers to a high ethical ideal: "Therefore you are to be perfect, as your heavenly Father is perfect" (Matt. 5:48). As we know, God is holy, just, and good, and his law serves as a transcript of his character so that it, too, is "holy, just, and good" (Rom. 7:12).

8. The very next mention of "the law and the prophets" as an ethical summation occurs later in the same Sermon: "Therefore, however you want people to treat you, so treat them, for this is the Law and the Prophets" (Matt. 7:12). This clearly speaks of ethical conduct: the Golden Rule involves how we treat people. Several commentators note that Matthew 5:17 forms an *inclusio* with Matthew 7:12. For instance: "Mention of 'the law and the prophets' takes the reader back to 5.17 and thereby establishes an *inclusio* within which Matthew has treated of the Torah (5:17-48)."[22]

---

[22] W. D. Davies and Dale C. Allison, Jr., *The Gospel According to Saint Matthew* (ICC) (Edinburgh: T & T Clark, 1988),1:685. Cp. 484. See also: Hagner, *Matthew 1-13*, 105, 176; Keener, *A Commentary on the Gospel of Matthew*, 249. Carson, "Matthew," 144.

9. The leading concern in the whole Sermon on the Mount (wherein Matt. 5:17-21 is set) is not prophecy fulfillment, but ethical obligation, kingdom righteousness. Allison and Davies note of Matthew 7:12: "Although the so-called 'golden rule' sums up in brief the *right conduct* towards others and therefore appropriately closes 6.19-7.11, a section on social behaviour, 7.12 is not simply the conclusion of 6.19-7.11 (or of 7.1-11). Rather does it bring to a climax the entire central core of the sermon on the mount, 5.17-7.11)."[23] Morris concurs: The "therefore" opening Matthew 7:12 "probably refers to the whole of the preceding sermon, not simply to the immediately foregoing."[24] As does Hendriksen: "Therefore" serves to "link the present passage with the entire large division introduced by 5:17"[25] Ridderbos observes: "In these sayings the religious and ethical demands are worked out to a consequence and depth which not only explain the remarkable impression which the Sermon must directly have created on its first hearers, but which also explain why subsequent hearers speak of the *problem* of the Sermon on the Mount, the problem of its purpose and purport as an ethical commandment, and the problem of its practicality."[26] Consider a few obvious samples from the Sermon:

• "For I say to you, that unless your *righteousness surpasses* that of the scribes and Pharisees, you shall not enter the kingdom of heaven" (Matt. 5:20).
• "Beware of practicing your *righteousness* before men to be noticed by them; otherwise you have no reward with your Father who is in heaven" (Matt. 6:1).
• "The lamp of the body is the eye; if therefore your eye is clear, your whole body will be full of light. But if your eye is *bad*, your whole body will be full of darkness. If therefore the

---

[23] Davies and Allison, *Matthew*, 1:685.
[24] Morris, *Matthew*, 172.
[25] Hendriksen, *Matthew*, 365.
[26] Herman N. Ridderbos, *When the Time Had Fully Come* (Grand Rapids: Eerdmans, 1957), 29.

light that is in you is darkness, how great is the darkness!" (Matt. 6:22-23).

• "Seek first His kingdom and His *righteousness*, and all these things shall be added to you" (Matt. 6:33).

• "Therefore, however you want people to treat you, *so treat them*, for this is the Law and the Prophets" (Matt. 7:12).

• "Not everyone who says to Me, 'Lord, Lord,' will enter the kingdom of heaven; but *he who does the will of My Father* who is in heaven" (Matt. 7:21).

• "Therefore everyone who hears these words of Mine, and *acts upon them*, may be compared to a wise man, who built his house upon the rock" (Matt. 7:24).

10. Besides all of this, it would be incredible to suppose that someone would claim Jesus was teaching that he had come to abolish the *prophecies* about the Messiah! After all, he is here warning his hearers against misconstruing his teaching: "*Do not think* that I came to abolish the Law or the Prophets; I did not come to abolish, but to fulfill" (Matt. 5:17). How could anything he taught be understood as denying his own Messiahship?

Gordon's argument is exaggerated. As Gordon concludes his rebuttal of Bahnsen's handling of "law and prophets," he shifts his Klinean argument into high gear:

Even in the two texts where the expression appears to focus on the ethical requirements of that administration, it is both the law and the prophetic administration of that law which are referred to.

The significance of this observation is profound in its consequences for exegesis. Biblically, 'law and prophets' are conjoined. They are together in their function, and the prophets are in fact executors of the Sinai covenant. Their anticipation of Messiah's arrival is part of their declaration of judgment on Israel for her unfaithfulness to the covenant, because only the Messiah will be able to deliver from the curses of the

Sinai administration. From a biblical perspective, if the Sinai legislation remains, then the prophetic office of preparing for the Messiah's arrival remains also. (CT, 29)

Gordon's observations regarding the meaning of the coming of Christ for Israel are surely on target — as a general redemptive-historical reality. Nevertheless, his covenantal analysis in this debate is mistaken and should be rejected for several reasons.

First, Gordon's position is basically that of Kline's peculiar redemptive-historical methodology. In Appendix 4 of the original edition of *Theonomy* itself Bahnsen ably dismantles Kline's "two canon" theology (which is clearly the backdrop of Gordon's argument).[27] Kline's approach not only differs from most evangelical theologians, but even most *covenant* theologians. Bahnsen points out that covenant theologians generally emphasize the continuity of the covenants, rather than their discontinuity (as does Kline). Bahnsen complains that Kline's argument "is *not* accompanied with any *scriptural* backing or exegesis" (TCE, 558): it is based on pure theological assertion rooted in his distinctive covenant model.

As noted previously, Gordon himself has to rebut the Westminster Confession of Faith over related issues. And doing so he shows the alignment of Theonomy with historic Reformed theology: "Theonomists are not the first to abstract legislation from the Sinai covenant. The Westminster Assembly appears to have done it beforehand" (CT, 40). Furthermore, of the theonomic movement he later notes: "It is also an intellectual movement, an extension (albeit extreme) of ideas already germinal in some dimensions of the Reformed tradition" (CT, 43).

Bahnsen's approach to the phrase "law and prophets" is the widely-held view of various evangelical schools of thought, as I pointed out above when citing France, Keener, Hendrikson, and Hagner. Any mainstream view should not be the one under suspicion; the unique perspective should arouse questions.

---

[27] Kline teaches "that the Old Testament is not the canon of the Christian church."Meredith G. Kline, *The Structure of Biblical Authority* (Grand Rapids: Eerdmans, 1972), 109. Cited in TCE, 556.

Second, the context of the phrase under consideration ("law and prophets") fails to confirm Gordon's position. Gordon holds that

> the significance of this observation is profound in its consequences for exegesis. Biblically, "law and prophets" are conjoined. They are together in their function, and the prophets are in fact executors of the Sinai covenant. Their anticipation of Messiah's arrival is part of their declaration of judgment on Israel for her unfaithfulness to the covenant, because only the Messiah will be able to deliver from the curses of the Sinai administration. (CT, 29)

Thus, Gordon sees Christ's use of "law and prophets" in this context as an indicator of a "declaration of judgment on Israel for her unfaithfulness."

Questions that should arise when considering Gordon's theological musings are: Is that what *Christ* was teaching *in the Sermon on the Mount* — just after the Beatitudes? How can this "declaration of judgment on Israel" be read into Jesus' use of the phrase "law and prophets" here? Is that not a lot of weight for this common phrase to bear — especially since it does not do so elsewhere (Gordon does not mention this interpretation as one of the three uses of the phrase)? Where are "the curses of the Sinai administration" touched on in the Sermon (CT, 29)?

Again, it is certainly true that in many contexts Christ openly and vigorously declares God's coming judgment upon Israel (e.g., Matt. 8:11-12; 10:1-23; 11:20–24; 23:34-24:34). But that is not *all* that he preaches; nor does it appear to be what he teaches *here*.

Nothing in Matthew 5 suggests Jesus is teaching his hearers about a change of covenantal administration. We see no denigration of ceremonial pride and confidence here, as we do in Isaiah's denunciation of Israel before her temple is destroyed (Isa. 1). The whole context exudes a strongly ethical concern regarding righteous living. He anticipates objections to his re-interpreting the law from the scribes and Pharisees and braces his audience for those objections: "Do not begin to think [significance of the aorist ingressive] I have come to destroy the Law or the Prophets" (Matt. 5:17). Besides, on Gordon's view, any Pharisaic complaint about his coming in order to effect a change in the Mosaic system would be legitimate and would not be denied by Christ.

Third, what is more, the very teaching of the passage in question contradicts Gordon. He claims on the basis of his theological method that "from a biblical perspective, if the Sinai legislation remains, then the prophetic office of preparing for the Messiah's arrival remains also" (CT, 29). Which means: While the Mosaic *law* is in effect the Old Testament *administration* remains operative, the prophetic office is in gear, and revelation is not final. Neither Gordon and the Klineans nor Bahnsen and the theonomists hold that the revelatory prophetic office and the Old Testament administration are still functioning. Consequently, if this reasoning were correct, Theonomy would indeed be contrary to the New Covenant.

Not only is his whole theology read into the Matthew 5:17-20 on a very tenuous basis, but his observation contradicts the very terms of the Lord's statement. Verses 19-20 read:

> Whoever then annuls one of the least of these commandments, and so teaches others, shall be called least in the kingdom of heaven; but whoever keeps and teaches them, he shall be called great in the kingdom of heaven. For I say to you, that unless your righteousness surpasses that of the scribes and Pharisees, you shall not enter the kingdom of heaven.[28]

We must note that the "kingdom of heaven" is that redemptive-historical reality resulting *because of* the coming of Christ (Matt. 3:2; 4:17, 23; Matt. 12:28), the one into which men then began "forcing their way" (Matt. 11:11-12) despite the resistance of the old covenant-oriented scribes and Pharisees (Matt. 23:13). After the coming of Christ the kingdom of heaven slowly unfolds in history (Matt. 13:31-33) until the end (Matt. 13:36-43). It is characterized in history by a now/not yet reality that shows it future orientation even in the Sermon on the Mount

---

[28] Another feature of the passage undermining Gordon's view is the Lord's declaring that the law stands "until heaven and earth pass away" (v. 18). Since Gordon elaborates on this phrase later in his argument (CT, 31-33), I will withhold comment until the proper place. But the argument I provide there should be brought to bear here, as well.

(cf. Matt. 6:10).[29] It is not a function of the old order, but of the new.

While dealing with Matthew 3:2 Leon Morris explains the Matthean concept of the kingdom of heaven: "The kingdom is closely connected with the person of Jesus, and this is what is in mind with John [Baptist's] use of the expression. He is pointing to the truth that Jesus will shortly appear, and with him the kingdom."[30] Alexander called the kingdom of heaven "the new dispensation or the reign of the Messiah."[31] Ridderbos points out its eschatological character and its focus on the coming of Christ.[32] He notes that the Sermon on the Mount is especially concerned with it: "It is clear from this that the Sermon on the Mount is only to be understood when there is a full recognition of the framework in which it appears, namely, the gospel of the Kingdom of God and of His mighty deed in His Son Jesus Christ."[33]

Van Gemeren puts it even more forcefully (even though he is not a theonomist[34]):

> Jesus did not come to free people from God's eternal law (5:17-20), binding for both Jews and Gentiles. . . . Childs has correctly stated, "The law of Moses is not a temporary measure that has now been superseded in the kingdom of heaven, but rather represents the eternally valid will of God."[35]

Consequently, Gordon's analysis is mistaken. Jesus urges keeping and promoting the details of "My law" (Jer. 31:33) as evidence of one's standing in this *New Covenant sphere of existence*: "whoever keeps and teaches them, he shall be called great in the kingdom of heaven" (Matt. 5:19). Murray notes of this passage that "our relation to the kingdom

---

[29] See Gentry in Kenneth L. Gentry, Jr., ed., *Thine Is the Kingdom: Studies in the Postmillennial Hope* (Vallecito, Calif.: Chalcedon, 2003), ch. 5.

[30] Morris, *Matthew*, 53.

[31] Joseph Addison Alexander, *The Gospel According to Matthew Explained* (Lynchburg, Vir.: James Family, rep. n.d., [1861]), 130.

[32] Ridderbos, *When the Time Had Fully Come*, 14ff.

[33] Ridderbos, *When the Time Had Fully Come*, 28.

[34] See: chapters by Willem A. Van Gemeren in Strickland, ed., *The Law, the Gospel, and the Modern Christian.*.

[35] Willem Van Gemeren, *The Progress of Redemption: The Story of Salvation from Creation to the New Jerusalem* (Grand Rapids: Zondervan, 1988), 330.

of heaven is defined in terms of our relation to the law." Regarding the matter of living in the kingdom (v. 19) and being excluded from the kingdom (v. 20), "the law is the norm in both cases, in the former case the criterion by which our relative position in the kingdom of God is determined, in the latter case the criterion by which we are excluded entirely from the kingdom. Hence there can be no escape from the conclusion that the law is directly relevant to membership in and station within the kingdom of God."[36]

Hendrikson concurs: "Although all is of grace and nothing whatever is *earned* by the citizen of the kingdom, yet his rank or position in that kingdom will depend on and be commensurate with his respect for God's holy law."[37] He notes regarding the "kingdom" that "Kingdom of God and church when used in this sense are nearly equivalent. This is the meaning in Matt. 16:18-1. '. . . and upon this rock will I build my church. . . . I will give unto you the keys of the kingdom of heaven.'"[38] William Loader writes: "The point of this instruction for Matthew is that he wants his community to know that it is still in force and will be until eternity. Hence 5:19 threatens severe demotion in the kingdom of God for any who teach modification of the least command."[39] Most commentators agree.[40] The Lord's statement regarding the "law and prophets" does *not* require that "from a biblical perspective, if the Sinai legislation remains, then the prophetic office of preparing for the Messiah's arrival remains also" (CT, 29).

---

[36] John Murray, *Principles of Conduct* (Grand Rapids: Eerdmans, 1957), 152, 153.

[37] Hendrikson, *Matthew*, 292.

[38] Hendrikson, *Matthew*, 250.

[39] William Loader, *Jesus' Attitude towards the Law: a Study of the Gospels* (Grand Rapids: Eerdmans, 1997), 169.

[40] See for example: Morris, *Matthew*, 110. John Calvin, *Harmony of the Gospels of Matthew, Mark, and Luke*, David W. Torrance, ed., (Grand Rapids: Eerdmans, 1972), 1:178. D. A. Carson, "Matthew," in *The Expositor's Bible Commentary*, 8:101. William Barclay, *The Gospel of Matthew* (DSBS) (2d. ed.: Philadelphia: Westminster, 1975), 126, 131. Robert H. Mounce, *Matthew* (NIBC) (Peabody, MA: 1991), 44. Heinrich August Meyer, *Critical and Exegetical Handbook to the Gospel of Matthew*, tran. by Peter Christie (Winona Lake, Ind.: Alpha, rep. 1883), 122-23. John A. Broadus, *Commentary on Matthew* (Grand Rapids: Kregel, rep. n.d., 1886), 100. Alexander, *Matthew*, [1861]), 125, 129. David Hill, *The Gospel of Matthew* (The New Century Bible Commentary) (Grand Rapids: Eerdmans, 1972), 118. Keener, *Matthew*, 177.

Fourth, contrary to Gordon's Klinean conception of covenantal canon and the removal of the Mosaic law as our ethical standard, Bahnsen demonstrates that even the nations around Israel were obligated to the law of God and were subject to prophetic denunciations based on that law. His chapter 18 is titled: "The Civil Magistrate in Nations Surrounding Israel" (TCE, ch. 18). In this chapter he specifically anticipates the Klinean objection:

> It might be supposed that because God was dealing with Israel in a covenant context of blessing (i.e., redeeming and intending to redeem these chosen people) and did not set His electing love upon all the other nations (cf. Amos 3:2), the standard of ethical obligation and moral uprightness differed between Israel and the nations. Should this be the case, then general discontinuity between the law governing Israel and the law governing her neighbors might extend even to matters of social morality and the magistrate's duty to promote justice. In that supposed case there would be a divergence of ethical standard at the civic level, and this could have bearing upon the answer to the question "ought the magistrate today (i.e., non-Israeli rulers) obey the law of God as revealed in the Older Testament?" (TCE, 331)

As usual, Gordon neither mentions nor interacts with Bahnsen's argument, leaving his unwary reader to imagine that Theonomy has no response to the objection. And this despite the fact that Bahnsen's original edition of *Theonomy* dealt with the alleged problem. In fact, he even seems unaware of Bahnsen's interaction with the Klinean argument particularly. Yet Bahnsen discusses the matter for over twenty pages in this chapter, in addition to numerous other places scattered throughout *Theonomy*, including an Appendix on Kline. Bahnsen also specifically deals with this issue in *No Other Standard* in chapter 7: "Israel's Theocratic Uniqueness." He carefully demonstrates that the Bible applies God's law — excluding the ceremonial features — to the peoples and nations outside of Israel.

Theonomists note that only the *ceremonial, ritual* directives in the law are covenantally-limited, as elements distinguishing Israel from the nations as a peculiar people. But the moral directives in the law of God (including the judicial features that enforce the moral law in the civil sphere) are universal in obligation. This is apparent from both the Old and New Testaments.

The Old Testament prophets never rebuke the nations around Israel for failing to be circumcised or eating pork or not keeping any of the ceremonial features of the law.[41] Yet those nations are reproached for various moral failures, such as in the cases of Sodom (Gen. 13:13; 18:20) regarding homosexual sins (Gen. 19:4ff; Lev. 18:22; 20:13; 2 Peter 2:6-8),[42] the Canaanite nations who fall under the same moral prohibitions as Israel (Lev. 18:24-28), the Chaldeans (Hab. 2:12; cp. Mic. 3:10), and Babylonia (Hab. 1:4; cp. Mic. 3:1-12).

Israel herself is obligated to distinguish moral obligations from ceremonial duties (1 Sam. 15:22; Psa. 51:14-17; Prov. 21:3; Hos. 6:6). For instance, the food laws are specifically set forth as a distinguishing feature of Israel's holiness (Lev. 20:22-26; Deut 14:1-21; Acts 10:9-43), whereas laws against murder, rape, and theft are not. Simply put, the law of God has *both* covenantally distinctive *and* generally common features.

In the later, post-resurrection New Testament the moral directives of the law are promoted among the Gentiles and in the New Covenant context, while the ceremonial elements alone are mentioned as distinguishing Jew and Gentile. We could note especially the Jerusalem Council in Acts 15 (TCE, 222-224), the "wall of separation" in Ephesians 2:14-15 (NOS, 103), the statement in 1 Corinthians 7:19 (TCE, 256), and

---

[41] Bahnsen will not allow escape from this problem by complaining of our difficulty in distinguishing ceremonial and moral laws in certain places: "to complain that the moral/ceremonial distinction makes things difficult for a theologian is only saying what could be said of many perfectly acceptable theological concepts (e.g., the Trinity, the hypostatic union, communication of attributes, the different elements and order of redemption). The distinction was not invented by theonomists; the warrant and necessity of drawing this distinction is granted by many authors who are not theonomists. Some laws are more difficult to handle than others, of course, because they incorporate both moral and ceremonial elements, but all responsible interpreters of the Biblical text must wrestle with such tough examples"(NOS, 96).

[42] These condemnations even appear in history before the Sinaitic covenant and its objective revelation through Moses. Remember: the moral law of God in Scripture is the natural law known to men as images of God.

more. In fact the ceremonial laws served to "tutor" men to Christ by teaching of redemption (Gal. 3:23-24; cp. 1 Cor. 9:20-21).[43] The New Testament declares that the law is "holy, just, and good" (Rom. 7:12; cp. Rom. 3:31; 8:4; 13:3-10; 1Tim. 1:8-11) and urges specific moral laws (2 Cor. 6:14; 9:9; 1 Tim. 5:18) but never ceremonial laws (Gal. 2:3; 5:2; Acts 15:1, 9-10).

Consequently, since the eschatological kingdom of heaven dawns in Christ, his words underscore the continuing relevance of the law of God in this final era of redemptive history. Gordon's objection is an anti-contextual theological objection, not an exegetical observation.

Gordon's Πληρῶσαι Argument

Gordon's second charge against Bahnsen's Matthew 5 exegesis relates to the verb πληρῶσαι. He sees the word as filling out his own previous objection to Bahnsen, which was based on the phrase "the law and prophets":

> The most daring dimension of Bahnsen's interpretation of Matt 5:17ff. is his argument that πληρῶσαι should be interpreted to mean 'ratify' rather than "fulfill." This interpretation is consistent with his interpreting the prophets out of the "law and the prophets," yet it is erroneous nonetheless. (CT, 29)[44]

I will take up his argument point for point, beginning with this comment and adding others as I progress.

Gordon's confession regarding Bahnsen's exegetical method. Unlike some other critics of Theonomy, Gordon recognizes that Bahnsen's argument "follows sound lexicographical considerations" (CT, 29). He notes further that:

---

[43] See my Appendix for a fuller discussion of 1 Cor. 9:20-21 in this regard. See also NOS, ch. 6: "Categories of Old Testament Law."

[44] Many critics are quick to attack Bahnsen's interpreting πληρῶσαι as meaning to "confirm, ratify." However, no less as reputable an exegete as D. A. Carson notes: "Not a few writers, especially Jewish scholars take the verb to reflect the Aramaic verb *Qum* ('establish,' 'validate,' or 'confirm' the law). Jesus did not come to abolish the law but to confirm it and establish it (e.g., Dalmon, pp. 56-58; Daube, *New Testament*, pp. 60f.; Schlatter, pp. 153f.; and esp. Sigal 'Halakah,' pp. 23ff.)." Carson, "Matthew," in *The Expositor's Bible Commentary*, 8:142.

Bahnsen is correct in attempting to interpret πληρῶσαι as functioning antithetically in this passage to catalase. This is not only required by the general context, but by the fact that 'law and prophets' is the direct object of each of the two verbs in question. He then argues that it would not make sense to speak of 'fulfilling' the law, but that it would make sense to speak of 'ratifying' the law (CT, 29).

He even goes so far as to admit: Bahnsen "is certainly right that this is plausible (CT, 29).

These are happy admissions much appreciated in the debate, since Bahnsen gives such extended, in-depth analysis of the passage. Of course, Gordon is convinced that Bahnsen's argument, though methodologically sound and interpretively plausible, "reaches erroneous conclusions, because some of the alternatives are not considered" (CT, 29). So we must continue.

Gordon's misinterpretation of Bahnsen's exegetical argument

Gordon makes a serious gaffe when he complains of Bahnsen that "he misunderstands the use of πληρόω in the passage to mean 'ratify' rather than 'fulfill'" (CT, 29). This is simply not true. Rather, Bahnsen notes that we have to understand the meaning of "fulfill" in this setting. What does Jesus *mean* by saying he came to "fulfill" the "law and the prophets"? This is especially important to determine since the idea of "fulfilling" the law is an uncommon notion. Had the statement declared that he had come to fulfill the prophecies of the Old Testament, there would be little need to dig into the meaning of "fulfill" since this would be a common use of the verb.[45]

In response to this common objection, Bahnsen noted elsewhere against a critic: "he focuses upon my translation of the word *plaroo* as 'to confirm in full measure.' However, Lightner grants that the word can and does mean this sometimes. He misconstrues the theonomic view as choosing this translation instead of 'to fulfill.' In fact, the question is rather which of the many senses of 'fulfill' is more precisely intended in this text?" (NOS, 275).

---

[45] See examples from Matthew: Matt. 1:22; 2:15, 17, 23; 4:14; 8:17; 12:17; 13:14, 35; 21:4; 26:54; 27:9.

To Fowler (the apparent source of Gordon's complaint, CT 28), he responded:

> Note the available senses of the Greek term and choose that translation which is the best functional equivalent (indicated by the syntactical use of the term and the English counterparts). The distinction between common words for 'confirm' and 'fulfill' which Fowler points to in Hebrew and Greek is utterly irrelevant, for this does nothing to preclude the use of one word as a precising definition of the other in suitable contexts. In every language there is more than one way to express the same thing, and any linguist knows that the combinations and distributions of senses for verbal tokens do not have a one-for-one correspondence or parallel between different languages. (NOS, 277-78)

Thus, Bahnsen simply does not choose *ratify* "rather than" *fulfill*. He argues that the multi-faceted word "fulfill" is used *in the sense of* "ratify." As Wenham expresses it: "Jesus' "thought is that of 'fulfilling and so establishing.'"[46]

Gordon's overstatement of Bahnsen's exegetical argument

The reader should be somewhat surprised with Gordon's rhetorical flourish here. He marvels at the "most daring dimension of Bahnsen's interpretation," but then immediately notes that this very argument by Bahnsen follows "sound lexicographical considerations" and that Bahnsen "is certainly right that this is plausible" (CT, 29). Why is a sound lexicography and plausible interpretation a "most daring" theological act? It seems that a "most daring" interpretation would be one that did *not* follow sound lexicography and was *not* "plausible."

In fact, in *Theonomy* itself Bahnsen presented a wealth of documentary evidence from a wide-range of exegetical scholars for declaring that πληρῶσαι can mean "confirm" (TCE, 70-74). He particularly cites Septuagintal evidence, the Apocrypha, and several New Testament passages, while providing the several scholarly witnesses who

---

[46] David Wenham, "Jesus and the Law: An Exegesis on Matthew 5:17-20," *Themelios* (April, 1979): 93. Cited in Bahnsen, NOS, 319.

interpret the verse as signifying Jesus' coming to "to confirm, ratify, or establish" the law: John Calvin, Hans Windisch, George Campbell, David Brown, Charles Spurgeon, Herman Ridderbos, W. C. Allen, and John Murray. Bahnsen's interpretation of the verb is *not* "daring," for "such a translation should not be regarded as novel in any way; it has well-established roots in the history of translation and commentary" (TCE, 73).

And we could add other witnesses, as well. For instance, William Loader's important, detailed, scholarly work *Jesus' Attitude towards the Law* states of Matthew 5:17: "The orientation of the statement is clear: it is in the opposite direction of abrogation; it is confirming and up-holding the validity of the Law and the Prophets."[47] He adds: "The opening section inevitably raised the question: how does God's author-ity in Jesus relate to God's authority in the Law and the Prophets. Mat-thew seems bent on saying: no conflict. In all it is God's authority; yet, given salvation history, Jesus brings something new. The new is not abrogation of the old. Matthew presents it rather as a matter of Jesus upholding the integrity of the Law and Prophets by giving them au-thoritative interpretation."[48]

Keener agrees: "*First, Jesus' language clearly affirms his commitment to the law of Moses.* When Jesus says that he came not to 'abolish' the law and prophets but to 'fulfill,' he uses terms that would have conveyed his faithfulness to the Scriptures. To 'fulfill' God's law was to 'confirm' it by obedience and demonstrating that one's teaching accorded with it."[49]

David Hill: "The meaning of *plerosai* is variously interpreted — 'confirm', 'validate', 'bring to actuality by doing', 'set forth in its true meaning', and therefore 'complete'. The interpretation must be guided by the context (especially verses 21-48), and by Matthew's use of the verb elsewhere in the Gospel, and these factors suggest that it be un-derstood as 'establish'."[50]

Herman Ridderbos concurs: "There can thus be no doubt what-ever that the category of the law has not been abrogated with Christ's advents, but rather has been maintained and interpreted in its radical sense ('fulfilled'; Matt. 5:17)."

[47] Loader, *Jesus' Attitude towards the Law*, 168
[48] Loader, *Jesus' Attitude towards the Law*, 168.
[49] Keener, *Matthew*, 177.
[50] Hill, *Matthew*, 117.

In a direct rebuttal to Bahnsen, Wayne Strickland admits: "It is, of course, lexically possible to adopt the meaning 'to confirm' for *plerosai*, since it takes this nuance in a few passages of the LXX and Apocrypha as well as three New Testament passages (Rom. 15:19; 2 Cor. 10:6; James 2:23)."[51]

Quite interestingly, Samuel Bolton (who is an important resource for Gordon, CT, 34-35) argues much like Bahnsen does: Speaking of Matthew 5:17-18, Bolton said, "this seems to be very full and very plain for the continuance of and obligation to the law," and he went on to buttress his observation by appeal to Romans 3:31; 7:12, 22, 25; James 28; and 1 John 2:4; 3:4. He continues:

> Therefore, since Christ, who is the best expounder of the law, so largely strengthens and confirms the law (witness the Sermon on the Mount, and also Mark 10: 19); since faith does not supplant, but strengthens the law; since the apostle so often presses and urges the duties commanded in the law of God in his mind, and that he was under the law of Christ (1 Cor. 9:21); I may rightly conclude that the law, for the substance of it, still remains a rule of life to the people of God. . . . If Christ and His apostles commanded the same things which the law required, and forbade and condemned the same things which the law forbade and condemned, then they did not abrogate it but strengthened and confirmed it. And this is what they did: see Matt. 5:19. . . . But he that breaks the law does sin, as says the apostle: 'Sin is the transgression of the law' (1 John 3:4). and 'Where no law is there is no transgression' (Rem. 4:15). Therefore Christians are bound, if they would avoid sin, to obey the law.[52]

Bahnsen is not out on a limb. He is not at all being "daring" in this. In fact, Reformed Old Testament scholar Willem Van Gemeren states the matter in a way quite acceptable to Bahnsen:

---

[51] Strickland, *The Law, the Gospel, and the Modern Christian*, 257.

[52] This Bolton reference is cited in Bahnsen, BTS, 173. It is taken from Samuel Bolton, *The True Bounds of Christian Freedom* (Edinburgh: Banner of Truth, rep. 1964 [1645]), 61, 62, 66.

Jesus did not come to free people from God's eternal law (5:17-20), binding for both Jews and Gentiles. . . . Childs has correctly stated, "The law of Moses is not a temporary measure that has now been superseded in the kingdom of heaven, but rather represents the eternally valid will of God."[53]

Gordon's continuing concern with "law and prophets"

He returns once again to his complaint that Bahnsen suppresses "the prophets" in the previously discussed phrase. Of Bahnsen's conclusion, he notes:

> This meaning of πληρῶσαι would not make much sense of the prophetic dimension of the equation; how would Jesus be "ratifying" the prophets? It would be better to find an understanding of both verbs, πληρῶσαι and καταλῦσαι, which makes sense of both of the direct objects.
>
> If we take the "law and prophets" together as a reference to the Sinai covenant, or the era in which God's people are governed thereby, then it makes sense to understand Jesus to be saying that he has not come (at least in his humiliated state) to abolish that covenantal administration, but to bring it to its conclusion. Since the other ἦλθον-statements of Jesus are routinely understood as being a reference to his humiliated state (his earthly ministry prior to his resurrection and ascension), there is also no conflict between such a statement and the reality that later he does terminate the one covenant administration and inaugurate a new one. (CT, 30)

Against this I would reply:

1. Gordon's conditional argument fails. His argument involves a conditional case. It requires that "*if* we take the 'law and prophets' together as a reference to the Sinai covenant," *then*

---

[53] Van Gemeren, *The Progress of Redemption*, 330. Van Gemeren is citing H. Henry Meeter, *The Basic Ideas of Calvinism* (Grand Rapids: Kregel, 1960 edition), 44.

such-and-such follows. But we do not. I have already responded at length to this approach to the passage, so I will not repeat that material here. I believe Gordon's proposed condition has been weighed in the balance and found wanting. Bahnsen's view *does* make sense of "both of the direct objects," in a manner widely held among exegetes, for the "law and prophets" is a familiar phrase referring to the whole Old Testament revelation. But here Gordon supplements his earlier material, requiring my further response.

2. Gordon's argument involves absurdity. Gordon strongly emphasizes "the prophets" as a direct object of two key verbs: "It would be better to find an understanding of both verbs, πληρῶσαι and καταλῦσαι, which makes sense of both of the direct objects" [i.e., "law and prophets"] (CT, 30).

Yet, the very way in which Christ presents his statement shows the absurdity of Gordon's objection. In Matthew 5:17 Jesus opens his comments on the law with these words: "Do not think that I came to abolish the Law or the Prophets; I did not come to abolish, but to fulfill." The ingressive aorist μή νομίσητε means: "Do not begin to think."[54] It therefore implies the possibility that some *would* think such: The grammatical form of the statement "presupposes the existence of the opinion that is denied."[55] Why would Jesus be leading people to believe he was *not* fulfilling Scriptures? Did he not point out that he fulfilled prophecy (Matt. 26:24; Luke 24:25-27; John 5:39; 10:33; 19:7)? He was, however, frequently accused of breaking the law of God (e.g., Matt. 19:3; 12:1-4; Luke 6:2; John 8:3-8;).

Alford notes of this prospect: "It is a question whether our Lord includes the *prophecies*, properly so called, in His meaning here. I think *not*: for no person professing himself to be the Messiah would be thought to *contradict the prophecies*."[56]

---

[54] Frank Stagg, "Matthew," in Clifton J. Allen, ed., *The Broadman Bible Commentary*, vol. 8: Matthew-Mark (Nashville: Broadman, 1970), 107.

[55] Hagner, *Matthew* 1:104.

Davies and Allison agree: "But 'to annul the prophets' does not make so much sense, and one wonders whether such an accusation was ever brought against Christians or their Lord."[57]

3. Gordon's argument is over-subtle. As is common with Klinean arguments, this one presses hidden issues not easily surmised by the average reader. And it certainly was not readily accessible to Jesus' original audience of common people.

Bahnsen argues at length and quite reasonably (and according to Gordon, even "plausibly"), that whatever Christ is declaring when he states "I have not come to abolish but to fulfill," he *cannot* mean that in the final analysis he actually *will* abolish the "law or prophets" (TCE, 57-60). After all, he announces *immediately* thereafter: "For truly I say to you, until heaven and earth pass away, not the smallest letter or stroke shall pass away from the Law, until all is accomplished" (Matt. 5:18).[58] And then he warns that one's status in the kingdom of the heaven (which he came to establish) depends upon one's keeping and promoting the law: "Whoever then annuls one of the least of these commandments, and so teaches others, shall be called least in the kingdom of heaven; but whoever keeps and teaches them, he shall be called great in the kingdom of heaven" (Matt. 5:19).

His original audience surely would not have believed he actually meant that he would not abolish the law while *in his humiliated state* for three and one-half years (as per Gordon). But just three years later when exalted he *would*, in fact, abolish it. Nothing in the context suggests it, and everything opposes it.

Bahnsen responds at length to objections that interpret πληρῶσαι in a way that allows the law's ending, invalidating, replacing, or setting aside (TCE, 57-62). These contrary views all fail by involving Christ in contradiction. All such interpretations simply speak of various *modes*

[56] Henry Alford, *Alford's Greek Testament: An Exegetical and Critical Commentary*, 7th ed. (Cambridge: University Press, 1874; Grand Rapids: Guardian, 1976), 1:42

[57] Davies and Allison, *Matthew*, 1:484.

[58] Again as stated before, I will hold off analysis of this statement until later when Gordon himself brings it into the discussion.

of removing the law in the very context wherein he declares *twice* that he has *not* come "to abolish" it (Matt. 5:17a, b). In the final analysis according to Gordon, Jesus *had* come to abolish the law, and he *must* abolish it if he is to establish a global, non-Jewish kingdom.[59]

David Wenham (a reputable evangelical exegete) argues against Robert Banks' understanding of Matthew 5:17 in such a way that confirms (!) Bahnsen's exegesis as over against Gordon's:

> We may agree with Banks that *plerosai* is normally used in Matthew to mean 'fulfill' (especially of the fulfillment of prophecy). . . . But whereas Banks believes that Matthew's thought is that of 'fulfilling and so transcending," the context suggests rather that the thought is that of "fulfilling and so establishing." The contrast in v. 17b, "I came not to abolish but to . . . ," favours this view: "abolish–fulfil/establish" are a more natural pair of opposites than 'abolish–fulfill/transcend.' And the subsequent context also favours this interpretation: the fact that Jesus is the fulfiller of the law leads on to the practical "therefore" of v. 19: Jesus' followers are to uphold and not abolish the law.[60]

William Loader concurs:

> For Matthew, Jesus stated categorically that he came to do the opposite of abolishing the Law and the Prophets. In the light of the preceding context, where Jesus demands good works, this most naturally means something like: they are to be taken with the utmost seriousness. Keep the whole Law! The verses which follow 5:17, namely 5:18-19, 20, and 21–48, confirm this. The orientation of the statement is clear: it is in the opposite direction of abrogation; it is confirming and upholding the validity of the Law and the Prophets.[61]

---

[59] Gordon warns: "From a biblical perspective, if the Sinai legislation remains, then the prophetic office of preparing for the Messiah's arrival remains also" (CT, 29).

[60] Wenham, "Jesus and the Law," 93. Cited in Bahnsen, NOS, 319.

Furthermore, regarding Gordon's note that ἦλθον-statements speak of his *incarnational* coming: they do not necessarily demand a focus on his humiliation and suffering of his incarnation *as over against* his consequent glorification and victory. After all, he was glorified *while on earth* and as a *consequence* of his coming and in his incarnate body. For instance, in Hebrews his becoming incarnate had as its *goal* his providing for our redemption and securing his own incarnational glorification (Heb. 2:9; cp. 2:14, 17). Hebrews 10 even emphasizes his coming as the instrument of our redemption and his establishing the New Covenant (Heb. 10: 5-9, 16-17). In other words, Jesus did come to abolish the old covenant; but he tells us himself he did not come to abolish "the law or the prophets."

And what shall we say regarding Gordon's statement that "there is also no conflict between such a statement [i.e., "I came not to destroy the law or prophets"] and the reality that later he does terminate the one covenant administration and inaugurate a new one" (CT, 30)? Here I believe Gordon is confusing categories. Theonomists recognize that the Lord terminates "the one covenant administration" in order to "inaugurate a new one." After all, we are Christians and not Jews! This is not the issue between us: we do not believe that we are under the Mosaic *administration* (the *old covenant*), rather than the Christic administration (the New Covenant). We believe that "when He said, 'A new covenant,' He has made the first obsolete. But whatever is becoming obsolete and growing old is ready to disappear" (Heb. 8:13).

Actually Gordon is engaged in conceptual confusion here. He is equating the Mosaic *administration* with the Mosaic *legislation*, thereby confusing form and content. Bahnsen's enumerated summary of Theonomic Ethics is helpful in drawing proper distinctions: "Changes in covenantal administration that are warranted by Scripture (cf. 4) are recognized with the coming of the new and better covenant in Christ (5). Relativism (situationism) is repudiated, and the divinely revealed ethic is not reduced to a parochial or tribal perspective in the evolutionary history of ethics; (6) God's word advances universal justice, not a double-standard of morality" (TCE, xxvii). He writes in *By This Standard*: "Thus the Old Covenant administration (sacrifices, covenant signs,

---

[61] Loader, *Jesus' Attitude towards the Law*, 166.

temple) can be set aside for the New Covenant realities, even though the Old Covenant moral law remains fundamentally the same" (BTS, 314).

As Philip E. Hughes argues on the basis of 2 Corinthians 3: "The law is an integral component of the new no less than it is of the old covenant."[62] Calvin's comments on 2 Corinthians 3:7 are helpful: "We must now examine briefly these attributes of Law and Gospel, bearing in mind that he is not speaking of the whole doctrine contained in the Law and the prophets nor of what happened to the fathers under the old testament but is taking note only of what belongs peculiarly to the ministration of Moses."[63] Bahnsen deals extensively with 2 Corinthians 3 showing that the old covenant legislation remains even when its administration changes (BTS, ch. 16).

The old covenant is certainly different from the New Covenant, for the Scripture itself compares and contrasts them (2 Cor. 3; Heb. 8-9). But as Bahnsen argues and common sense demands: it is not different in *every* respect (BTS, 324). Though the administrative form changes, the inherent morality remains. Is this not demanded by Jeremiah's revelation of the New Covenant: "'Behold, days are coming,' declares the Lord, 'when *I will make a new covenant* with the house of Israel and with the house of Judah, *not like the covenant which I made with their fathers* in the day I took them by the hand to bring them out of the land of Egypt, My covenant which they broke, although I was a husband to them,' declares the Lord. 'But *this is the covenant* which I will make with the house of Israel after those days,' declares the Lord, 'I *will put My law within them, and on their heart I will write it*'" (Jer. 31:31-33).

Gordon's argument from the Matthean fulfillment theme

Gordon writes:

As Vern Poythress has demonstrated, such a rendering is also much more consistent with the ordinary understanding of

---

[62] Philip Edgecumbe Hughes, *Paul's Second Epistle to the Corinthians* (NICNT) (Grand Rapids: Eerdmans, 1962), 96.

[63] John Calvin, *The Second Epistle of Paul the Apostle to the Corinthians and the Epistles to Timothy, Titus, and Philemon,* ed. by David W. Torrance and Thomas F. Torrance (Grand Rapids: Eerdmans, 1964), 44.

πληρόαι in contexts where the direct object is prophetic. Indeed, there is no evidence that the prophets were ever thought of as legislating, but there is evidence, within Matthew's Gospel, that the law was conceived of as prophesying: "For all the prophets and the law prophesied until John"(11:13). . . . This way of understanding the verb is consistent with how the verb is regularly related to "prophets"; it is consistent with Matt 11:13. (CT, 30)

His argument is intriguing, but unconvincing. Interestingly, Gordon's argument was effectively rebutted by Bahnsen long before he published it. I wonder if Gordon has read Bahnsen's extensive interactions with critics.

Consider Bahnsen's response to Poythress as evidence against Gordon:

Poythress wants to say that "fulfill" in Matthew 5:17 should be assimilated to the other uses of 'fulfill' in Matthew where it applies to prophecies of the Old Testament. But the specific context of the Sermon on the Mount simply does not deal with Old Testament prophecies (even though they are surely found elsewhere in Matthew's gospel). We get into real trouble when we overlook the obvious. Poythress (and others) who try to import prophetic, typological "nuances" into the word "fulfill" in Matthew 5:17 are doing just that — importing preconceived ideas into the text (and context), rather than reading them out of the text. Even when one's theological conclusions are orthodox, this is not exegesis. The violence done to the context of Matthew 5:17 by importing prophetic and typological objects of "fulfillment" is astounding, obvious to any simple reader. Jesus there deals with ethical directives and lifestyle among His followers. We must go elsewhere in Matthew's writing to find the typological and prophetic emphasis upon which Poythress chooses to focus. (NOS, 322-23)

And consider Bahnsen's rejoinder to Strickland:

The alert reader must cry out: 'Where is there *any* mention or discussion of Old Testament prophecies in this passage or its local context?' The fact is that there is not so much as a word about Old Testament prophecies to be found. . . . Any reader can see that Christ is not discussing prophecy but ethics, at this particular point — indeed, extending to the end of the sermon. . . . Notice that the word 'therefore' (*oun* in the Greek text; cf. NRSV) connects verses 18 and 19. Verse 29 is presented as an inference or application of the premise provided in verse 18. On the Strickland hypothesis, then, we have Jesus declaring that, because Old Testament *prophecies* must be fulfilled, anybody who breaks one of *"these commandments"* will be demoted in God's kingdom. This renders the word 'therefore' unintelligible, moving from a premise about prophecies to a conclusion about commandments! And Strickland's interpretation suppresses and ignores the demonstrative pronoun 'these' in verse 19: "Anyone who breaks one of the least of *these* commandments." Here Jesus refers back to the subject of his statement in vers 18: "not the smallest letter, not the least stroke of a pen, will . . . disappear from the law." "These" are *not* the prophecies of the Old Testament, as Strickland strains to maintain, but rather the commandment.[64]

Furthermore, we must recall that the phrase "law and prophets" most often refers to the Old Testament revelation *en toto*, as the full body of divine revelation available to the first century Jew. Therefore, we do not have a situation where "the direct object is prophetic" *in the sense Gordon's view demands* (CT, 30). In fact, in Matthew itself the phrase can refer to the Old Testament revelation with an emphasis upon ethics (as per Bahnsen): "Therefore, however you want people to treat you, so treat them, for this is the Law and the Prophets" (Matt. 7:12). "On these two commandments depend the whole Law and the Prophets" (Matt. 22:40). The "prophets," then, simply fill out the designation of

---

[64] Bahnsen in Strickland, *The Law, the Gospel, and the Modern Christian*, 299-300.

the Old Testament, which here is called "the law and/or prophets." Thus, Bahnsen's interpretation (not *translation*) of "confirm, ratify" is perfectly suitable.

In addition, I am not sure why Gordon writes: "there is no evidence that the prophets were ever thought of as legislating, but there is evidence, within Matthew's Gospel, that the law was conceived of as prophesying" (CT, 30). Theonomists do not claim that prophets "legislated" anything. Nor that Jesus in Matthew 5 was legislating. Gordon knows this, for he speaks of Bahnsen's understanding of πληρσαι as meaning "ratify" (CT, 29, 30), not "legislate." Gordon makes an interesting statement, but one irrelevant to the issue at hand. Ratifying and/or confirming are not equivalent to legislating. Besides this, "to prophesy" does not necessarily mean "to predict in advance." To "prophesy" means "tell forth" not just to "forth tell," that is, it means to speak the mind of God by direct revelation. Jesus' statement in Matthew 11:13 ("For all the prophets and the Law prophesied until John") simply declares that "both indeed conveyed the authentic word of God."[65]

Gordon's "exhaustive detail" response

Bahnsen's most vigorously challenged position is his assertion that in Matthew 5:17-20 Jesus affirmed the law "in exhaustive detail." And Gordon does not fail to object to it:

> Bahnsen attempts to establish a thesis that Jesus, in Matthew 5, reiterates for all time the validity of the entire Mosaic law, not merely the "moral" law, and that he does so "in exhaustive detail." Such an interpretation, if correct, would necessarily either condemn Paul and the other apostles or destroy Theonomy. Paul not only relaxes one, but several of the Mosaic laws, and not merely the "least," but several of the major laws, to wit, circumcision, the Jewish calendar, and the dietary laws. (CT, 30).

But again, Gordon is too late, for Bahnsen has already responded to this objection. He directly deals with this sort of challenge noting

---

[65] Morris, *Matthew*, 283.

that it is not a protest against himself, but against Christ. In a debate book on Christian political theory he answers an evangelical authority:

> The theonomic interpretation of Matthew 5:17-19 cannot be correct, reasons Strickland, because it "would not allow for *any* abrogation of *any* portion of the Mosaic law." Once again, however, he has badly misread. As a matter of linguistic and exegetical fact, Christ does not offer any qualifications to his absolutistic endorsement of the law's validity specifically in Matthew 5.[66]

Theologian John Frame objects similarly, noting that Bahnsen's view is "a fine brash hypothesis which dies the death of a thousand qualification." Bahnsen responds:

> But [my expression] meant only to summarize the teaching of Jesus Himself in the particular text at Matthew 5:17-19. Did it not do so correctly? Jesus spoke of the "validity" of the law ("Do not think that I came to abrogate"). Jesus spoke of it "abiding" ("until heaven and earth pass away"). And Jesus spoke of it in exhaustive detail ("not one jot or tittle," "the least of these commandments"). But when Jesus spoke, then of the abiding validity of the law in exhaustive detail, was it "a fine brash hypothesis" just because the general principle would be qualified by Biblical teaching elsewhere? (NOS, 26)

Clearly then, it is not Bahnsen who "attempts to establish a thesis" that "reiterates for all time the validity of the entire Mosaic law." Christ did so. Bahnsen is only summarizing Jesus' teaching. If Bahnsen were to say simply "until heaven and earth pass away, not the smallest letter or stroke shall pass away from the Law," would that be one of *Bahnsen's* "attempts to establish a thesis" that "reiterates for all time the validity of the entire Mosaic law"? Those are *directly* the words of Christ; Bahnsen's short-hand phrase "exhaustive detail" is functionally equivalent. It differs little from Hengstenberg's statement regarding Matthew

---

[66] Bahnsen in Strickland, *The Law, the Gospel, and the Modern Christian*, 299.

5:17-19: "There the Lord asserts, in the strongest expressions, the eternal duration of the whole law, to its very smallest detail, and its binding power for the members of the new covenant."[67]

Bahnsen explains regarding the changes effected by the coming of the New Covenant:

> The theonomist maintains just here that there is a controlling presumption which should affect our conclusions about the New Testament view of the validity of Old Testament commandments — and that controlling hermeneutical assumption is mandated by no less than the authority of the Lord of the covenant Himself, speaking directly to the very question of the law's continuing validity (Matt. 5:17-19). The New Testament teaches us that — unless exceptions are revealed elsewhere — Old Testament commandment is binding, even as the standard of justice for all magistrates (Rom. 13:1-4), including every recompense stipulated for civil offenses in the law of Moses (Heb. 2:2). From the New Testament alone we learn that we must take as our operating presumption that any Old Testament penal requirement is binding today on all civil magistrates. The presumption can surely be modified by definite, revealed teaching in the Scripture, but in the absence of such qualifications or changes, any Old Testament penal sanction we have in mind would be morally obligatory for civil rulers.
>
> *Given this presumption*, the *silence* of the New Testament about any particular civil punishment would actually give *support* to its continuing validity, rather than detract from it. This is a logically inescapable conclusion." (NOS, 68-69)

Furthermore, Bahnsen's Preface to the second edition of *Theonomy* speaks directly to the issue of theonomic tolerance of change, even referencing Kline's approach as one source of complaint in this matter:

---

[67] E. W. Hengstenberg, *A History of the Kingdom of God Under the Old Testament* (Cherry Hill, N.J.: Mack, 1972, rep. 1871), 1:326.

Before offering an outline, we must be warned that some people have been kept from an accurate analysis of theonomic ethics—sometimes by the author's manner of expression, sometimes because the order of discussion (especially qualifications) is not that expected by some readers, and sometimes because the book has simply not been read, or read completely, or read at a safe distance from distorting preconceptions and prejudices. For instance, a combination of such factors has misled some to maintain that Theonomy, because it often speaks of our obligation to the exhaustive details of God's law ("every jot and tittle"), cannot allow any change or advance over the Old Testament at any point, even by God Himself, and must follow without exception every single Old Testament precept strictly, literally (even the cultural trappings necessitate verbatim application), and without qualification or modification.

These false depictions cannot be justified from a careful reading of the book. There are no fewer than seventy pages that refer to the progress of revelation and redemptive history, God's right to change the law, exceptions to general continuity, laws which are laid aside, or advances over the Old Covenant. I mentioned "radical differences," "legitimate and noteworthy discontinuities," and laws which have "become obsolete." What is championed is "the presumption" of moral continuity between the Testaments. It was clearly spelled out that "if we are to submit to God's law, then we must submit to every bit of it (as well as its own qualifications)." Because "only God has the authority and prerogative to discontinue the binding force of anything He has revealed," we should live by the Old Testament law "except where expressly indicated otherwise." (TCE, xxiii-xxiv)

But allow me to interact a little more with Gordon on this point. Let us apply this sort of objection in another context. Suppose Bahnsen taught: "Whoever divorces his wife and marries another woman commits adultery against her." This absolutistic statement does not allow for any justification for a divorced person remarrying. Would Bahnsen be guilty of condemning Christ who declares: "I say to you, whoever divorces his wife, *except for immorality*, and marries another woman commits adultery" (Matt. 19:9)? The first statement is absolutistic; the second allows a qualification. We know, of course, that Bahnsen would not be contradicting the Lord, for both of these statements come from Christ himself: the first statement was Christ's own teaching in Mark 10:11. Does *Jesus* engage in teaching that "dies the death of a thousand qualifications"?

Actually, Christ's absolutistic statement in Matthew 5:17-19 does *not* die the death of a thousand qualifications. Neither does *Bahnsen's summary of it* by the phrase "exhaustive detail." It no more does so than the statement "there is only one God" dies by qualifying that Jesus is God, the Father is God, and the Spirit is God because God is a Trinity, Jesus exists in hypostatic union with God, and so forth. Bahnsen's understanding of Christ's teaching shows that Gordon's ceremonial law objection fails: "Jesus says in Matthew 5:17 that He came to confirm and restore the full measure, intent, and purpose of the Older Testamental law" (TCE, 67). If Christ is confirming and restoring the "full measure, intent, and purpose" of the law, we must then ask: "What *is* the "intent and purpose" of the *ceremonial* law? We know the "full measure, intent, and purpose" of the *moral* law: it served as a standard of righteousness, a standard destroyed by scribal tampering which Jesus was correcting (Matt. 5:21-48).

The fact is, the ceremonial law — the "restorative law" (TCE, ch. 9) — of the Old Testament was a "tutor" to point to Christ. It was "put out of gear" (TCE, 207, 210) after Christ came (Gal. 3:24-25; cp. Eph. 2:14-16). The shadows always anticipated the reality in Christ (Heb. 7:11-12; 8:1-7; 9:6-12, 15, 23-26; 10:1-18). The ceremonial laws no longer operate as they did in the Old Testament — not because they were abrogated, but because they reached their *designed end or goal* in pointing to a coming Savior and the finalization of redemption in him. And Bahnsen clearly teaches this in *Theonomy*:

> The meaning and intention of these laws is equally valid under the Older and New Covenants, even though the former manner of observation is now "out of gear." The restorative law of the Older Testament declared that there is no remis-

sion of sin apart from the shedding of blood (Lev. 17:11; Heb. 9:22). The truth of this law, its axiomatic content, could not be set aside, even though the way in which it is observed could. The meaning was secure. 'Therefore, it was necessary' that the Older Testament copies be cleansed with blood because they anticipated the cleansing of the heavenly things by Christ's sacrifice(Heb. 9:23-24). Christ did not cancel the requirement of the restorative ceremonies; He once and for all kept them so that we might observe them in Him. He is our sacrificed passover (1 Cor. 5:7), our redemptive lamb (1 Pet. 1:19), etc. It is 'impossible' to be saved now by any other sacrifice (Heb. 10:4). (TCE, 210)

But Gordon continues his principial objection by offering what he deems to be an appropriate *reductio ad absurdum*:

If the law requiring a bloody rite (circumcision) can be fulfilled by a non-bloody rite (baptism), then where would Bahnsen's arguments for capital punishment necessarily go? Would we wash criminals today who commit capital crimes? If we would not, then why not? If we fulfill the requirement of not eating with Gentiles by eating with Gentiles, then do we fulfill the requirement of not murdering by murdering? If we fulfill the requirement of eating a feast on the day of atonement by not eating a feast on the day of atonement, then do we fulfill other mosaic laws by not doing them? If this were so, what would be left of Theonomy? How could the mosaic law possibly function as a guide for civil governments today, if the mosaic laws could be properly applied by not following them? (CT, 30-31).

This certainly would either destroy Theonomy by transforming its absolutistic character into relativistic nonsense, or by demonstrating its methodological absurdity. But it does neither.

Gordon challenges Bahnsen's argument: "Would we wash criminals today who commit capital crimes? If we would not, then why not?" The answer is easy: We would not because the Scripture provides neither principle nor precept directing us to do so. God's Word informs us that ceremonial law has a terminus in Christ, and must be approached differently today (see above). It provides us parallels between Old Testament and New Testament ceremonies, for example: circumcision/baptism (Col. 2:11-12), Passover/Lord's Supper (Luke 22:15-20; 1 Cor. 5:7). It applies Old Testament ceremonial words to New Testament spiritual realities, for example: "sacrifice" (Rom. 12:1; Phil. 2:17; 4:18; Heb. 13:15) and "temple" (1 Cor. 3:16; 6:9; Eph. 2:21). It encourages our *ceremonial* but not our *moral* transformation.

Gordon's refusal to recognize ceremonial law as categorically distinct from moral/judicial law would lead *him* into moral absurdities if he were consistent with his method in this *reductio*. He would be led to confess: "Forbidding murder and rape Thou hast not desired; My ears Thou hast opened; prohibiting theft and kidnaping Thou hast not required" (cp. Psa. 40:6). Or he could expect God to complain: "'What are your multiplied works of righteous obedience to Me?' says the Lord. 'I have had enough of your keeping a just weight and balance, and your surely putting to death he that strikes a man that he die'" (cp. Isa. 1:11). You see, the Scriptures clearly allow that *ceremonial* faithfulness (though important in its place) is not comparable to *moral* obedience (which is *always* obligatory). Gordon, therefore, is comparing apples and oranges when he equates ceremonial law and judicial law.

So Gordon's complaint is wrong-headed: "How could the mosaic law possibly function as a guide for civil governments today, if the mosaic laws could be properly applied by not following them?" (CT, 31). The answer is: The mosaic laws are *not* "properly applied by not following them." We must understand the meaning of the laws as God designed them: ceremonial law pointed to a time of completion, whereas moral/judicial law does not.

Gordon's final comment in this matter is:

> Of course, we believe the paint on the bottom of Bahnsen's shoes was self-applied, as soon as he left the corner into which he had painted himself. Had the "law and prophets" been correctly understood as a reference to the entire revelation within the Sinai administration, Jesus' intention would have

been clear: he would not abrogate any of the requirements or promises of that covenant administration until he had brought it to its fulfillment and had established a new covenant. (CT, 31)

Certainly, it is true that all the Old Testament revelation was given "within the Sinai administration," for Moses wrote the first books of the Bible and those writers and prophets following him lived under the Sinaitic covenant. But there are several problems with Gordon's conclusions.

I have already shown that it is unlikely Jesus was referring to the Sinai administration as such. Rather, he was referring to the sum total of the Old Testament Word of God. And the New Testament clearly endorses "all Scripture" as "inspired by God and profitable for teaching, for reproof, for correction, for training in righteousness" (2 Tim. 3:16), which included the Old Testament. The overwhelming majority of evangelical scholars recognize "law and prophets" as representing the Old Testament revelation, not the "Sinai administration."

After all, Jesus says nothing here that would lead his followers to suspect he was speaking only of a fading administration of God's dealings with man. He can and does make such statements elsewhere, but not here. For instance, in John we read: "Jesus said to her, 'Woman, believe Me, an hour is coming when neither in this mountain, nor in Jerusalem, shall you worship the Father'" (John 4:21). In Matthew we hear Jesus' lament: "O Jerusalem, Jerusalem, who kills the prophets and stones those who are sent to her! How often I wanted to gather your children together, the way a hen gathers her chicks under her wings, and you were unwilling. Behold, your house is being left to you desolate!" (Matt. 23:37-38). Several of his parables warn of the coming redemptive-historical change, such as the Parable of the Landowner (Matt. 21:33-45) and the Parable of the Marriage Feast (Matt. 22:1-14). For instance, in the Parable of the Wineskins we read: "But no one puts a patch of unshrunk cloth on an old garment; for the patch pulls away from the garment, and a worse tear results. Nor do men put new wine into old wineskins; otherwise the wineskins burst, and the wine pours out, and the wineskins are ruined; but they put new wine into fresh wineskins, and both are preserved" (Matt. 9:16-17). These fit well with the great commission which engages a world-wide mission that could not be focused on a local temple (Matt. 28:18-20). Thus, Jesus can easily state that a change is coming. But he does not do that in Matthew 5.

In fact, he speaks of the perpetuity of the law of God in such a way in Matthew 5 that his hearers could never have even imagined that the law was nearing the end of its administration: "For truly I say to you, until heaven and earth pass away, not the smallest letter or stroke shall pass away from the Law, until all is accomplished" (Matt. 5:18). I will leave fuller consideration of this important verse until my next section.

So then, not only is Jesus silent about a coming revocation of the law, but he leaves the exact opposite supposition. And we should remember that the law was directly related to the kingdom of heaven which he was preaching. How could anyone have thought the kingdom of heaven would have nothing to do with the law?

Gordon's "Temporal Clause" Response

Earlier in his article Gordon summarily stated his objection to Bahnsen's understanding of Matthew 5:18: "he fails to appreciate the genuinely temporal character of the parallel temporal clauses, 'until heaven and earth pass away,' and 'until all things come to pass'" (CT, 29). When he finally gets to this part of his response, he opens with these words:

> The strongest apparent exegetical case for Bahnsen's viewpoint resides in his taking the two temporal clauses as metaphors which, when negated, mean "never." Thus, the passage would be interpreted as teaching that all of the requirements of the Sinai administration continue forever. However, if these two temporal clauses can be demonstrated to be non-metaphors, and actual temporal clauses, then all that can be proven by Matthew 5 is that the Mosaic covenant, both in its prophetic and legal aspects, abides temporarily, until God changes it by causing heaven and earth to pass away, and by bringing 'all things' to pass. (CT, 31)

How shall we respond to this rebuttal of Bahnsen's "strongest apparent exegetical case"? A number of problems beset Gordon's critique.

Gordon misreads Bahnsen's argument. Here I am very disappointed with Gordon's rebuttal. He seriously mis-interprets *Theonomy* making it appear to me that he may only have read select passages from it. I can at least state that in my view he has not read it *carefully*. And the problem I raise is not that he has simply confused some obtuse sentence which Bahnsen heavily leans on in his book. Rather he wrenches a statement from its clarifying context, radically misconstrues it, and then builds his whole response on this unrecognizable misconstruction. Let me explain the error before I respond to his lengthy ensuing argument.

Gordon writes: "The strongest apparent exegetical case for Bahnsen's viewpoint resides in his taking the two temporal clauses as metaphors which, when negated, mean 'never'" (CT, 31). In the footnote attached to this sentence Gordon quotes Bahnsen's offending sentence: "Given the cultural-literary milieu it is quite likely that this phrase was a graphic and strong way of saying 'never'" (CT, 31 n10). This is the *only* quoted material from Bahnsen on this *major* point in Gordon's rebuttal which consumes two full pages.

Immediately upon making this observation, Gordon drives home the basic argument given above. He complains that: (1) Bahnsen interprets the phrases "until heaven and earth pass away" and "until all things comes to pass" as *metaphors* and not as "genuine temporal clauses," which are "non-metaphors" (CT, 31). And (2) Bahnsen requires that the phrases "mean 'never,'" so that he demands that the law of God last forever into all eternity. Neither of these two assertions is true; in fact, both are patently false.

Gordon has focused on one sentence divorced from its contextual setting, and has interpreted it very narrowly at that. But Bahnsen does *not* demand that the phrases in question mean *"never" in the sense Gordon implies*, that is, as meaning absolutely never, ever. We must consider the sentence in its actual context. I will italicize Bahnsen's statements that show that he only demands that the law will last "as long as history lasts," that is, until the Second Coming. In fact, this is all Bahnsen need argue, since theonomy deals with ethics in time and on earth: "the thesis of this treatise has been that the law is valid and unchanged *until the end of the world*" (TCE, 224).

Now notice Bahnsen's offending sentence in its actual interpretive setting:

The "heaven and earth" was a regular allusion for stability (e.g., Eccl. 1:4; cf. Baruch 3:32) and thus the cosmic order stood as a standard for comparison—especially of the durability of God's word and covenant love (e.g., Ps. 119:89-92; Isa. 40:8; 51:6; 54:9-10; Jer. 31:35-36; 33:20-21, 25-26). Jesus contrasts the passing away of the heaven and earth to the immutability of His word (e.g., Matt. 24:35), and Luke 16:17 actually expresses the thought of Matthew 5:18 in terms of such comparison ("It is easier for heaven and earth to pass away than for one tittle of the law to fall"). Thus we can see what Christ is stating. *He states that the law will remain valid at least as long as the physical universe lasts, that is, until the end of the age or world.* Given the cultural-literary milieu it is quite likely that this phrase was a graphic and strong way of saying 'never.' Christ certainly taught that heaven and earth would pass away (e.g., Matt. 24:35); yet the idiomatic use of the phrase for strong comparison should not be overlooked in understanding His words. *Christ was not likely discoursing on the exact status of the law in the consummation age here but simply emphasizing its continual validity during this age by means of a strong literary device.* Even when we do take into account the actual ending of heaven and earth we see that Scripture teaches it to be at the return of Christ: there will be a great conflagration and noise (2 Peter 3:10) and separation of mankind into those who no longer experience death and those who experience the second death eternally (Rev. 21:1-8; cf. Isa. 66:22-24). *At least until that point the details of the law will remain.* (TCE, 79, emphasis mine)

Bahnsen means "never" in a relative historical sense, *not* in the absolute *eternal* sense. He would agree with Carson's interpreting it as "never, as long as the present world order persists."[68] Hagner encourages the relative rather than absolute sense of the clause: "The words of the first clause . . . are not simply a popular way of saying 'never' (contra Montefiore; Strecker, *Sermon*). They refer instead to the end of time as we know it."[69] Or as Hill puts it: "**till heaven and earth pass away:** i.e.

---

[68] Carson in Gaebelein, *The Expositor's Bible Commentary*, 8:145.

[69] Hagner, *Matthew 1-13*, 107.

for ever, until the end of the world."[70]

In fact, the reader should note that Bahnsen's offending sentence has "never" in quotation marks. The reason is that he is simply quoting renowned exegete John A. Broadus from his commentary on Matthew 5:18. Broadus writes: "Till heaven and earth pass away, is a proverbial expression which would popularly signify *never*, and is probably designed to be so understood here."[71] Gordon has to throw out preceding and following statement by Bahnsen himself in order to get to Bahnsen's citation of Broadus.

Warfield's views on Matthew 5 are strikingly similar to Bahnsen's. He points out that the Lord himself "tells us explicitly that his mission as regards the law was, not to abrogate it, but 'to fulfill it,' that is to say, 'to fill it out,' complete it, develop it into its full reach and power. The law, he declares, in the most solemn manner, is not susceptible of being done away with, but shall never cease to be authoritative and obligatory. . . . So long as time endures, the law shall endure in full validity, down to its smallest details. . . . So long as the world stands no iota of the law shall pass away — till all that it prescribes shall be performed."[72]

Furthermore, in the broader context of his lengthy discussion of Matthew 5:18, Bahnsen repeatedly states that the law will endure temporally until the end of time, without demanding that it continue into eternity (emphases mine):

- "The reason why Jesus could not presume to invalidate the law is that *the law remains binding until the end of the world*" (TCE, 75).
- "His statement is broader and more absolute—there is absolutely nothing which could be supposed to invalidate the law (not even the Messianic advent!) *until the very end of the world and final consummation*" (TCE, 76).
- "Not even the very least extensive number of the very least significant aspect of the Older Testamental law will become

---

[70] Hill, *Matthew*, 118.

[71] John A. Broadus, *Commentary on Matthew* (Grand Rapids: Kregel, rep. n.d., 1886), 100.

[72] B. B. Warfield, *Selected Shorter Writings of Benjamin B. Warfield* (Phillipsburg, N.J.: P & R, rep. 1970), 1:313, 314.

invalid until heaven and earth pass away! This statement is underscored in its importance by the double negative (οὐ μή) and use of ἀμήν at the head of the sentence. It is hard to imagine how Jesus could have more intensely affirmed that *every bit of the law remains binding in the gospel age*" (TCE, 76).

• "Jesus is saying that the exhaustive particulars of God's law have "imperishable validity *for all time*"" (TCE, 80).

• "Allen's summary of Christ's teaching on the law is to the point: '*So long as the world lasted* its [the law's] authority was to be permanent.' Every single stroke of the law must be seen by the Christian as *applicable to this very age between the advents of Christ*" (TCE, 84).

• "Consequently, the Messiah-Prophet declares that every written stroke of God's law *continues in force until the consummation of all things*" (TCE, 84-85).

• "The Son of God does not break with the word of His Father; what Jesus teaches in Matthew 5:18 is in full accord with the prescription, praise, and prophets of the Older Testament. *Until the world draws to an end* not one slightest stroke of the law shall be invalidated" (TCE, 85).

• "B. B. Warfield's summary was also right on the mark: 'it is asserted with an emphasis which could not be made stronger, that the law in its smallest details remains in undiminished authority *so long as the world lasts*'" (TCE, 86).

Bahnsen continually reiterates throughout his massive work this theme of historical continuance of the law of God:

• "Calvin maintained that 'a perfect pattern of righteousness stands forth in the law . . . one everlasting and unchangeable rule to live by'; this holy standard 'is just as applicable to every age, even *to the end of the world*.'" (TCE, 2)

• "Based on Matthew 5:17 f., the thesis of this treatise has been that the law is valid and unchanged *until the end of the world*." (TCE, 224)

• "It harmonizes with Christ's words in Matthew 5:17 f. to the effect that every jot and tittle of God's law remain valid *until the end of the world*." (TCE, 229)

• "Of course what he fails to mention in conjunction with this is that the law of God which commands us to love our neighbors holds validity up to the point when heaven and earth pass away (Matt. 5:18)—which is to say that God's law prescribes proper ethical relationships for *the period from creation to consummation.* Since the law itself obtains a different status when the period for which it specifies moral guidance has ceased, the alteration of relationships which ensues at *the end of history* simply does not amount to a change in the law. The end of the period in which the law is to be used does not constitute an amendment of the law. Moreover, it would be illegitimate to infer that because the law will not be used *when history ends,* we are not obligated to keep a portion of the law while history is still in process!" (TCE, 562)

How could Bahnsen be more clear? How could Gordon have been more mistaken? This is a totally unnecessary error on Gordon's part — and an error made while challenging what he deems "the strongest apparent exegetical case for Bahnsen's viewpoint" (CT, 31). It would seem that engaging another's "strongest" argument would require great care and diligence. Bahnsen's complaint that too many critics have not carefully read his work has been proven a legitimate concern time and again in Gordon's article.

Bahnsen affirms Gordon's basic demand. Gordon argues that the two phrases "until heaven and earth pass away" and "until all things come to pass" are "non-metaphors, and actual temporal clauses." This is supposedly contrary to Bahnsen's position which Gordon (for some unknown reason) thinks is: "the passage would be interpreted as teaching that all of the requirements of the Sinai administration continue forever" (CT, 31).

But as shown in citations above, Bahnsen is *not* arguing for a metaphorical understanding of these clauses. Nowhere does he state that these are "metaphors." In fact, he is expressly and repeatedly declaring that they are temporal clauses that demand that the law remain in affect until the Second Coming of Christ when history ends.

In addition to the above material which *assumes* a temporal understanding of the clauses, Bahnsen clearly states: "In order to properly understand Christ's declaration about the *temporal length* of the law's validity in exhaustive detail it is helpful to look at the common Jewish teaching on that same point" (TCE, 77, emphasis mine). What could be more clear?

Bahnsen's citation of Broadus suggesting that the phrase is "a graphic and strong way of saying 'never'" (TCE, 79) does not require that "never" be understood in an absolute sense. That is, the connotation of "never" does not demand that the law continue into eternity forever and ever. Amen. This is obvious in that Jesus does not use the word "forever" in this context, though this is a word which he used frequently enough (Matt. 6:13; John 6:15, 58; 8:35; 12:34; 14:16). But he does declare the law remains "until heaven and earth pass away," which is a temporal designate. This phrase means "never" according to common parlance in a temporal sense, that is, while the current historical order remains.

Surprisingly, just two paragraphs after claiming Bahnsen's view denies the temporal meaning of the clauses, Gordon cites Bahnsen's clear affirmation of the temporal nature of the phrases: "It is thus not farfetched for Bahnsen to say regarding this verse that 'the law will remain valid at least as long as the physical universe lasts'" (CT, 31). His claiming that Bahnsen denies temporality and his admission that he affirms it are on the same page of Gordon's article.[73]

---

[73] Gordon writes: "True, within a modern cosmology, it is difficult to believe that 'heaven and earth' can pass away" (CT, 31). He neglected to mention that "within a modern cosmology" it is also difficult to believe that God created the Universe and that it is upheld and controlled by his providential word. But his statement is really quite surprising. After all, there are several models proposed by physicists that teach that the universe will ultimately pass away, whether by Helmholtz's theory of the universe's gradual disintegration under the forces of the second law of thermodynamics, or by the "Big Crunch" which expects the Universe to collapse into a gravitational singularity, or by the "Big Rip" which rips apart the universe by dark matter gravitational fields, or by the "Big Bounce" concept in quantum loop gravity theory which expects a series of expanding and contracting universes, or by its violent and sudden collapse into a wormhole, or by other hypothetical means. I do not know why he would say that modern cosmology finds such to be difficult. See P. C. W. Davies, *The Last Three Minutes: Conjectures About the Ultimate Fate of the Universe* (New York: Basic, 1997). Charles Seife, *Alpha & Omega: The Search for the Beginning and End of the Universe* (New York: Viking, 2003). C. R. Kitchin, *Journeys to the Ends of the Universe: A Guided Tour of the Beginnings and Endings of Planets, Stars, Galaxies, and the Universe* (Philadelphia: Hilger, 1990).

Gordon's interpretation is complicated. After chastising Bahnsen on the basis of a misreading of his argument, Gordon provides his own interpretation of Christ's statement. His argument goes through several steps before reaching its point.

Gordon argues that Peter speaks of God's judgment upon man in the Noahic Flood, which in a covenantally significant way causes the "heavens" and the "earth" to "perish":

> For when they maintain this, it escapes their notice that by the word of God the heavens existed long ago and the earth was formed out of water and by water, through which the world at that time was destroyed, being flooded with water. But the present heavens and earth by His word are being reserved for fire, kept for the day of judgment and destruction of ungodly men. (2 Peter 3:5-7)

For Gordon this opens the prospect that the passing-away-of-heaven-and-earth language does not require the coming of the end of time. Rather, this language can have another pre-consummational referent: "The 'destruction' or 'passing away' of heaven and earth is also then spoken of when God *judges* its inhabitants. Cosmologically, the heaven and earth were not annihilated in the flood. Covenantally, however, the inhabitants thereof were judged by God, and the judgment was spoken of as perishing or 'destruction' (CT, 32).

This interpretation of the biblical phraseology is certainly possible.[74] With this alternative theological understanding as covenantal background, Gordon offers his interpretation of Matthew 5:18. He suggests that the "judgment/destruction of the heavens and the earth . . . took place with the death of Jesus," although in another sense "it will take place at his return" (CT, 32). He parallels the darkness and the resurrections associated with Christ's crucifixion (Matt. 27:45, 50-53) with the events surrounding his future return (Matt. 24:29) (CT, 32). Thus, the death of Christ can be a passing away of heaven and earth in Gordon's understanding.

---

[74] I agree that the Scriptures can apply "end of world" language to pre-consummational events. See: Kenneth L. Gentry, Jr., *Perilous Times: A Study in Eschatological Evil* (Texarkana, Ark.: CMF, 1999), 77-79.

Finally, he draws all of this together as evidence against Bahnsen:

> For our purposes, then, the expressions in Matt 5:17ff. which suggest that the "law and prophets" will never pass away, nor any part thereof, must be understood as in fact genuine temporal expressions, indicating that they will not pass away *until* all the matters prophetically anticipated come to pass, as D. A. Carson and others have argued. From both an OT and a gospel perspective, OT prophecies are seen as coming to fulfillment at a single moment, which "moment" the remainder of the NT writings divide into two. Only the apostolic, post-resurrection instruction enables us, with any confidence, to determine which aspects are fulfilled in the first coming of the Messiah, and which in his second coming. And such instruction plainly indicates that many of the "jots and tittles," not the least of which are circumcision, the calendar, and the dietary code, have indeed passed away. (CT, 32-33)

So here we have Gordon's full-blown Klinean scheme before us. I will respond to Gordon at several levels.

Gordon holds a minority position. I would point out that (as usual) Gordon is swimming against the stream of evangelical exegesis. This, of course, does not prove him wrong, but it does once again remind us of his Klinean tendency to adopt peculiar, complex interpretive approaches. I will cite just a few exegetes who concur with Bahnsen's interpretation of the "heaven and earth" language in Matthew 5:18, which, as Hagner notes, is the view of "the majority of commentators."[75] Each of these scholars understand Christ to be speaking of the end of history, not of the crucifixion of Christ.

• Calvin: "It is quite enough to understand that sooner will heaven crash, and all the fabric of the earth dissolve, than the fixity of the Law shall be shaken."[76]

---

[75] Hagner, *Matthew 1-13*, 107.
[76] Calvin, *Matthew* 1:180-181.

• Lenski: "'Until the heaven and the earth passes away' means until the end of time."[77]

• Hendrikson: "Not until the universe in its present form disappears (Ps. 102:25; Isa. 34:4; 51:6; Matt. 24:35; Rom. 8:21; Heb. 1:12; II Peter 3:7, 10-13; Rev. 6:14; 21:1-3)."

• Hill: "**till heaven and earth pass away:** i.e. for ever, until the end of the world. The eternity of the Law is constantly asserted in Jewish writings."[78]

• Davies and Allison: "The law — in contrast to Jesus words (cf. 24.35 . . .)— therefore only endures until the havens and the earth are gone. It is not eternal."[79]

• Hagner: The words refer "to the end of time as we know it and the beginning of eschatology proper, that is, the time of the regeneration of the created order. . . . In other words, the law, as interpreted by Jesus, will remain valid until the close of this age."[80]

• Morris: "*Until heaven and earth pass away* points to the end of created things . . . the totality of creation."[81]

• Loader: "The emphasis on obedience to commandments in 5:16 and 17 and in 5:19-20, not to speak of 5:21-48, precludes reading ἕως ἀν πάντα γένηται as implying the temporary validity of Torah until it is changed by Jesus or until it is fulfilled in Jesus' ministry or his death and resurrection. The point of the instruction for Matthew is that he wants his community to know that it is still in force and will be until eternity."[82]

• Keener: "Matthew declares that nothing will pass from the law 'until all is accomplished' (5:18), meaning until the consummation of the kingdom, when heaven and earth pass away (24:34; cf. Jer 31:35-37; Ps-Philo 11:5; Sib. Or. 3:570-72). The idea that Jesus' death and resurrection is the 'goal of the world,'

---

[77] R. C. H. Lenski, *The Interpretation of St. Matthew's Gospel* (Peabody, Mass.: Hendrickson, 1998, rep. 1943), 208.

[78] Hill, *Matthew*, 118.

[79] Davies and Allison, *Matthew*, 1:490.

[80] Hagner, *Matthew 1-13*, 107.

[81] Morris, *Matthew*, 109.

[82] Loader, *Jesuss' Attitude towards the Law*, 169.

thus allowing the law to be set aside as fulfilled, violates the whole thrust of the passage." He then notes that Overmann "rightly calls 'such hermeneutical gymnastics . . . excessive . . . tortured' and 'contrived.'"[83]

Gordon contradicts himself. Earlier in his article he states in amusement that "we believe the paint on the bottom of Bahnsen's shoes was self-applied, as soon as he left the corner into which he had painted himself" (CT, 31). Nevertheless, he himself has a worse foot problem than paint on the shoe, for he shoots himself in the foot here.

We must remember that he criticizes Bahnsen for taking these temporal clauses as "metaphors" (CT, 31). Now, after a vigorous assertion that "until heaven and earth pass away" and "until all is accomplished" are "genuine temporal clauses" and are "non-metaphors" (CT, 31), Gordon explains that "until heaven and earth pass away" does not mean what it actually declares. Instead, it functions — *as a metaphor* (!) — for divine judgment upon men even when "the heaven and earth were not annihilated" (CT, 32). In fact, Gordon states: "I believe there is a sense in which this took place with the death of Jesus" (CT, 32). The "sense" in which this occurs is metaphorical!

Interestingly then, Bahnsen's interpretation not only is *not* metaphorical despite Gordon's complaint, but it actually requires that the phrase be "genuine temporal clauses" (Gordon's language) in order to argue that the law remains binding upon men, whereas Gordon's interpretation, despite his earlier statement, *is* metaphorical.

Gordon's interpretation is contra-contextual. Even though the heavens-and-earth-pass-away language could theoretically be a metaphor for God's judgment upon men, it clearly does not function so in Matthew 5. The phrase does not stand alone but is supplemented by another temporal clause that demands it speak of the actual end of history.

Jesus states: "For truly I say to you, *until heaven and earth pass away*, not the smallest letter or stroke shall pass away from the Law, *until all is accomplished*" (Matt. 5:18). As Davies and Allison observe: both phrases stand "in synonymous parallels: both refer to the outstanding consummation. . . . The objection that this makes for unnecessary redundancy fails because 'until all things are accomplished' adds two things:

---

[83] Keener, *Matthew*, 178.

it (1) introduces the idea, absent from the preceding ἔως clause, of God's prophetic promises and redemptive purpose . . . and (2) eliminates the possibility of interpreting 'until heaven and earth pass away' as being the rhetorical equivalent of 'never': rather is a define end to the law set forth."[84] Thus, these conjoined temporal clauses speak of one event: the end of history. Then and only then "all is accomplished," every prophecy fulfilled, every act of history completed.

Bahnsen ably argues for the synonymous parallel between these two temporal clauses, with both of them reflecting the end of the world (TCE, 80-84). Of the phrase πάντα γένηται ("all things come to be") he notes that the neuter πάντα ("all things") cannot refer back to the masculine νόμος ("law"), so must be alluding to something else. And unlike Matthew 24:34 ("all *these* things") the πάντα in Matthew 5:18 is "unparticularlized," having no "definite referent and antecedent" (TCE, 81), so that it is not referring to "these things," i.e., "the law or prophets." Furthermore, it is anarthous which makes it "absolutely general," referring to "all things, everything," as in Matthew 18:26; 22:4; Mark 4:34; Luke 1:3; and other passages (TCE, 83). As a matter of fact, if πάντα γένηται speaks of the law and prophets coming to pass, then it is tautological. It would be stating: "The law and prophets will not come to pass until the law and prophets come to pass." In the final analysis, Gordon's view wrongly implies that γένηται basically means the same thing as πληρόω.

Gordon's interpretation strains the text

Gordon claims that the "moment" of prophetic fulfilment is divided "into two," that is, at the first coming of Christ and at his second coming. He presents a case for understanding the *crucifixion* as a judgmental passing away of the heavens and earth, while holding that the *second coming* will witness the final, consummational event. However, not all prophecies of "the law and prophets" (the Old Testament) can be sorted into these "two" moments. That is, not all prophecy focuses *only* on Christ's death and on his return. Indeed, Matthew's gospel uses the fulfillment motif to show that prophecy is being fulfilled all along his incarnational life, from birth to resurrection (Matt. 1:22; 2:15, 17, 23; 4:14; 8:17; 12:17; 13:14, 35; 21:4; 26:54, 56; 27:9).

---

[84] Davies and Allison, *Matthew*, 1:495.

Gordon might possibly respond by arguing that: "The two 'big moments'—the pivots—of prophetic fulfillment are the crucifixion and the return of Christ. But certain prophecies will be fulfilled between his crucifixion and his return, according to Acts and other New Testament references." However, if we associate those post-crucifixion prophecies with the Second Advent, then these prophecies are connected by a span of 2000 years thus far. This hardly seems to be a "moment." And the prophecies fulfilled in Acts surely cannot be deemed tantamount to the passing away of heaven and earth.

As cited earlier, Keener deems such an interpretation as proffered by Gordon out of the question: "The idea that Jesus' death and resurrection is the 'goal of the world,' thus allowing the law to be set aside as fulfilled, violates the whole thrust of the passage." He then notes that Overmann "rightly calls 'such hermeneutical gymnastics . . . excessive . . . tortured' and 'contrived.'"[85]

Gordon's interpretation is counter-intuitive. His view requires that the passing away of heaven and earth has a double-fulfillment: "The only remaining issue, then, is *when* such judgment/destruction of the heavens and the earth will take place. Within a NT eschatology, I believe there is a sense in which this took place with the death of Jesus, and another sense in which it will take place at his return. " (CT, 32)

Is it really plausible that Christ is teaching in this one verse (Matt. 5:18) that the "heavens and the earth passing away" is a metaphor for the judgment of the world, which occurs *both* in his death *and* at his return? This interpretive maneuver expects us to believe that this passage (which does not appear to be speaking of judgment at all) is actually pointing to judgment at Christ's death and at his return, and all of this simultaneously. Christ was *clarifying* his position on the law and the Prophets in Matthew 5, not attempting to confound his hearers with double-meanings: "Do not think that" (Matt. 5:17); "You have heard that the ancients were told . . . but I say unto you" (Matt. 5:21-47).

Had Gordon argued that since the passing away of heaven and earth can be a metaphor for God's judgment at the cross, therefore this judgment language in Matthew 5:18 speaks of that event *alone*, he might have had a less strained argument. He would have had a strained argu-

---

[85] Keener, *Matthew*, 178.

ment on other grounds, to be sure, but not an unbearably strained one leaning too heavily on this double-fulfillment requirement.

Gordon's interpretation is overly-subtle. His interpretation is overshadowed by Bahnsen's strongly exegetical approach. Bahnsen demonstrates the clear, accessible, internal consistency of the whole context of Jesus' teaching, while undermining Gordon's complex, counter-intuitive approach (see: TCE, 80-83). The Lord opens by urging his hearers to understand that "I came not to abolish the Law or the Prophets; I did not come to abolish but to fulfill" (Matt. 5:17). Note Jesus' emphasis on the continuing validity of the law:

- He declares *twice* that he has *not* come to "abolish" the Law or Prophets: μή νομίσητε ὅτι ἦλθον καταλῦσαι τόν νόμον, οὐκ ἦλθον χαταλάσε (Matt. 5:17).
- He employs an explanatory γάρ which introduces the *opposite* conclusion of what some (including Gordon!) might think: "*For* truly I say to you, until heaven and earth pass away, not the smallest letter or stroke shall pass away from the Law, until all is accomplished" (Matt. 5:18).
- He employs ἀμῆν to accent the truthfulness of his statement (Matt. 5:18).
- His truthful declaration emphatically endorses the "smallest letter or stroke" of the law (Matt. 5:18).
- He vigorously stresses the matter by repeating "one" before each element: "not *one* (ἐν) small letter or *one* (μία) stroke" (Matt. 5:18).
- He declares these will "*not* pass from the law" by a strong means of denial, employing the double negative (οὐ μη) (Matt. 5:18).
- He warns that any who would diminish even "the least of the commandments" would themselves be diminished in his "kingdom" which he had come to establish (Matt. 5:19).
- He demanded that the righteousness of his followers must "surpass" (περισσεύση) that of the Scribes and Pharisees, the supposed champions of the law (Matt. 5:20).

• He then intensifies the proper application of the law for a full twenty-six verses (Matt. 5:21-27).

With all this emphasis who would think that the law would soon be "passed away" (CT, 32)? Jesus certainly does not seem here to teach that the law would pass away at his crucifixion, which finally establishes the kingdom of heaven by effecting redemption. Gordon's argument is necessarily complex because the simple reading of the Lord's teaching here in Matthew 5 cannot be easily overthrown.

Gordon contradicts himself again. He complains against Bahnsen's argument that "had the 'law and prophets' been correctly understood as a reference to the entire revelation within the Sinai administration, Jesus' intention would have been clear: he would not abrogate any of the requirements or promises of that covenant administration until he had brought it to its fulfillment and had established a new covenant" (CT, 31).

Now Gordon believes (as we do) that the New Covenant was finally and fully established in Christ's death. We know this because he informs us that his suggested meaning for πληρῶσαι "is consistent with the portrait of Christ elsewhere in the NT as functioning within the Sinai covenant *until* he *established* the new *by his death and resurrection*, and therefore [in Matthew 5 Christ is] requiring his disciples to obey the Mosaic law *until the New Covenant was inaugurated*" (CT, 30, emphasis mine). He also states: "If we take the 'law and prophets' together as a reference to the Sinai covenant, or the era in which God's people are governed thereby, then it makes sense to understand Jesus to be saying [in Matt. 5:17] that he has not come (at least in his humiliated state) to abolish that covenantal administration, but to *bring it to its conclusion*" (CT, 30, emphasis mine). Consequently, the *whole* "law and prophets" ("the Sinai administration") has been "brought to its fulfillment" because the New Covenant has been established at the death of Christ.

But now the problem arises. He later writes: "For our purposes, then, the expressions in Matt 5:17ff. which suggest that the 'law and prophets' will never pass away, nor any part thereof, must be understood as in fact genuine temporal expressions, indicating that they will not pass away *until* all the matters prophetically anticipated come to pass" (CT, 32). Gordon clearly teaches us that not "any part" of the law and prophets will "pass away" until "*all* the matters prophetically anticipated come to pass." Yet in the very next two sentences, he writes: "From both an OT and a gospel perspective, OT prophecies are seen as coming to fulfillment at a single moment, which 'moment' *the remainder of the NT writings divide into two*. Only the apostolic, post-resurrection instruction enables us, with any confidence, to determine *which aspects are fulfilled in the first coming* of the Messiah, and *which in his second coming*" (CT, 33). Thus, on the one hand, not "any part" of the law will pass away until "*all* the matters prophetically anticipated come to pass," while on the other hand, "the NT writings divide into two" the prophetic fulfillments so that some do not come to pass until "his second coming." Thus, if not "any part" of the law passes until "all the matters" transpire, how can he be opposed to Theonomy?

Conclusion

In *Theonomy in Christian Ethics* Bahnsen offers a full fifty pages of exegesis of Matthew 5:17-20. Obviously Gordon did not have the space available to offer a point-by-point rebuttal in his article. Nevertheless, his presentation was disappointing in that it appears that he did not realize that Bahnsen had already answered most of his counter observations in at least two other books (*No Other Standard* and *By This Standard*), various articles, and public debates and lectures. Several of his main counter interpretations were rooted in his distinctive Klinean convictions and are subject to scrutiny on that basis alone. Bahnsen's exegesis continues to be more compelling than his critics' counter analyses.

Chapter 4
The Argument from Covenant Theology
(Part 1)

We come now to Gordon's third main argument against Theonomic Ethics. His first argument involved philosophical concerns (the argument from necessity covers three pages in his presentation). I showed how this argument was both misguided and irrelevant. Gordon based his presentation on unpublished conversations with un-named individuals while admitting he could not find the problem in Bahnsen, who was the focus of his critique. His second argument engaged exegetical considerations (the argument from Matthew 5 covers five and one-third pages). This was unnecessarily innovative and open to easy counter analysis. I noted that Bahnsen's exegesis is supported by numerous exegetes and Gordon's analysis is virtually unique due to Klinean peculiarities inherent in it.

Gordon's final complaint against theonomy is his *theological* argument rooted in the demands of covenantalism. He titles this section of his critique: "The Theonomic Understanding of Covenant Theology." This is obviously his most important argument in that he provides eleven pages of argument on this point, which is more than both of his preceding points combined, consuming 55% of his critique. This argument is especially relevant in that it is rooted in Bahnsen's own Reformed theology and brings into sharp relief the systemic differences between Bahnsen and Gordon.

Given the seriousness of this argument, I will first briefly summarize Gordon's main points in order to quickly orient the reader to his specific concerns. Then I will state my general disappointments with his presentation, thereby quickly dispatching those matters without deeper consideration so as not to distract us from the fundamental issues. Finally, I will return to his main points, responding at length to the substance of his covenantal critique.

Gordon's Position Summarized

Reformed theology is covenant theology. Regarding the centrality of the covenant in Reformed theology, Gordon's mentor Meredith Kline writes: "Reformed theology has long prized the covenant as a structural concept for integrating all that God has so diversely spoken unto men of old time and in these last days."[1] Karlberg agrees: "It is this doctrine of the covenant that distinguishes Reformed theology from all other theological traditions" and "Covenant theology has long been identified as the hallmark of the Reformed tradition."[2] In the present section under consideration, Gordon's theological critique of Bahnsen focuses on what he believes are foundational errors involving theonomy's "failure" to understand the implications of covenant theology. Thus, these (alleged) problems are system errors in the theonomic proposal, not tangential mistakes or detail irrelevancies.

The centrality of the covenant in Gordon's critique is evident in that he mentions the covenant in each one of his major sections (including his introduction and conclusion) and on almost every page of his article. In fact, the word "covenant" (in noun, adjective and adverb forms) appears 164 times in his twenty page article, averaging more than eight times on each page (by contrast "theonomy" in its various forms appears only seventy-five times).

Gordon recognizes theonomy as a species of covenant theology, and rightly so. But he argues that "Theonomy would indeed establish the extreme end of the covenant theology spectrum" (CT, 42). This is because "Theonomy does not wish merely a return to a biblical ethic, or a Judeo-Christian ethic, but to the ethic of the Sinai covenant" (CT, 23). Thus, theonomy is a form of hyper-covenantalism, an extremist abuse of covenant theology. Consequently, his first point in this section on the covenant is titled: "Historical-theological considerations." I will briefly engage his historical argument in a section later.

---

[1] Meredith G. Kline, *By Oath Consigned: Reinterpretation of the Covenant Signs of Circumcision and Baptism* (Grand Rapids: Eerdmans, 1968), 13.

[2] Mark W. Karlberg, *Covenant Theology in Reformed Perspective: Collected Essays and Book Review in Historical, Biblical, and Systematic Theology* (Eugene, Ore.: Wipf & Stock, 2000), 74.

Certainly covenantalism is the theological context from which Bahnsen operates. In his original introduction to *Theonomy in Christian Ethics* Bahnsen engages the matter of covenantal setting of the Mosaic law as he counteracts dispensationalists: "In the notes for this Bible Scofield quite plainly assigns the law of God to the temporally-limited fifth dispensation which extends from Sinai to Calvary, concluding 'The Christian is not under the conditional Mosaic Covenant of works, the law, but under the unconditional New Covenant of grace'" (TCE, 21).

Bahnsen mentions his covenantal concerns in his Preface to the second edition of *Theonomy*: "This summary highlights the fact that Theonomic Ethics, proceeding in terms of salvation by grace alone, (1) is committed to developing an overall Christian world-and-life view (2) according to the regulating principle of sola Scriptura (3) and to the hermeneutic of covenant theology" (TCE, xxvii). He even provides an entire chapter titled: "Covenantal Unity" (Ch. 8). He later states:

> Because the Apostle Paul acknowledged the unity of God's covenantal dealings throughout the Older Testamental period he could speak of the "covenants of the promise" (Eph. 2:12). Covenantal grace was central to all of God's administrations. There was one underlying promise which formed the core for all the diverse administrations of covenant relationship; God's purpose was not divided, His intentions were not dichotomized. (TCE, 479)

In *By This Standard* he speaks of his covenantal methodology involving presumed continuity within the unfolding covenant of grace: "This is, in a sense, the heart of 'covenant theology' over against a dispensational understanding of the relation between Old and New Testaments" (BTS, 3). He also offers three full chapters focusing particularly upon covenantal issues: "The Covenant's Uniform Standard of Right and Wrong" (ch. 5). "Continuity Between the Covenants of the Law" (ch. 15) and "Discontinuity Between the Covenants of the Law" (ch. 16).

It is surely appropriate then for Gordon to analyze the theonomic scheme covenantally. Were Bahnsen alive today he would welcome such an in-house critique. As it turns out, Gordon's covenantal critique leans heavily on four important Klinean emphases (which I will quickly introduce at this point). I will frame them as objections against theonomy.

The Problem of Covenant Duties

Gordon argues that covenantal duties oblige only the *express parties* to the covenant and that the Mosaic law (so important to theonomy) is inextricably bound up in the Sinaitic Covenant *with Israel*. God gave his law in covenant to Israel, and to no other nation.

> If there is a hermeneutical commitment evident in Theonomy (despite the genuine differences on many particular exegetical points within Theonomy) it is the belief that the Sinai legislation, even in its judicial dimensions, is legislation which is well-suited for, and intended to be observed by, all nations and peoples. Now plainly, the duties of a given covenant are only obligatory on those who are parties to the covenant. For Theonomy, however, all peoples in all times are obliged to these duties, unless there is some instruction somewhere else in Scripture exempting particular peoples from particular duties. The Theonomic approach, then, abstracts the legislation from its covenantal context. Apparently, for Theonomy, a covenant really was made at Sinai, but the legislation was a peripheral, incidental dimension of the covenant itself; or, a covenant was really made at Sinai, and the covenant itself continues until the return of Christ. (CT, 39-40)

Gordon is certainly correct that Bahnsen and theonomists believe that " the Sinai legislation, even in its judicial dimensions, is legislation which is well-suited for, and intended to be observed by, all nations and peoples." Thus for Gordon, since only Israel is under covenantal obligations, Theonomic Ethics is misdirected as an ethical obligation, being invalid on biblico-theological principle.

The Problem of Covenantal Discontinuity

Gordon complains that theonomy suppresses the discontinuity between covenantal administrations:

Whether due to the direct influence of Dabney and Murray or not, it is without doubt that Theonomy's approach to biblical covenants tends toward mono-covenantalism. What is distinctive about Theonomy is its resistance to recognizing discontinuity in the legislation of the various covenants.

What's in a word? Well, in this case, plenty. Theonomy's resistance to recognizing covenantal distinctions as they are represented in Scripture goes even so far as to change conventional Christian nomenclature. Throughout *Theonomy in Christian Ethics*, Bahnsen promotes the neologistic "older covenant" and "newer covenant." (CT, 39)

Thus, Gordon deems Bahnsen's (alleged) failure to recognize distinctions between the various divine covenants is a serious error in his theonomic program.

The Problem of Legalistic Element

As Gordon argues, the Sinaitic covenant involves a strongly legalistic character which is part-and-parcel to the Mosaic law code as delivered to Israel in the Sinaitic covenantal administration. This legalism is inappropriate to our New Covenant age thereby rendering the contemporary application of the Mosaic law out of keeping with the overarching covenant of grace.

His history-of-doctrine section (CT, 33-39) points out the difficulty presented by the Sinaitic Covenant, a difficulty caused by the apparent legalistic element characterizing the Mosaic law. Gordon notes that historically the unity of the covenant of grace "became a problem when discussing the Sinai administration, which apparently all conceded had both legal and gracious aspects." He argues that "Sinai was indeed difficult to describe, precisely because it continued the covenant of grace while also retaining (for typological reasons) a 'legal' element," which led to a "widespread willingness to concede a legal dimension to the Sinai administration" (CT, 34).

Gordon considers John Murray's covenantal perspective to be a forerunner to Bahnsen's theonomic method. In responding to Murray, he observes:

111

Paul, by contrast, describes covenants in terms of their administration and their stipulations or requirements, and thus contrasts the promissory character of the Abrahamic and *the "works" character of the Sinai covenant* in e.g., Galatians 3. The earliest covenant theologians of the sixteenth and seventeenth centuries appear to have employed the term 'covenant' more as Paul did, including both the stipulations and the effects of varying covenants, and this is why for them (more than for Murray) the Sinai administration could be perceived as having a *genuinely legal/works dimension*, although not with regard to salvation but with regard to inheriting and prospering in Canaan. (CT, 38, n24, emphasis mine)

As Mark Karlberg (a Klinean author whom Gordon appreciates[3]) states: "The Mosaic Covenant is to be viewed in *some sense* as a covenant of works."[4] Therefore, for Gordon (and Kline and Karlberg) the law's legalistic design renders its ethical strictures inapplicable in the purely gracious setting brought about by the cross work of Christ.[5]

---

[3] Karlberg calls Kline "one of the leading, yet often neglected, Reformed interpreters of our day." Karlberg, *Covenant Theology in Reformed Perspective*, 14. In some ways, Gordon's covenantal critique of theonomy appears to be a summary of the work of Karlberg, a disciple of Kline. See reference to Karlberg in Gordon's defense of Lee Irons in T. David Gordon, "Historic Reflections on the Continuity between Sinai Covenant and New Covenant, and therefore between the Law of Moses and Christian Duty. A Presentation by T. David Gordon to the Advisory Committee (AC-10A) of the 70th GA of the OPC Re. the Irons Appeal (June 26, 2003)."

[4] Mark W. Karlberg, "Reformed Interpretation of the Mosaic Covenant," *Westminster Theological Journal*, 43:1 (Fall, 1980): 1.

[5] Karlberg's work — a book which is much larger than Gordon's brief article (418 pp. v. 20 pp.) — focuses more at length on the problem of legalism inherent in the Sinitic administration: "The special focus of this volume is the Calvinistic teaching concerning the Mosaic Covenant as anticipatory of the New Covenant established through the shed blood of Jesus Christ." He notes that "the critical exegetical-theological debate centers upon the interpretation of Lev 18:5 ('do this and live'), in which biblical text the apostle Paul identifies the principle of *inheritance by works*, as opposed to *inheritance by faith*" (*Covenant Theology in Reformed Perspective*, 13). He frequently mentions Theonomic Ethics, its error in not recognizing this legalistic problem, and its defenders Bahnsen, Gary North, and R. J. Rushdoony.

The Problem of Decalogue Abstraction

Gordon points out that even the Ten Commandments themselves are relevant and applicable *only* in their Mosaic *environment*. They are, therefore, the unabstractable heart of the Sinaitic covenant.

> The evidence becomes even greater when we recognize throughout the Scriptures the close relation between the ten commandments and the Sinai covenant. Biblically, far from being "abstractable" from that covenant administration, the ten commandments are the *heart* thereof. The biblical authors can speak, at least by synecdoche, of the Sinai covenant as *being* the ten commandments. (CT, 40)

The Decalogue is a prominent feature of the Mosaic administration of the old, legalistic covenant. In Gordon's view, then, the Decalogue is intricately bound up with Israel's covenantal administration. Consequently, we may not abstract even it from that setting for our use in this New Covenant era.

Gordon's Weaknesses Noted

In order to keep focused on the more important differences between Gordon and Bahnsen later, I will quickly state a few secondary problems in Gordon's presentation. As I did in dealing with his two other main arguments, I must first thrash through this troublesome undergrowth before I can begin lumber-jacking in Gordon's actual forest.

Gordon's Citation Failure

As he criticizes theonomy's failure in the matter of the covenant, I must note once again a citation vacuum on his part. In his first major argument (the argument from necessity), he presented a view that he could not find in Bahnsen, even though he expressly claimed to be focusing on Bahnsen's formulation of theonomy (CT, 25). In this section his covenantal rebuttal never cites Bahnsen at all. Bahnsen's work is strongly committed to covenant theology, and he had a lot to say about God's covenants regarding God's law. I would think Gordon ought at least to quote one or two of Bahnsen's own relevant observations, but he does not.

113

Gordon's Hesitant Approach

Despite his vigorous denunciations of theonomy (as noted in my first chapter above), I was surprised that when Gordon's arguments finally appear they frequently become quite hesitant. And especially here, since he declares that "one of the most profound ironies has been the failure of covenant theologians (with some exceptions) to critique Theonomy on this point," i.e., covenant theology (CT, 40). You would think vigorous denunciations and profound ironies would lead to bold opening salvos.

His first paragraph in his covenantal critique, however, actually *cedes ground* to theonomists (at least theoretically):

> Not surprisingly, there has not been complete unanimity in understanding the relations among the various covenantal administrations in the Bible, even among those who consider themselves "covenant theologians". . . . For centuries, there has been discussion about how best to describe the similarities and dissimilarities between the various biblical covenants and the various redemptive epochs. Although I embrace one of those viewpoints, what follows is designed more to set the discussion of Theonomy within a history-of-doctrine framework, than to promote the viewpoint I hold. (CT, 33)

Though he is preparing to challenge theonomy on a "history-of-doctrine" approach, he opens by effectively confessing that he is entering territory which historically has allowed several acceptable options ("there has not been complete unanimity"), noting that this situation has prevailed "for centuries," and admitting that his own view is (allegedly) not crucial to state in his presentation ("although I embrace"). My temptation was simply to declare that theonomy holds an acceptable view in this field of possibility — even on Gordon's own analysis! — , and let it go at that. Again, given his scathing denunciations of theonomy (CT, 42, 43; IS, 22), why is he so hesitant?

Later he writes: "Interestingly, as early as the seventeenth century, the Sinai covenant was considered to be perhaps the most difficult covenant administration for covenant theologians to come to terms with" (CT, 33). By admitting this, his history-of-doctrines approach fails to nail down an *historically relevant* covenantal case against Bahnsen's theonomy. This centuries-long debate might explain why other (more cautious) covenantal theologians do not resolve "one of the most profound ironies" perplexing Gordon, which is their "failure . . . to critique Theonomy on this point" (CT, 40). Apparently, others recognize theonomy as a live option in the covenantal debate.

Gordon's Defensive Posture

As we read his critique we discover that Gordon's Klinean commitments put him on the defensive. While he argues his covenantal case, Gordon feels he must defend Kline against widespread concerns about his theological innovations. Although he makes only a brief comment in this regard, it is important in that his argument *assumes* a Klinean theology throughout. His aside shows the sting he feels in challenges to Kline's views. It is hard to criticize another theologian (Bahnsen) when one of your favorite theologians (Kline) has his own public relations problem. Gordon writes:

> Perhaps the most celebrated example [of reluctance to admit covenantal discontinuities] has been the tendency to perceive Meredith G. Kline's views as unusual or novel, when they are in fact virtually identical (in broad stroke) with the views discussed by Bolton in the early 1640s. It is not my intention to explicate or defend Kline's views here, but to remind that his views are not at all novel; they are over 350 years old. His views have been *perceived* as unusual in the context of a generation in full reaction against dispensationalism. (CT, 36)

We must note that Gordon is admitting a "tendency" (which implies a widespread concern) to deem "Kline's views as unusual or novel." Consequently, he is inadvertently confessing that Kline's views are being viewed with some suspicion in our contemporary theological environment, for Kline's "views *have been* perceived as unusual" (my emphases).

Even Kline enthusiasts recognize his tendency to innovation. In commending Kline's article, "Space and Time in the Genesis Cosmogony," Henri Blocher comments that Kline is "not afraid to leave the beaten track." As Blocher also notes of Kline's 1957 article based on Genesis 2:5: he "has thrown into the arena a new argument."[6] Kline's publisher comments on the back cover copy of *Images of the Spirit*: "Ground-breaking research has come to be a hallmark of Meredith G. Kline." The publisher of *The Structure of Biblical Authority* wrote: "Here is a distinctive approach to an old and fundamental question of the Christian faith: '*What is the Bible?*'" Bruce Waltke recently wrote: "M. Kline broke fresh ground when he modified 'sons of God' to mean 'divine' kings" in Genesis 6.[7]

Mark Karlberg speaks of Kline's "*insights* into the meaning of the biblical text that are invaluable for the contemporary *restatement* and *reformulation* of Reformed systematic theology."[8] He later writes: "Adoption of Kline's interpretations leads inevitably to a number of significant *modifications* of traditional dogmatic exposition."[9] And: "Kline's recent formulations are not only *provocative*, but they are crucial to contemporary theological debate."[10] Thus, the tendency to see "Kline's views as unusual or novel" prevails *even among his devotees.*

Strangely though, we do not have to poll other theologians and publishers regarding their recognizing novelty in Kline. Kline frequently informs us himself! In fact, one of his better known works draws attention to his innovation in his own sub-title: *By Oath Consigned: A Reinterpretation of the Covenant Signs of Circumcision and Baptism* (1968). In his rather abstruse *Images of the Spirit* (1980) he writes of his own work: "It would still appear that there is some breaking of fresh ground in the following pages."[11] He admits that his observation on a certain "foundational and pervasive theme" of Scripture is "overlooked" by other theologians: "Overlooked though it has been, the idea of creation in the image of the Glory-Spirit is, in fact, a foundational and pervasive theme in the Scriptures."[12]

---

[6] Henri Blocher, *In the Beginning: The Opening Chapters of Genesis* (Downers Grove, Ill: InterVarsity, 1984), 53.

[7] Bruce K. Waltke and Cathi J. Fredricks, *Genesis: A Commentary* (Grand Rapids: Zondervan, 2001), 116.

[8] Karlberg, *Covenant Theology in Reformed Perspective*, 338. Emphases mine.

[9] Karlberg, *Covenant Theology*, 357. Emphasis mine.

[10] Karlberg, *Covenant Theology*, 358.

[11] Meredith G. Kline, *Images of the Spirit* (Grand Rapids: Baker, 1980), 10.

[12] Kline, *Images*, 11.

In a published study on Romans 5, Kline once again leaves traditional interpretation behind, when he writes: "As I see it, the customary interpretations of Rom 5:13-14, irrespective of theological perspective, are alike in one respect: their failure to account satisfactorily for the particular segment of history Paul selects to make his point."[13] In another article he speaks of the chronological sequence view of Genesis 1 which has "long been traditional," noting that "these traditional interpretations continue to be dominant in orthodox circles." Consequently, he brings a "generally overlooked" interpretation to the debate.[14]

In his "Space and Time in Genesis Cosmogony" article Kline distances himself from the "more traditional types of exegesis,"[15] offering instead: "My apologia concludes then with a claim of adding something somewhat fresh to the old debate."[16] He closes his article noting that "our conclusion is then that the more traditional interpretations of the creation account are guilty not only of creating a conflict between the Bible and science but, in effect, of pitting Scripture against Scripture."[17]

In his Preface to *The Structure of Biblical Authority* he writes: "The initial concern with the canonical aspect of Scripture led inevitably to reexamination of the formal character of Scripture as such." 'What is the Bible?' became a central question, and it receives here a somewhat distinctive answer, in line with the new direction taken in the formulation of biblical canonicity."[18] In the book itself he offers his own "somewhat fresh formulation" of ethics: "our thesis is that this Old Testament ethical pattern is an aspect of intrusion."[19]

---

[13] Meredith G. Kline, "Gospel Until the Law: Romans 5:13-14 and the Old Covenant," *Journal of the Evangelical Theological Society*, 34:4 (December 1991): 433.

[14] Meredith G. Kline, "Because It Had Not Rained." *Westminster Theological Journal* 20 (May, 1958): 146.

[15] Meredith G. Kline, "Space and Time in the Genesis Cosmogony," *Perspectives on Science and Christian Faith* 48:1 (March 1996): 11.

[16] Kline, "Space and Time," 2.

[17] Kline, "Space and Time," 14.

[18] Meredith G. Kline, *The Structure of Biblical Authority* (Grand Rapids: Eerdmans, 1972), 7.

[19] Kline, *Structure of Biblical Authority*, 154, 160.

So then, while Gordon himself laments the *"tendency* to perceive Meredith G. Kline's views as unusual or novel," we must understand why such a tendency exists. Some who even agree with Kline recognize he is "not afraid to leave the beaten track" or to throw "into the arena a new argument" (Blocher), or to effect "modifications" in Reformed theology (Karlberg), or to move into "fresh ground" (Waltke). His publishers mention as a "hallmark" his tendency to "ground-breaking research" and his "distinctive approach" to issues. Even Kline himself delights in offering his own "re-interpretation" of theological themes, pursuing "fresh ground," establishing "overlooked" observations, leaving behind "customary interpretations," rebutting views that have "long been traditional," while presenting "something somewhat fresh" and urging "reexamination" of texts as he offers "a somewhat distinctive answer." No wonder there is a tendency to "perceive" Kline as offering "unusual or novel" positions!

Gordon's Historical-Theological Argument

I will now return to a matter I mentioned in my introduction to the present work. But here I not only will reiterate it, but expand upon it due to the significance Gordon gives to the covenantal critique of theonomy, the "hermeneutical commitment evident in Theonomy" (CT, 40). Oddly, on the one hand he attacks theonomy as an "extreme viewpoint" (CT, 42, cf. also 43) that misunderstands covenantal principles by following an "a-covenantal hermeneutic" (CT, 42). But then he admits on the other that it falls within an acceptable mainstream view of Reformed orthodoxy. The critics of theonomy need to be made aware of their own history-of-doctrine problem in this regard (theonomic methodology is not a bizarre novelty in theological history), while theonomists themselves should recognize their own acceptable place in the Reformed tradition.

Here I will recall his extreme denunciation of theonomy in a later article:

Theonomy is not merely an error, though it has manifestly been regarded as erroneous by the Reformed tradition. It is the error du jour, the characteristic error of an unwise generation. It is the error of a generation that has abandoned the biblically mandated quest for wisdom on the assumption that the Bible *itself* contains all that we need to know about life's various enterprises. It is the proof-textual, Bible-thumping, literalist, error par excellence. (IS, 22)

He does not go that far in the article before us.[20] But he does lean that way by concluding that theonomy is "partly" an "outrageous or extreme viewpoint" (CT, 42), a "psychological phenomenon" arising from "authoritarian personalities" (CT, 43). Gordon is obviously not trying to follow Dale Carnegie in an effort to "win friends and influence people" in the theonomic movement.

Gordon Discounts Particular Reformed Theologians

In order to attack theonomy, Gordon has to criticize several noteworthy Reformed schools and theologians along the way. He criticizes the Westminster divines en masse (CT, 40, 42[21]), as he does Scottish Presbyterianism (CT, 38). He also vigorously rejects the views of Robert L. Dabney (CT, 34-35, 38) and John Murray (CT, 36-38). His critique of the divines is especially interesting in that both he and Bahnsen took ministerial vows swearing to "sincerely receive and adopt" the Westminster Standards which the divines authored.

After criticizing the "errors" of these Reformed theologians, Gordon then concludes:

> It may not be merely coincidental, then, that many of the more ardent proponents of Theonomy are influenced by the same tradition that influenced (and possibly culminated in) John Murray. If Dabney, Murray, et al. were uncomfortable recognizing fundamental differences in the stipulations of the Mosaic covenant and other biblical covenants, it would not

---

[20] The newer article suggests he has hardened himself in his views. He states: "If anything has changed, then, it is that I would now argue with equal zeal for the *in*sufficiency of Scripture in other than religious or covenantal areas." (IS, 22). Consequently, the more denigrating language betrays his more "mature" thinking on the subject.

[21] Karlberg, a Klinean theologian and a resource for Gordon, writes: "Certain elements in the *Confession* indicate an orientation toward 'theonomic politics." Karlberg, *Covenant Theology*, 67.

be surprising if those influenced by them would be uncomfortable recognizing fundamental differences in the *legislation* within the various covenants. (CT, 38)

Gordon Disagrees with Classic Reformed Theologians

Gordon's views are also contrary to many other Reformed authorities who tend to be closer to theonomy than to his peculiar Klinean covenantalism. Many Reformed theologians of note accept the Mosaic law as a pattern for New Covenant ethics and political theory. Oddly enough, though Gordon charges theonomy with being on "the extreme end of the covenant theology spectrum" (CT, 42), it actually would appear that Klinean theology is on the extreme end of the scale. In other words, a "history-of-doctrine" approach hurts Gordon's own position rather than Bahnsen's — especially in light of the names omitted from his survey. Let us consider several notable samples from the Reformed tradition.

John Calvin (1509-64) Theologians point to the strong tendency in Calvin toward covenantal continuity and the endorsing of the contemporary relevance of God's law. Andrew Hoeffecker complains in this regard about Calvin: "Calvin did not distinguish sharply enough between the way God related to Israel in the Old Testament (especially through the theocracy) and the church in the New Testament."[22] Alister McGrath agrees with Hoeffecker's understanding of Calvin: "Nevertheless, it will be clear that his stress upon the unity of the Old and New Testaments raises a very serious difficulty: there appears to be no fundamental difference between the old and new covenants, save that of clarity of expression."[23] The *Encyclopedia of the Reformed Faith* sets Calvin over against Luther regarding the place of the law: "For Luther [the law] generally connotes something negative and hostile; hence his listing the law along with sin, death, and the devil. For Calvin, the law was viewed primarily as a positive expression of the will of God whereby

---

[22] W. Andrew Hoeffecker, ed., *Universe, Society, and Ethics*, vol. 2, *Building a Christian Worldview* (Phillipsburg, N.J.: Presbyterian and Reformed, 1986), 239.

[23] Alister E. McGrath, *A Life of John Calvin: A Study in the Shaping of Western Culture* (Grand Rapids: Baker, 1990), 161.

God restores the image of God in humanity and order in the fallen creation."[24]

Regarding the Decalogue, the modern editor's "Introduction" to Calvin's study on the Ten Commandments reads: "By the moral law [Calvin] meant the Decalogue, which he defined as 'the true and eternal rule of righteousness' for all men and nations 'who wish to conform their lives to God's will."[25] Andrew Hoeffecker notes the practical impact of Calvin's view of the law: "Calvin was also deeply involved in organizing social life in Geneva. To him the Ten Commandments, especially the last six, were the norm for all social activity."[26]

These statements well summarize Calvin's views on this issue, demonstrating his strong commitment to covenant continuity and, therefore, the continuing relevance of the Mosaic law. At this juncture I will simply list a few relevant citations from Calvin himself supporting this observation:

> He [God] willed for the law to be written "down" and preserved that it might not simply serve one age, but that it might retain its vigor and authority until the end of the world.[27]

> Now in particular he wanted to write . . . [the law] on two tablets of stone that it might endure, for it was not given [to last] for just a brief period [of time] as something transient. . . . The truth and substance of the law were not [confined] to one age; they constitute something permanent which shall abide forever.[28]

> It is appropriate for you to observe this law, since it has been established to be permanent, to endure age after age, and to be preached until the end of the world.[29]

---

[24] I. John Hesselink, in Donald K. McKim, ed., *Encyclopedia of the Reformed Faith* (Louisville: Westminster, 1997), 215.

[25] Benjamin W. Farley, *John Calvin's Sermons on the Ten Commandments* (Grand Rapids: Baker, 1980), 24.

[26] Hoeffecker, *Universe, Society, and Ethics*, 241.

[27] Calvin, *Sermons on the Ten Commandments*, 238.

[28] Calvin, *Sermons on the Ten Commandments*, 25.

[29] Calvin, *Sermons on the Ten Commandments*, 48.

It is true that the law with regard to its ceremonies has been abolished, but with regard to its substance and doctrine which it contains, it always has virtue; it never decays. Thus let us note that although we did not live in the time of Moses, that does not mean that we can scorn the remonstrances which he made and which are contained in the law. Why? Because he was speaking to us; he was not simply speaking to that multitude which was assembled on the mountain of Horeb. In general, he was speaking to the whole world.[30]

3. The Law of God Alike for All. Because there is one only Lord and Master who has dominion over our consciences, and because his will is the only principle of all justice, we confess all our life ought to be ruled in accordance with the commandments of his holy law in which is contained all perfection of justice, and that we ought to have no other rule of good and just living, nor invent other good works to supplement it than whose which are there contained, as follows: Exodus 20: 'I am the Lord thy God, who brought thee,' and so on. (From Calvin's "Genevan Confession."[31])

Certain ignorant persons, not understanding this distinction, rashly cast out the whole law of Moses, and bid farewell to the Two Tables of the Law .... Banish this wicked thought from our minds! (*Inst.* 2:7:13)

The covenant made with all the patriarchs is so much like ours in substance and reality that the two are actually one and the same. (*Inst.* 2:10:2)

The moral law (to begin first with it) is contained under two heads. ... It is the true and eternal rule of righteousness, prescribed for men of all nations and times, who wish to confirm their lives to God's will. For it is his eternal and unchangeable will that he himself indeed be worshiped by us all, and that we love one another (*Inst.* 4:20:15).

Clearly Gordon is out of step with Calvin, whereas Bahnsen is much closer to Calvin's covenantal social theory.

---

[30] Calvin, *Sermons on the Ten Commandments*, 49.

[31] J. K. S. Reid, *Calvin: Theological Treatises* (Philadelphia: Westminster, 1954), 26.

Other early Reformers

Huldrych Zwingli (1484-1531). Lillback quotes *An Exposition of the Faith* by Zwingli: "We preach the law as well as grace. For from the law the faithful and elect learn the will of God and the wicked are also affrighted so that they either serve their neighbour through fear or reveal all their desperation and unbelief."[32] He points out that Zwingli's argument for infant baptism, which was rooted in the Old Testament, was vigorously denounced by Anabaptists: "This type of interpretation was illegitimate . . . because the Old Testament was promised only to the Jews and not to the heathen."

John Oecolampadius (1482-1531) and Heinrich Bullinger (1504-75). Lillback also notes that the Reformer Oecolampadius argued that "the Christian stands in the same covenant with the Jews."[33] Bullinger remarked that "the things which are agreeable to the law of nature and the Ten Commandments, and whatsoever else God has commanded to be punished, must not in any case be either clean forgotten, or lightly regarded."[34]

Later Reformers

John Knox (1514-71). Knox writes: "Of these two places it is evident, that principally it appertains to the king, or to the chief magistrate, to know the will of God, to be instructed in his law and statutes, and to promote his glory with his whole heart and study, which are the chief points of the first table."[35] Elsewhere he states: "The moral law is the constant and unchangeable will of God, to which the Gentile is no less bound than were the Jews."[36]

Samuel Bolton (1606-54). Sounding almost like Bahnsen himself, Bolton (an important source cited by Gordon, CT, 34-38), wrote of

---

[32] Peter A. Lillback, *The Binding of God: Calvin's Role in the Development of Covenant Theology* (Grand Rapids: Baker, 2001), 76.

[33] Lillback, *The Binding of God*, 85.

[34] Heinrich Bullinger, *The Decades*, ed., Thomas Harding (Cambridge: University Press, 1849), 3:280. Cited in Karlberg, *Covenant Theology*, 62.

[35] John Knox, *Selected Writings of John Knox* (Dallas, Tex.: Presbyterian Heritage, 1995), 409.

[36] Knox, *Selected Writings*, 410.

Matthew 5:17-18: "This seems to be very full and very plain for the continuance of and obligation to the law." And he went on to buttress his observation by appeal to Romans 3:31; 7:12, 22, 25; James 2:8; and 1 John 2:4; 3:4. He continues:

> Therefore, since Christ, who is the best expounder of the law, so largely strengthens and confirms the law (witness the Sermon on the Mount, and also Mark 10:19); since faith does not supplant, but strengthens the law; since the apostle so often presses and urges the duties commanded in the law of God in his mind, and that he was under the law of Christ (1 Cor. 9:21); I may rightly conclude that the law, for the substance of it, still remains a rule of life to the people of God. . . . If Christ and His apostles commanded the same things which the law required, and forbade and condemned the same things which the law forbade and condemned, then they did not abrogate it but strengthened and confirmed it. And this is what they did: see Matt. 5:19. . . . But he that breaks the law does sin, as says the apostle: 'Sin is the transgression of the law' (1 John 3:4). and 'Where no law is there is no transgression' (Rom. 4:15). Therefore Christians are bound, if they would avoid sin, to obey the law.[37]

> My work is to show the chief and principle ends for which the law was promulgated or given. There are two main ends to be observed, one was political, the other theological or divine. The political use is hinted at by the apostle in I Tim. 1:8-9. . . . It was made for them [sinners] in such fashion that, if it were not their rule, it should be their punishment. Such is the political use of the law.[38]

James Durham (1622-58). The popular Puritan writer James Durham wrote: "The first conclusion that we take for granted is, that this law (as it is moral) ties even Christians and believers now, as well as of old. . . .

---

[37] Samuel Bolton, *The True Bounds of Christian Freedom* (Edinburgh: Banner of Truth, rep. 1964 [1645]), 61.

[38] Bolton, *True Bounds*, 78.

Christ was so far from destroying this law in its authority, and Paul so
far from making it void by the doctrine of faith, that our Lord tells, he
came to fulfill it (Matt. 5:17), and Paul shows that his preaching of faith
was to establish it (Rom. 3:31). Which truth being confirmed by them
both in their practice and doctrine shows that the breach of the holy
law of God is no less sinful to us now, than it was to them before us."[39]

God added "the law on mount Sinai, as a help to the covenant
made with Abraham (Gen. 17) which was a covenant of grace, and was
never altered as to its substance." Indeed, "the duties called for here are
to be performed as a part of the covenant of grace, and of the obligation that lies upon us thereby."[40]

George Gillespie (1613-48). Westminster divine, George Gillespie, responded against the "the Arians, Ebonites and Socinians, who argued
that "in controversies, or questions of religion, we must not argue from
the Old Testament, but from the New": "Our orthodox protestant
writers condemn as well the Anabaptists who reject and scorn at arguments brought against them from the Old Testament, as the Manichees
who did repudiate the Old Testament as having proceeded from an evil
God. . . . By the same principle they must deny that an oath (be it never
so just and necessary) may be imposed by authority, or that the magistrate ought to put to death a blasphemer, an incestuous person, an
adulterer, a witch, or the like (the scriptural warrants which make them
crimes capital being in the Old, not in the New Testament). Saith not
the Apostle, 2 Tim. iii. 16, 'All scripture (and consequently the lawful
examples and laudable precedents of the Old Testament) is given by
inspiration of God, and is profitable for doctrine, for reproof, for correction, for instruction in righteousness.'"[41]

---

[39] James Durham, *Practical Exposition of the Ten Commandments*, ed. by Christopher
Coldwell, *Practical Exposition of the Ten Commandments* (Dallas: Naphtali, rep. 2002 [1675]),
53.

[40] Durham, *Ten Commandments*, 53.

[41] George Gillespie, *The Works of George Gillespie* (Edmonton, Alb.: Still Waters
Revival, rep. 1991), 2:67-68. I should note that modern theonomists do not necessarily agree with his exegesis and application, but we do respect his reformational reflex
in endorsing the continuing validity of God's law in the realm of civil discourse.

Gordon Contradicts General Reformed Theology

Gordon's peculiar Klinean views (i.e., the Mosaic law was intended solely and exclusively for Israel, the Ten Commandments cannot be "abstracted" from the Sinaitic Covenant, a radical discontinuity separates the Mosaic economy from other divine covenants) are contrary to the general convictions of historic Reformed orthodoxy.

The Law in the Believer's Life. Lillback speaks of "the Reformed emphasis upon the law in the believer's life."[42] Berkhof observes that "the Heidelberg Catechism devotes not less than eleven Lord's Days to the discussion of the law."[43] In this regard, Jones well summarizes the matter of the Ten Commandments: "The catechetical tradition of the Christian church — continued and expanded by both Protestants and Catholics after the Reformation— puts the Ten Commandments (with some variations in enumeration) alongside the Apostles' Creed and the Lord's Prayer to provide the primary pedagogical tools for communicating the cognitive structure of the Christian faith."[44]

The Three-fold use of the Law. The well-known three-fold use of the law contradicts Gordon's summary dismissal of the law from Christian ethics. As David C. Jones observes: "Eventually the different functions of the law became standardized as civil or political, convictional or pedagogical, and normative or didactic. To summarize: The civil use of the law is as a bridle to restrain sin and to promote justice in society. The pedagogical use of the law is a mirror to convict of sin and to show the need of a Savior. The third or directional use of the law is as a map to guide believers in their new obedience."[45] Louis Berkhof agrees: "It is customary in theology to distinguish a three-fold use of the law"[46]

---

[42] Lillback, *The Binding of God*, 76.
[43] Berkhof, *Systematic Theology*, 615.
[44] Jones, *Biblical Christian Ethics*, 104.
[45] David Clyde Jones, *Biblical Christian Ethics* (Grand Rapids: Baker, 1994), 120.
[46] Louis Berkhof, *Systematic Theology* (Grand Rapids: Eerdmans, 1941), 614.

The Political Use of the Law. Calvin even applies Paul's statement in 1 Timothy 1:8ff to the political use of the law (*Inst.* 1:358-59). Jones reminds us that "the first use [of the law] is political or civil. . . . The civil restraint of the law is appointed by God for public peace and preservation of the social order so that the gospel may make its way unhindered by those in the grip of Satan."[47] The *Encyclopedia of the Reformed Faith* states: "A distinctive characteristic of the Reformed view of the law is its emphasis on the third use of the law. For John Calvin, this function of the law as a norm and guide for the believer is its 'proper and principal' use."[48] Berkhof comments on "a *usus politicus* or *civilis.* The law serves the purpose of restraining sin and promoting righteousness."[49]

Klinean theologian Mark Karlberg admits that: "since the time of the Reformation there has been a Reformed consensus that there is an interconnection between OT laws, personal Christian life, and national public policy."[50] He even notes that:

> those of the magisterial wing of the Reformation were committed to the implementation and enforcement of Christian principles of morality, if need be by use of the sword. They believed that the Mosaic civil legislation regulative of the ancient Israelite theocracy was at the same time compatible with natural law implanted in human reason by virtue of creation in God's image. Though the law of Moses was not the meritorious basis of temporal or eternal salvation, nevertheless it provided a *model* (not a norm) for civil duty. Thus, the civil code of Moses was instructive in the public ordering of life and society in every nation, especially the Christian commonwealth. This was, in traditional Protestant terminology, the 'first use' of the law of God. . . . [T]he law of God was normative for Christian living, good works being the fruit of justifying faith.[51]

---

[47] Jones, *Biblical Christian Ethics*, 118.

[48] *Encyclopedia of the Reformed Faith*, 215.

[49] Berkhof, *Systematic Theology*, 614.

[50] Karlberg, *Covenant Theology*, 59.

[51] Karlberg, *Covenant Theology*, 114.

Karlberg even comments that "in the latter half of the seventeenth century ... the Puritans viewed the Mosaic civil code as normatively binding on all nations everywhere" and "the Puritans gave further room for theonomic politics. Over time the Puritan civil enactments conformed more and more to the old Mosaic legislation with its accompanying sanctions."[52]

Gordon Disputes Contemporary Reformed Theology

Gordon's peculiar Klinean views are contrary to the general convictions of more recent Reformed scholars.

Benjamin B. Warfield (1851-1921). Warfield observed in his writings that "there is no duty imposed upon the Israelite in the Ten Commandments which is not equally incumbent upon all men, everywhere. These commandments are but the positive publication to Israel of the universal human duties, the common morality of mankind. The law, he declares, in the most solemn manner, is not susceptible of being done away with, but shall never cease to be authoritative and obligatory."[53] He writes further: "So long as time endures, the law shall endure in full validity, down to its smallest details. ... Now, the law of which our Lord makes this strong assertion of its ever-abiding validity, includes, as one of its prominent constituent parts, just the Ten Commandments."[54]

Geerhardus Vos (1862-1949). Vos is the father of biblical theology and exercises a strong influence over Kline's method which is adopted by Gordon. In fact, Gordon's article expresses appreciation for Vos on three occasions: On page 2 he directs the reader to others who have "ably discussed" the particular matter under consideration, including Vos. On page 33 he speaks of "developing a theology of the covenants, or a biblical theology (in the Vosian sense)." On page 39 (note 26) he makes an observation important to his position on covenantal discontinuity: "Geerhardus Vos . . . recognizes in his biblical theology not

---

[52] Karlberg, *Covenant Theology*, 67.

[53] B. B. Warfield, *Selected Shorter Writings of Benjamin B. Warfield* (Phillipsburg, N.J.: P & R, rep. 1970), 1:312.

[54] Warfield, *Selected Shorter Writings—I*, 314.

only what he called the 'organic principle' (his label for continuity), but also what he called the 'principle of periodicity' (his label for discontinuity)."

As it turns out, regarding the Ten Commandments Vos would *disagree* with Gordon, for Gordon discounts the Ten Commandments as our authority today:

> Theonomists are not the first to abstract legislation from the Sinai covenant. The Westminster Assembly appears to have done it beforehand, though on a much smaller scale and in a more ambiguous manner. The divines at Westminster appear to have abstracted the decalogue from the Sinai covenant, and to have understood the ten words as timeless and, if you will, "covenant-less." ... We [must] recognize throughout the Scriptures the close relation between the ten commandments and the Sinai covenant. Biblically, far from being "abstractable" from that covenant administration, the ten commandments are the *heart* thereof. (CT, 40)

Now consider the following statements by Vos on the contemporary authority of the Decalogue. Vos directly contradicts Gordon's hermeneutic:

> It may be observed, that, while the words are primarily addressed to Israel, this was due entirely to the circumstances of the historical situation, and can never prove the existence in the mind of the legislator of a double standard, rendering a thing sinful when done to a fellow-Israelite, and condonable when done to non-Israelites.
>
> The primary application to Israel in no wise interferes with a world-wide application in all ethical relationships. . . . Certain features at first sight would seem applicable to Israel alone, for instance what is said of the deliverance from the Egyptian bondage. . . . The historical adjustment does not detract from the universal application, but subserves it.[55]

---

[55] Geerhardus Vos, *Biblical Theology: Old and New Testaments* (Grand Rapids: Eerdmans, 1948), 147.

If we may apply the term 'Christian' thus retrospectively to the Decalogue, we should say, what it contains is not general but Christian ethics.[56]

Elsewhere Vos comments on the law of God as an aspect of the eschatological orientation of the covenant of works:

> The truth of the matter is that in the covenant of works the natural relationship was made to serve a positive purpose. It is not set aside, but incorporated into something higher. From this it follows that, where the higher becomes powerless and falls away, the natural relationship nevertheless remains. As a creature man is subject to God, and, had it not pleased God to reward the keeping of the law with eternal life, the requirement would still be effective. "Do this!" is still valid, even if it is not followed by: "You shall live." Thus, it is that in the covenant of grace, too, the participants are exempt from the demand of the law as the condition for eternal blessedness, but not from its demand as being normative for their moral life.[57]

Herman Ridderbos (1909-). Dutch theologian Ridderbos writes:

> The law is the norm appointed by God for man's relationship to God and for true manhood. . . . When Paul uses 'law' in this sense . . . he means in general the law of Moses (cf. 1 Cor. 9:9; Rom. 10:5). He speaks of it in an undifferentiated sense, i.e., without expressly distinguishing between its various constituent parts, but in doing so he has the moral demands of the law especially in view, in particular those of the decalogue (cf. Rom. 13:8-10; Gal. 5:14; Rom. 2:17-22). It is the special privilege of Israel to have received this law, a matter to which Paul

---

[56] Vos, *Biblical Theology*, 148.

[57] Geerhardus Vos, *Redemptive History and Biblical Interpretation: The Shorter Writings of Geerhardus Vos*, ed. by Richard B. Gaffin, Jr., (Phillipsburg, N.J.: Presbyterian and Reformed, 1980), 244.

draws attention or alludes in a great many connections (cf. Rom. 2:17ff.; 9:4; et al.).

Yet the knowledge of the law is not confined to Israel. Very closely bound up with the view of man as creature of God is the fact that to the gentiles as well all knowledge of the law cannot be denied (Rom. 2:14ff). . . . He thereby speaks very definitely of the law and by that means qualitatively the same law as that which has been given to the Jews. . . . [I]t is true above all that the law of which Paul speaks in this whole context is the law of God.[58]

So far as the law of Moses is concerned, when Paul gives expression to the continuing demand of the law, he cites the decalogue specifically. One can hardly make contrasts here between "Moses" and "Christ," nor between "the law" and "the law of Moses." And this holds, too, for the qualification "the commandments." However true it is that Christ has abolished "the law of commandments, consisting in ordinances" (Eph. 2:15; Col 2:14), this does not alter the fact that it is said elsewhere that what really matters is the keeping of God's commandments (*entolon*; 1 Cor. 7:19), and that in concrete cases an explicit appeal can be made to an individual "ordinance" in the law of Moses (Eph. 6:2; 1 Cor. 9:9ff.). Also the contrast between the unity (of the law of Christ) and the multiplicity (of the law of Moses), however meaningful this distinction may be in a specific context (cf. Mark 12:32ff), must be rejected as false, if it is intended to oppose the continuing significance of Moses.

As for (c), if one asks himself what the material content is of the expression "bound to the law of Christ" (2 Cor. 9:21), the answer will lie in the fact that Christ *suo modo* represents the law of God and thus the law of Moses. . . . There can thus be no doubt whatever that the category of the law has not been abrogated with Christ's advent, but rather has been maintained and interpreted in its radical sense ("fulfilled"; Matt. 5:17).[59]

---

[58] Herman Ridderbos, *Paul: An Outline of His Theology* (Grand Rapids: Eerdmans, 1975), 106.

[59] Ridderbos, *Paul*, 285.

O. Palmer Robertson (1937-present):

Are we to conclude that all the various covenantal administrations of the Old Testament find continuing significance for believers today with the single exception of the Mosaic covenant? Are we to presume that the covenant of law alone among divinely-initiated covenants has lost its binding significance?

To the contrary, presumption would favor the continuing significance of the Mosaic covenant for the believer today.[60]

Albert M. Wolters (1942-present):

What makes the light of Scripture so helpful and indispensable is that it spells out in clear human language what God's law is. Even without Scripture we have some notion of the requirements of justice, but Moses and the prophets, Jesus and the apostles put it into clear, unmistakable imperatives.[61]

David C. Jones (1937-present):

If the Ten Commandments are the covenant God made with Israel, how can they be universal norms of human conduct? . . . That the ten words are still operative appears also from Jesus' exposition of the moral law in the Sermon on the Mount.

The authority of the Decalogue is thus presupposed in Jesus' teaching. . . . The reason the Ten Commandments are directives for the people of God under the new covenant as well as the old is because they represent the essential will of God for human beings as such.[62]

The Ten Commandments are universal moral norms because they represent the will of God for human nature as he created it . . . ; they are ground in his purposes and instruction for human beings always and everywhere.[63]

---

[60] O. Palmer Robertson, *The Christ of the Covenants* (Phillipsburg, N.J.: P & R, 1980), 183.

[61] Albert M. Wolters, *Creation Regained: Biblical Basics for a Reformation Worldview* (Grand Rapids: Eerdmans, 1985), 33.

[62] Jones, *Biblical Christian Ethics*, 106, 107, 109.

[63] Jones, *Biblical Christian Ethics*, 116.

Gordon Misreads Reformed Samples

Though I must bypass much of his "history-of-doctrine" analysis due to space limitations, I was quite surprised to see Gordon — a capable and experienced theologian and a clear and effective writer — stumbling here. I will focus on only one sample: his misrepresentation of Robert Lewis Dabney. In one respect it is not necessary that I challenge him on his mistaken interpretation of Dabney, since I am defending Bahnsen. Yet in another, it helps us to see that Gordon (like many other critics of theonomy[64]) can be incautious, not just in his occasional vitriol against theonomy, but also in his reading of theology. This should alert us to the dangers of a being overzealous in theological discourse. I will not deal at length with his stumblings here, but I will provide enough information on this one sample so that my reader may sense the frustration theonomists feel and so that he may look into the matter further if interested.

In his article Gordon misstates Dabney's views regarding three fundamental matters[65]: (1) He claims Dabney believed that a covenant "was *either* gracious *or* legal" so that he did not recognize a "legal dimension" existing at Sinai (CT, 35). (2) He claims Dabney held "a genuine error on his part," which was that God's "unchangeable character [was] not capable, apparently, of revealing 'new elements' to subsequent covenant-administrations, but only of revealing 'developments of existing features'" (CT, 35). (3) He claims Dabney's view "essentially affirms moral law to exist in the universe apart from the volition of the Creator," so that he believes there are 'intrinsic and eternal' moral laws in the universe, prior to God's volition, which God does not establish but only recognizes?" (CT, 36 n19). He is wrong on each of these points.

Dabney on Sinai Legislation

Gordon thinks Dabney does not recognize a "legal dimension" in the Sinaitic legislation (CT, 35). Gordon argues:

---

[64] See Bahnsen, *No Other Standard: Theonomy and Its Critics.* See especially chapters 3 ("Spurious Targets and Misguided Arrows") and 4 ("Theological and Logical Fallacies").

[65] Oddly the three matters Gordon misrepresents Dabney on are the three main reasons he disputes Dabney! In other words, all three of his reasons for criticizing Dabney are mistaken.

Dabney's disagreement was partially due to a misunderstanding. Dabney apparently believed that a covenant was *either* gracious *or* legal. Believing this, and rightly recognizing that there were true saints under the Sinai administration, who would profit from the gracious atoning work of Christ, Dabney could not describe such an administration as 'legal.' What he appears to have misunderstood is that the legal dimension recognized by many at Sinai was only *one dimension*. That is, other orthodox theologians had not argued that the Sinai administration was exclusively, or even primarily, legal; they had argued that there was a legal dimension, related to the inheritance of the land of Canaan. (CT, 35)

Actually, Dabney can speak of various "aspects" (i.e., dimensions) of the Sinai Covenant: "It is the Covenant of Sinai viewed in one of its limited aspects only, which is here [in Jer 31] set in antithesis to the Covenant of Grace: It is the secular theocratic covenant, in which political and temporal prosperity in Canaan was promised, and calamity threatened."[66]

Unfortunately for Gordon, Dabney continues in a direction that Gordon overlooks. Dabney does, in fact, consider a view very close to Gordon's conception (which sees the legal dimension as an aspect of the typological character of the Sinaitic administration). Dabney points out that the French Reformed theologian Moise Amyraut (1596-1664) held such a view:

> The French divines, Camero and Amyraut, proposed an ingenious modification of the legal theory of Moses' covenant: That in it a certain kind of life was proposed (as in the Covenant of Works,) as a reward for an exact obedience: But that the life was temporal, in a prosperous Canaan, and the obedience was ritual. This is true, so far as a visible church-standing turned on a ritual obedience. But to the Hebrew, that tempo-

---

[66] Robert L. Dabney, *Lectures in Systematic Theology* (Grand Rapids: Zondervan, 1973 [rep. 1878]), 456.

ral life in happy Canaan was a type of heaven; which was not promised to an exact moral obedience, but to faith. Were this theory modified, so as to represent this dependence of the Hebrew's church-standing on his ritual obedience, as a mere type and emblem of the law's spiritual work as a 'schoolmaster to lead us to Christ,' it might stand.[67]

For this stringency was designed to be, to the Israelite, a perpetual reminder of the law which was to Adam, the condition of life, now broken, and its wrath already incurred, thus to hedge up the awakened conscience to Christ.[68]

We must note, then, contrary to Gordon, Dabney *does* recognize a legal dimension in the Sinaitic covenant. Of Amyraut's legal, Covenant of Works view he writes: "*This is true*, so far as a visible church-standing turned on a ritual obedience" (emphasis mine). And he even notes the purpose of this legal dimension: it was "a perpetual reminder of the law which was to Adam, the condition of life, now broken, and its wrath already incurred, thus to hedge up the awakened conscience to Christ." So Dabney *does* accept a legal *dimension* within the Mosaic law.

Dabney on Covenantal Changes

Gordon charges Dabney with "a genuine error" in holding that God's "unchangeable character [was] not capable, apparently, of revealing 'new elements' to subsequent covenant-administrations, but only of revealing 'developments of existing features'" (CT, 35). Gordon misunderstands and therefore badly misrepresents Dabney here. Gordon does not understand and explain *in what sense* God's unchangeable character forbids "new elements." To the unwary reader it appears that Dabney has an ironclad principle that new elements may not appear in developing covenantal transactions because God is unchanging. But this is simply not Dabney's view.

Gordon's full statement in this regard reads:

[67] Robert L. Dabney, *Lectures in Systematic Theology* (Grand Rapids: Zondervan, 1973 [rep. 1878]), 453.

[68] Dabney, *Lectures in Systematic Theology*, 454.

Dabney's disagreement was also due, however, to a genuine error on his part, one which would not remain confined to him. Note that Dabney considered it "untenable" for Sinai to be legal, because this would be "inconsistent with God's spiritual and unchangeable character." For Dabney, an unchangeable character is not capable, apparently, of revealing "new elements" to subsequent covenant-administrations, but only of revealing "developments of existing features." For Dabney, covenants (and laws) are reflections of the character of the one establishing the covenants (and laws) and thus are no more changeable than the character of the one so establishing them. (CT, 35)

Now we must notice the reason for Gordon's confusion: it lies in his only partially quoting Dabney. Gordon quotes Dabney as follows: "The Covenant of Sinai has seemed to many to wear such an aspect of legality, that they have supposed themselves constrained to regard it as a species of Covenant of Works.... This is untenable; because it is inconsistent with God's spiritual and unchangeable character, and with His honour" (CT, 35).

The ellipsis leaves out vitally important material. I will cite Dabney's whole sentence to show the serious failure in Gordon's representing the matter: "The Covenant of Sinai has seemed to many to wear such an aspect of legality, that they have supposed themselves constrained to regard it as a species of Covenant of Works; and, therefore a recession from the Abrahamic Covenant, which, we are expressly told, (John viii: 56; Gal. iii: 8,) contained the gospel."[69] Dabney's full sentence, then, shows that his problem with seeing Sinai as a legal covenant was *not* rooted in God's unchangeable character per se, but in God's unchangeable character allowing a *retrogression* in redemptive history, away from the gospel back to the Covenant of Works legal principle. On page 453 Dabney continues (note that Gordon's ellipsis picks up with the last sentence in this material): "so that had the transactions of Sinai been a *regression* from the 'Gospel preached before unto Abraham,' to a Covenant of Works, it would have been a most signal curse poured out on

---

[69] Dabney, *Lectures in Systematic Theology*, 452.

a chosen people. This is untenable; because it is inconsistent with God's spiritual and unchangeable character, and with His honour" (Emphasis mine).

Dabney's problem is not with new features per se, but with *retrogressive* movement. That is, the unchanging character of God will not have him moving from a gracious covenant back to legal covenant, then on forward once again with the gracious covenant. I have already shown in my first objection that Dabney will allow a legal *dimension* as a typological element in the Mosaic covenant.

Interestingly, Dabney follows a similar line of argument as does Samuel Bolton (who is highly commended by Gordon as an historical resource on the development of covenant theology):

> If God had introduced the law as a covenant, it would have disannulled the promise. It would also have declared God to be changeable, which cannot be, for, as the apostle says, 'God is one' (Gal. 3:20). . . . If God set this up as a covenant after He had given the promise, either this would have showed mutability in God's will, or contradiction in His acts, which cannot be. Therefore the law could not be a covenant of works.

Bolton further adds:

> There is, however, a second opinion in which I find that the majority of our holy and most learned divines concur, namely, that though the law is called a covenant, yet it was not a covenant of works for salvation; nor was it a third covenant of works and grace, but it was the same covenant in respect of its nature and design under which we stand under the Gospel, even the covenant of grace, though more legally dispensed to the Jews. It differed not in substance from the covenant of grace, but in degree, say some divines, in the economy and external administration of it, say others.[70]

---

[70] Bolton, *The True Bounds of Christian Freedom*, 91-92.

And both Dabney and Bolton are effectively following Calvin in this regard. Calvin comments:

> Now, as to the *new* covenant, it is not so called, because it is contrary to the first covenant; for God is never inconsistent with himself, nor is he unlike himself. He then who once made a covenant with his chosen people, has not changed his purpose, as though he had forgotten his faithfulness. It then follows, that the first covenant was inviolable; besides, he had already made his covenant with Abraham, and the Law was a confirmation of that covenant. As then the Law depended on that covenant which God made with his servant Abraham, it follows that God could never have made a new, that is, a contrary or a different covenant. . . . These things no doubt sufficiently shew that God has never made any other covenant than that which he made formerly with Abraham, and at length confirmed by the hand of Moses.[71]

Dabney on Moral Foundations

Gordon claims Dabney believes "there are 'intrinsic and eternal' moral laws in the universe, prior to God's volition, which God does not establish but only recognizes" (CT, 36 n19). This is a careless reading of Dabney. And his mistake is worsened by the fact that *while criticizing* Dabney he *accidentally* mentions Dabney's actual view — apparently *without even realizing it.* Let me explain.

Consider Gordon's (partial) citation of Dabney in this regard:

> These (moral distinctions) are intrinsic in that class of acts. They are not instituted solely by the positive will of God, but are enjoined by that will because His infinite mind saw them to be intrinsic and eternal. In a word: Duties are not obligatory and right solely because God has commanded them; but He has commanded them because they are right.... Just so; it is admitted that the basis of the moral distinction is *a priori* to all volition of God. (CT, 35)

---

[71]John Calvin, *Commentaries on the Prophet Jeremiah and the Lamentation,* transl. John Owen (Grand Rapids: Baker, rep. 2003), 3:126.

As quoted it would appear that Gordon has caught Dabney in an indefensible ethical position for a Christian theist. But looks are deceiving. Because partial citations are misleading.

Actually, Gordon is in error, not only in misrepresenting Dabney (which is bad enough and absolutely destructive of his argument[72]), but in falling into the medieval error of Voluntarism while (wrongly) accusing Dabney of its opposite, Intellectualism. The medieval scholars Averroes (aka Ibn Roschd), Thomas Aquinas, and Meister Eckhart held to Intellectualism, which asserts that the choices of the will result from intellectually *recognizing* that which is good. Consequently, if God looked outside himself to a moral law of nature he would be operating on the Intellectualist principle. Dabney does not hold this view, as I will show. Whereas in Voluntarism — promulgated by Avicebron (aka Ben Jehuda Ben Gebirol), Duns Scotus, and William of Ockham — the will determined that which is good. Therefore, in reference to God, good would be determined not by a principle outside of himself, but by the exercise of his sovereign will.

Gordon appears to commit the Voluntarist error in two statements in his article.[73] In the first one, he complains that in Dabney's view "it is admitted that the basis of the moral distinction is *a priori* to all volition of God" (CT, 35). In the second one, he writes: "Such a view as Dabney's essentially affirms moral law to exist in the universe apart from the volition of the Creator" (CT, 36 n19). Thus, Gordon appears to hold that moral distinction is rooted *in* the "volition of God." This is the Voluntarist view.

Simply put: Dabney does *not* believe there are "intrinsic and eternal" moral principles that exist *independently* of God. What he argues — and what all theists should argue, especially Reformed, Van Tillian theists — is that morality exists in the very *character* of God, which is intrinsic to his own eternal being. That is, eternal moral principles derive from the *being* of God rather than from either external moral principles

---

[72] Gordon inadvertently condemns himself when he writes: "Space does not permit a refutation of this brand of natural law theory here, though any theist can quickly perceive the direction such a refutation would take" (CT, 35). If "any theist" could "quickly" perceive the problem, why does Gordon himself fail here?

[73] I will not devote space to engage the debate over Voluntarism, but Dabney ably rebuts it in the very context Gordon cites. See: *Lectures in Systematic Theology*, 352-53.

existing independently of God in the universe or from a sovereign, arbitrary act of divine volition. After all, God's volition flows from and is directed by his *character*.

Note two problems for Gordon in this regard:

(1) Dabney clearly and frequently declares that principles of morality derive from God's character rather than any source outside of God himself. In his *Lectures in Systematic Theology* (LST) — in the very context from which Gordon cites — Dabney writes (emphases mine):

> • "The Scriptures represent God Himself, at least in one particular, as bound by this distinction of right and wrong, 'God cannot lie;' that is, *the eternal perfections of His own mind* so regulate His own volitions that His will certainly, yet freely, refuses all error." (LST, 352).
>
> • "If there were no cause, save God's mere will, why moral distinctions were drawn as they are, He might have made treachery a virtue, and truth a crime, &c. Against this every moral intuition revolts. Why might not God have done this? The only answer is, that *His own unchangeable moral perfections made it impossible.* Just so; it is admitted that the basis of the moral distinction is a *priori* to all volition of God; which is substantially my proposition."[74] (LST, 352)
>
> • "But the view I have given of the Law, as *the necessary and unchanging expression of God's rectitude*, shows that its authority over moral creatures is unavoidable." (LST, 353)
>
> • "Just these precepts are *the inevitable expression of a will guided by immutable perfections.*" (LST, 353)
>
> • "First, the Law must remain, under every dispensation, *the authoritative declaration of God's character.*" (LST, 353)

Gordon embarrassingly asks a rhetorical question that he should have avoided: "Can it possibly be that there are 'intrinsic and eternal' moral

---

[74] The reader should note that the last sentence of this statement from Dabney is quoted by Gordon after an ellipsis. The last sentence in that ellipsis (as I cite in my text) contradicts Gordon's whole point.

laws in the universe, prior to God's volition, which God does not establish but only recognizes?" (CT, 36) The answer is: Yes! Those principles prior to God's *volition* derive from his own eternal *character* which he possesses and recognizes in himself prior to and apart from all volition (1 Cor. 2:11b).

(2) One of Gordon's own statements shows that he is aware of Dabney's view, but somehow does not perceive the implications of it. Thus, even while he is confusing Dabney's presentation, he is contradicting himself (emphases mine): "For Dabney, covenants (*and laws*) are *reflections of the character* of the one establishing the covenants (and laws) and thus are *no more changeable than the character of the one* so establishing them" (CT, 35). Surely Gordon would not declare that God's moral character is changeable, would he? And yet he here recognizes "for Dabney" there are "laws" which are "reflections" of "the character" of God that are "no more changeable than the character of" God himself.

Again, space constraints (long since breached!) forbid a fuller discussion of Gordon's history-of-doctrine analysis. I must now move on to consider Gordon's primary criticism of Bahnsen and theonomy: the argument from the covenant. I will lay out this material in a separate chapter.

141

Chapter 5
The Argument from Covenant Theology
(Part 2)

Having laid the groundwork for responding to Gordon, I now must directly respond to his covenantal argument. Due to his reliance upon Kline's views, I will also have to engage Kline on some of the matters that do not actually appear in Gordon's article, but lay beneath it as theological presuppositions.

Gordon is convinced he has stumbled upon a devastating argument against Theonomy that almost all other covenant theologians have surprisingly overlooked: "One of the most profound ironies has been the failure of covenant theologians (with some exceptions) to critique Theonomy on this point. One would think that covenant theologians would have some idea of what a covenant is. Do covenants have parties, or do they not? Do covenants have obligations and sanctions, or do they not? If a covenant has parties, how is it that non-parties are obliged to its duties?" (CT, 40). It seems to me, though, that Gordon's peculiar Klinean commitments might better explain why this "profound irony" exists. Mainline covenant theologians do not see this matter in the same light as Gordon, and certainly do not follow his theological conclusions (such as the Decalogue not being applicable in the New Covenant era).

That covenant theologians generally do not see things as does Gordon may be seen in his criticism of the venerable Westminster Confession of Faith. Gordon not only finds it ironic that other theologians have not levied similar complaints against Theonomy, but he even expresses disappointment with the Westminster Confession of Faith for also failing in this matter of the covenant: "Theonomists are not the first to abstract legislation from the Sinai covenant. The Westminster

Assembly appears to have done it beforehand, though on a much smaller scale and in a more ambiguous manner. The divines at Westminster appear to have abstracted the decalogue from the Sinai covenant, and to have understood the ten words as timeless and, if you will, 'covenant-less.'" (CT, 40) The Westminster divines, Gordon argues, developed a covenantal theology that was "completely without any biblical evidence" and was "contrary to some of the evidence in Scripture" (CT, 40). In other words, this first creedal document to embody covenantalism did so "completely" devoid of evidence and even against the evidence in Scripture.[1]

In that his argument tends to meander, I have chosen to summarize it, break it down into four key components, and organize them in a logical progression. Given the nature of Gordon's position and my summary re-ordering of it, some overlap between these four points will necessarily occur. I summarily presented these in the opening of this chapter; I now will subject them to a theonomic critique.

The Question of Covenant Duties

The foundational component of Gordon's argument can be stated as a general principle: "Covenant duties oblige only the *express parties* to the covenant." He then applies that general principle to the specific question of the universal relevance of the Mosaic law (so important to Theonomy) by arguing that the Mosaic legislation is inextricably bound up in the Sinaitic Covenant *with Israel*. According to Gordon's reasoning, then, God gave his law in covenant to Israel, and to no other nation. Consequently, the Mosaic law cannot be urged upon nations beyond old covenant Israel, and after the coming of the New Covenant.

Gordon's complaint is capsulized in the following statement:

> If there is a hermeneutical commitment evident in Theonomy (despite the genuine differences on many particular exegetical points within Theonomy) it is the belief that the Sinai legislation, even in its judicial dimensions, is legislation which is well-suited for, and intended to be observed by, all nations and

---

[1] See evidence of the Confession's ground-breaking covenantalism in statements from B. B. Warfield, Geerhardus Vos, and Mark Karlberg in the discussion below.

peoples. Now plainly, the duties of a given covenant are only obligatory on those who are parties to the covenant. For Theonomy, however, all peoples in all times are obliged to these duties, unless there is some instruction somewhere else in Scripture exempting particular peoples from particular duties. The Theonomic approach, then, abstracts the legislation from its covenantal context. (CT, 39-40)

Elsewhere he vigorously criticizes Murray: "Murray, has not only failed to describe that covenant administration adequately, but, ironically, he has disserved his own attempt to describe accurately the *relational* dimension of biblical covenants, since one feature of that relation is that it is *exclusively a relation between God and his people*" (CT, 37, emphasis mine).

The key arguments he employs to this end are: (1) The Old Testament often speaks of the Sinaitic law summarized on the two tablets of stone as the "tables of the covenant" (Exo. 5:2-3; 31:18; 34:27-29; Deut. 4:13; 9:9, 11) (CT, 41). (2) God established Old Testament Israel as a theocracy in order to typify the eschatological kingdom (CT, 38). (3) The Gentiles are "described by the apostle Paul as 'outside of the law' (ἀνόμως)" and therefore could not "possibly be obliged to the law" (CT, 40). (4) The New Testament expressly declares that "the covenants and the giving of the Law" belong only to Israel (Rom. 9:4) (CT, 40). (5) The New Testament also notes that "sin was indeed in the world before the law" (Rom. 5:13), showing that the law came later in history even though sin existed much earlier (CT, 40).

The Tables of the Covenant

Theonomists do not deny that God made a specific covenant with Israel (Exo. 19:5; 24:7-8; cp. Eph. 2:12; Rom. 9:5).[2] Or that Israel is a "peculiar people" distinguished from the nations by distinctive laws which set Israel off from the Gentile environment (e.g., Lev. 5:2-3; Deut. 14:1-2, 21). Bahnsen himself writes: "God made a unique covenant with Israel, ruled uniquely in Israel, made Israel a holy nation, and specially revealed Himself to it — all very true" (NOS, 114).

---

[2] In fact, we do not even deny that the New Covenant was expressly made with Israel and Judah: "'Behold, days are coming,' declares the Lord, 'when I will make a new covenant with the house of Israel and with the house of Judah'" (Jer. 31:31).

Nor do we doubt that the tables of stone represent the heart of that covenantal relationship, even serving as the publicly identifiable cornerstone of that relation (Deut. 4:13; 9:9, 11; Exo. 31:18; 34:27-29). Again Bahnsen affirms this reality:

> The law can epitomize or stand for the covenant itself. We read in Genesis 17:10, 14 that circumcision could represent the very covenant itself that God made with Abraham. In like manner, the stipulations of the Mosaic law could be used to stand for the covenant itself, as in Exodus 24:3-8 (cf. Heb. 9:19-20). Just as circumcision is the covenant, so also is the law God's covenant. This is why the tables of law and commandments which God gave to Moses on Mount Sinai (Ex. 24:12) can actually be called 'the tables of the covenant' (Deut. 9:9, 11, 15). (BTS, 145)

We would note, however, that though Israel was under a special, public *covenantal obligation* to keep the divinely revealed law, the *moral obligations* within that covenant were not uniquely applicable to Israel alone. After all, the law in its moral dimension is a transcript of God's righteous character (Rom. 7:12) and God created man in his own image (Gen. 1:26) to function under God's rule (Psa. 115:3) in God's world (Psa. 24:1) — surely according to God's eternal, moral standard. It is inconceivable that God would employ a double standard of morality in his world.

Israel's covenantal advantage. Actually the moral obligations expressly written on the tables of the covenant gave Israel a *greater advantage* in specifically allowing her to know the will of God in an objective fashion. Those obligations that were morally focused did not give Israel a *unique* morality governing her conduct in a peculiar way.[3] As Paul states it: "What advantage has the Jew? Or what is the benefit of circumcision?

---

[3] Theonomy does recognize a genuine discontinuity in the experience of the old covenant saint and the New Covenant. That which truly distinguishes the new from the old covenant is freedom from what theologians have historically designated "ceremonial law." And in recognizing this, Bahnsen is affirming the Westminster Confession of Faith and its view of the new-found freedom of the New Covenant era (e.g.,

Great in every respect. First of all, that they were entrusted with the oracles of God" (Rom. 3:1-2). Note that he emphasizes the Jewish "advantage" by stating that it is "great in every respect." And the "first" advantage above all others is that "they were entrusted with the oracles of God." Though the world at large received God's general revelation (Rom. 1:18-21), Israel enjoyed the inscripturated "oracles of God." As Leon Morris puts it, Paul "speaks of the great, supreme privilege of the Jew, that of being entrusted with God's revelation to mankind."[4]

An important part of that advantageous entrustment of the divine revelation of the "oracles of God" was the Mosaic law from God. Israel's advantage in receiving this law appears elsewhere in Scripture: "What great nation is there that has statutes and judgments as righteous as this whole law which I am setting before you today?" (Deut. 4:8). "Indeed, ask now concerning the former days which were before you, since the day that God created man on the earth, and inquire from one end of the heavens to the other. Has anything been done like this great thing, or has anything been heard like it? Has any people heard the voice of God speaking from the midst of the fire, as you have heard it, and survived?" (Deut. 4:32-33). For this reason, the psalmist urged Israel to "Praise the Lord!" (Psa. 147:1, 7, 12) because the Lord

---

Acts 15:1, 10; Gal. 4:9-10; 5:2-3, 6). Our freedom is not in the disannulment of the moral sanctions of God's law through Moses, but rather through our freedom from the ceremonial aspects of the law: "under the New Testament, the liberty of Christians is further enlarged, in their freedom from the yoke of the ceremonial law, to which the Jewish Church was subjected" (WCF 20:1). However, the ceremonial law is necessarily temporary and subject to being put out of gear because it symbolically points forward to Christ. Once he has come, the ceremonies are fulfilled. But once Christ has come, our obligation not to kill or steal, or the civil magistrate's obligation to punish criminals is not fulfilled and put out of gear. The "weak and beggarly elements" (Gal. 4:9-10) of the law are the temporary, forward looking ceremonies. See: NOS, 87ff. The New Testament clearly states that these "middle wall of separation" elements have been broken down (Eph. 2:14) and that they were mere shadows that no longer obligate New Covenant Christians (Col. 2:17, 20). The old covenant era with its ceremonial features was vanishing away (Heb. 8:13), even though its moral directives for individuals and states remain (Rom. 3:19, 31; 1 Tim. 1:8-11). Jones agrees: "The way in which they [the ceremonial laws] have been rendered non-binding is by redemptive accomplishment rather than by legislative repeal." David Clyde Jones, in *Biblical Christian Ethics* (Grand Rapids: Baker, 1994), 110.

[4] Leon Morris, *The Epistle to the Romans* (Grand Rapids: Eerdmans, 1988), 153.

"declares His words to Jacob, His statutes and His ordinances to Israel. He has not dealt thus with any nation; and as for His ordinances, they have not known them. Praise the Lord!" (Psa. 147:19-20).

The Gentiles, however, groped in darkness in God's world (Isa. 9:1-2; cp. Acts 13:47). Though they will stand before him on Judgment Day, they did not have the objective, propositional revelation of his righteous standards that the Jew had: "For even though they knew God, they did not honor Him as God, or give thanks; but they became futile in their speculations, and their foolish heart was darkened" (Rom. 1:21). As Paul reminds the Ephesian converts regarding their former paganism: "This I say therefore, and affirm together with the Lord, that you walk no longer just as the Gentiles also walk, in the *futility of their mind*, being *darkened in their understanding*, excluded from the life of God, because of the *ignorance that is in them*, because of the hardness of their heart" (Eph. 4:17-18; cp. 2:2; 4:22). Paul preaches at Athens regarding the Gentile groping: "He made from one, every nation of mankind to live on all the face of the earth, having determined their appointed times, and the boundaries of their habitation, that they should seek God, if perhaps they might grope for Him and find Him, though He is not far from each one of us" (Acts 17:26-27).

So then, no other nation had heard God speak (Deut. 4:32-33). The Gentiles did not have access to this objective revelation of the law of God (Rom. 2:14). This is why the covenant is associated with the summary moral obligations found in the Decalogue: The "tables of stone" were a *permanent* presentation of the *objective* moral revelation of God that established and demonstrated Israel's advantage in knowing the express will of God.

Israel's covenantal responsibility. But God's establishing covenant with Israel was not only an advantage to her in which she could delight. It also made her *more responsible*, and therefore subject to divine chastisement for failing to live in terms of his clearly known law. After all, "to whom much is given, much is required." The Lord warns Israel in this regard: "You only have I chosen among all the families of the earth; *therefore, I will punish you* for all your iniquities" (Amos 3:2).

In the context of Paul's mentioning Israel's "advantage" regarding God's objective revelation, he rebukes the Jews for failing in this covenantal trust (Rom. 3:2; cp. 9:4) from God. They were "entrusted" (ἐπιστεύθησαν) with the oracles of God *in order to deliver them to others.* The word "entrust" carries this sense when in the passive voice followed by an accusative (cf. 1 Cor. 9:17; Gal. 2:7; 1 Thess. 2:4; 1 Tim. 1:11).[5] Paul complains: You are Jews who "know His will, and approve the things that are essential, being instructed out of the Law, and are confident that you yourself are a guide to the blind, a light to those who are in darkness, a corrector of the foolish, a teacher of the immature, having in the Law the embodiment of knowledge and of the truth, you, therefore, who teach another, do you not teach yourself? You who preach that one should not steal, do you steal?" (Rom. 2:18-21).

In fact, Scripture justifies the extermination of the Canaanites on the basis of their moral defilement, an objective moral defilement which Israel should clearly know due to her possessing the express, written law of God: "Do not defile yourselves by any of these things; for by all these the nations which I am casting out before you have become defiled. For the land has become defiled, therefore I have visited its punishment upon it, so the land has spewed out its inhabitants. But as for you, you are to keep *My statutes and My judgments*, and shall not do any of these abominations, neither the native, nor the alien who sojourns among you (for the men of the land who have been before you have done all these abominations, and the land has become defiled)" (Lev. 18:24-27). This is a frequent theme in the Pentateuch:

- "Moreover, you shall not follow the customs of the nation which I shall drive out before you, for they did all these things, and therefore I have abhorred them." (Lev. 20:23)
- "It is not for your righteousness or for the uprightness of your heart that you are going to possess their land, but it is because of the wickedness of these nations that the Lord your God is driving them out before you, in order to confirm the oath which the Lord swore to your fathers, to Abraham, Isaac and Jacob." (Deut. 9:5)
- "For whoever does these things is detestable to the Lord; and because of these detestable things the Lord your God

---

[5] For Israel's duty to promote God's law among the nations, see: Psa. 119:46; Isa. 2:3; 42:6; 49:6; 51:4; Mic. 4:2.

will drive them out before you." (Deut. 18:12)

Notice that the Canaanites were expelled from the land due to their defiling ways. Egypt's and Canaan's "statutes" differed from Israel's (Lev. 18:3), exposing them to the judgment of God for failing to meet up to his moral standard. Israel was warned to keep God's "statutes and judgments" so that they themselves would not commit *those* defilements and come under the *same* wrath of God (Lev. 18:24-17). The moral defilement of the Canaanites which merited God's wrath included breaching God's moral standards contained in "My statutes and My judgments" which were embodied in his covenant (Lev. 26:15; 1 Kgs. 11:11; 2 Kgs. 17:15; 23:3; 2 Chron. 34:31; Psa. 50:16; Isa. 24:5).

The world's obligation. Moving further along in our response to Gordon's argument about the "tables of the covenant," we must note that the Bible itself applies the law of God outside of Israel's borders. In fact, Bahnsen argues this at length in *Theonomy in Christian Ethics* (TCE, chs. 17-19) — though Gordon *never* alludes to this line of argumentation.

In Deuteronomy 4:6 Moses urges Israel: "So keep and do them, for that is your wisdom and your understanding *in the sight of the peoples* who will hear all these statutes and say, 'Surely this great nation is a wise and understanding people.'" Law abiding Israel was to be a model for the nations, exhibiting the objective righteousness of God which was rooted in "these statutes," a righteousness that should be praised by the nations. Surely that which is praiseworthy is being commended to the nations, just as that which breaches the morality of God's statutes and judgments can serve to condemn a pagan people (Lev. 18).

Indeed, God calls Israel to this very task of promoting his law-defined justice among the nations: "Pay attention to Me, O My people; and give ear to Me, O My nation; for a law will go forth from Me, and I will set My justice for a light of the peoples" (Isa. 51:4). The New Testament speaks of the absolute justness of the penalties contained in the law of God: "For if the word spoken through angels proved unalterable, and every transgression and disobedience received a *just recompense*" (Heb. 2:2) in that it is "good" (Rom. 7:12, 16; 1 Tim. 1:8).

David proudly wrote to this end: "I will also speak of Thy testimonies before kings, and shall not be ashamed" (Psa. 119:46). The prophets looked to a day wherein this conclusion would be reached among the nations: "Many peoples will come and say, 'Come, let us go up to the mountain of the Lord, to the house of the God of Jacob; that He may teach us concerning His ways, and that we may walk in His paths.' For the law will go forth from Zion, And the word of the Lord from Jerusalem" (Isa. 2:3). Isaiah laments: "The earth is also polluted by its inhabitants, for they transgressed laws, violated statutes, broke the everlasting covenant" (Isa. 24:5).

Bahnsen cogently summarizes this line of thinking: "The Mosaic law was a standard by which *unredeemed* Canaanite tribes were punished (Lev. 18:24-27) and which 'non-theocratic' *rulers* were called to obey (Ps. 119:46; Prov. 16:12) or prophetically denounced for violating (Isa. 14:4-11; Jer. 25:12; Ezek. 28:1-10; Amos 2:1-3; etc.)" (TCE, xxviii).

The New Testament "Apostle to the Gentiles" (Rom. 11:13; Acts 9:15; 18:6; 22:21; Gal. 2:9) declares that the whole world is accountable to God through his law: "Now we know that whatever the Law says, *it speaks to those who are under the Law*, that *every mouth* may be closed, and *all the world* may become accountable to God" (Rom. 3:19). This verse is speaking of the law of God summarized in the Ten Commandments which were contained on the "tables of the covenant" (see brief exposition of Romans 2 below), after all he expressly lists several of the specific commandments from the Decalogue in this section (Rom. 2:21-22). He also states in the very next verse that "through the law comes the knowledge of sin" (Rom. 3:20), which Paul in Romans 7:7 refers to the Ten Commandments (at least): "What shall we say then? Is the Law sin? May it never be! On the contrary, I would not have come to know sin except through the Law; for I would not have known about coveting if the Law had not said, 'You shall not covet'" (Rom. 7:7).

Paul even notes the moral obligation (and inability) of the carnal mind regarding the law: "The mind set on the flesh is hostile toward God; for *it does not subject itself to the law of God* [moral obligation], for it is not even able to do so [moral inability]; and those who are in the flesh cannot please God" (Rom. 8:7-8). The Gentiles were unable to keep God's law due to the "weakness of the flesh," whereas Christians are empowered to keep God's law: "For what the Law could not do, weak as it was through the flesh, God did: sending His own Son in the likeness of sinful flesh and as an offering for sin, He condemned sin in the flesh, in order that the requirement of the Law might be fulfilled in us, who do not walk according to the flesh, but according to the Spirit" (Rom. 8:3-4).

151

Paul even commends the law of God to Christians in the first century as sound doctrine supporting the gospel: "But we know that the Law is good, if one uses it lawfully, realizing the fact that law is not made for a righteous man, but for those who are lawless and rebellious, for the ungodly and sinners, for the unholy and profane, for those who kill their fathers or mothers, for murderers and immoral men and homosexuals and kidnappers and liars and perjurers, and whatever else is contrary to sound teaching, according to the glorious gospel of the blessed God, with which I have been entrusted" (1 Tim. 1:8-11).

What is more, Gordon's position appears to the Theonomist as unacceptable on its face: Surely the *content* of the Ten Commandments is not distinctive to Israel alone — though they alone possessed the actual God-carved stones (Exo. 31:18; Deut. 9:10)! And yet Gordon speaks of the "tablets of the covenant" which contain the "Ten Commandments" thus: "the ten commandments are the *heart* thereof. The biblical authors can speak, at least by synecdoche, of the Sinai covenant as *being* the ten commandments. Further, the 'tablets' engraved at Sinai are often qualified as the tablets 'of the covenant'" (CT, 40-41). According to Gordon, the distinctive, Jewish-limited, "Sinai covenant" can be spoken of as "*being* the ten commandments." Surely the nations outside Israel are forbidden to murder, to steal, and to commit adultery!

And surely God expects men organized in societies to punish the evil doers according to a righteous standard of judgment. After all, God himself ordains civil government (Rom. 13:1; 1 Pet. 2:14; cp. Gen. 9:6; Prov. 8:15) and considers the civil ruler to be a "minister of God" who is to be "an avenger who brings wrath upon the one who practices evil" (Rom. 13:4). This avenging wrath meted out by the civil authority is *God's* wrath, for he not only is a "minister of God," but the preceding text states: "Never take your own revenge, beloved, but leave room for the wrath of God, for it is written, 'Vengeance is Mine, I will repay,' says the Lord" (Rom. 12:19).[6] Romans 13:1-4 show how God repays those who afflict men. God's wrath is governed and directed by his moral standard, which is revealed to us in his law (Rom. 7:12; 1 Tim. 1:8-11). Even Klinean scholar Karlberg admits that "since the time of

---

[6] See: Bahnsen, *TCE*, ch. 19. See also: Kenneth L. Gentry, Jr., "Civil Sanctions in the New Testament," in Gary North, ed. *Theonomy: An Informed Response* (Tyler, TX,: Institute for Christian Economics, 1991, ch. 6.

the Reformation there has been a Reformed consensus that there is an interconnection between OT laws, personal Christian life, and national public policy."[7] He also confesses that "all can agree that the Mosaic law serves as a 'pattern' for public policy. But what does one mean by that term? Is the Mosaic pattern a guide or a standard? On that question the Reformed tradition was divided."[8]

God does not have a double-standard for men, he does not engage in moral duplicity. He does not have two standards of morality, one for Gentiles, the other for Jews (e.g., Lev. 24:22; Num. 15:16). In fact, Judgment Day proceeds on the principle of God's law: "For when Gentiles who do not have the Law do instinctively the things of the Law, these, not having the Law, are a law to themselves, *in that they show the work of the Law written in their hearts*, their conscience bearing witness, and their thoughts alternately accusing or else defending them, on the day when, according to my gospel, God will judge the secrets of men through Christ Jesus" (Rom. 2:14-16). As Bahnsen puts the matter: "Kline's major conceptual error is to speak as though civil 'justice' in the same kind of case can be completely different in two cultures ('cultural relativism')" (TCE, xxxiii).

Elsewhere Bahnsen writes:

Therefore, one should not come to the testimony of Scripture predisposed toward the idea that there is discontinuity between the ethical standards governing Israel and those which God uses to judge the nations. Had the law not been specially revealed to Israel, its inhabitants would nevertheless have been culpable (as in the case of its neighbors) for rebelling against the clear revelation of God (and His requirements) in nature and conscience (Rom. 1:18 ff.; 2:14-15). Thus the fact that the written law was primarily addressed to Israel certainly cannot be used to imply a double standard of morality between her and the surrounding nations! (TCE, 333)

---

[7] Mark W. Karlberg, *Covenant Theology in Reformed Perspective: Collected Essays and Book Review in Historical, Biblical, and Systematic Theology* (Eugene, Ore.: Wipf & Stock, 2000), 59.

[8] Karlberg, *Covenant Theology in Reformed Perspective*, 72.

Summary conclusions

So then, while it is true that God expressly established his covenant with Israel and presents her with the "tables of the covenant" as a distinctive evidence of his blessing, and though that covenant focused on her faithfulness to God's revealed law, it does not follow that the law of God in its moral — not ceremonial (see later discussion) — strictures itself is inapplicable to the nations. After all, many elements within that law are clearly obligatory on those outside of old covenant Israel. Those moral obligations are not inapplicable simply because they were written on tables of stone and given to Israel in order to govern her special relationship with God. As Robertson puts it: "While the summation of law in an externalized form may remain as the distinctive property of the Mosaic era, the presence of law throughout the history of redemption must be recognized."[9]

Consequently, Theonomists would agree with Geerhardus Vos regarding the Ten Commandments delivered on the tables of stone:

> It may be observed, that, while the words are primarily addressed to Israel, this was due entirely to the circumstances of the historical situation, and can never prove the existence in the mind of the legislator of a double standard, rendering a thing sinful when done to a fellow-Israelite, and condonable when done to non-Israelites.
>
> The primary application to Israel in no wise interferes with a world-wide application in all ethical relationships. . . . Certain features at first sight would seem applicable to Israel alone, for instance what is said of the deliverance from the Egyptian bondage. . . . The historical adjustment does not detract from the universal application, but subserves it.[10]

In the final analysis, Gordon (following Kline) argues that the Mosaic law is tied to the Mosaic Covenant and is not transferable outside of that old covenant administration into the New Covenant, and

---

[9] O. Palmer Robertson, *The Christ of the Covenants* (Phillipsburg, N.J.: P & R, 1980), 175.

[10] Geehardus Vos, *Biblical Theology: Old and New Testaments* (Grand Rapids: Eerdmans, 1948), 147.

that the Mosaic law involves a re-publication of the covenant of works. I would summarily respond that the moral strictures of the law itself are *not* covenantally limited in that: (1) The Ten Commandments represent the moral law re-published from natural revelation.[11] (2) There is nothing in the moral directives (including the judicial principles as a sub-set of moral obligations for redressing social evil) that presents an inherent problem in publishing God's righteous law (rooted in his eternal, unchanging character) as a moral obligation outside the Old Covenant administration. (3) The Old Testament itself, in fact, requires lawful obedience of the nations outside of Israel, just as the New Testament re-publishes the law and endorses it. (4) The only portion of the old covenant law that is Israel-confined and covenantally-constrained are the ceremonial features which demarcate Israel from the nations (see discussion later). (5) Even if the covenant of works itself is re-published in the Sinaitic administration, that does not mean that the moral standard and ethical obligation cannot be applied in the New Covenant era. It simply would not be applied as a covenant of works for those redeemed in Christ. (See discussion below on the legalistic dimension of the Mosaic law.)

The Typological Character of Israel

Gordon asks a rhetorical question that demonstrates for him where Theonomists go astray in this matter: "Was that theocracy a model for all civil government, or was it a type of the eschatological kingdom? Any good 'crown and covenant' Scottish Presbyterian (and Murray was a good one) tends to answer this differently than a good American Presbyterian." (CT, 38) Elsewhere Gordon quotes Vos approvingly: "The chief end for which Israel had been created was not to teach the world lessons in political economy, but in the midst of a world of paganism to teach true religion. . . . The theocracy typified nothing short of the perfected kingdom of God, the consummate state of heaven."[12] He

---

[11] As Gordon puts it: "The assembly asserted that God gave the ten commandments (or the equivalent thereof) to Adam, and then gave the same law to Moses" (CT, 40). Karlberg notes of Bullinger's position: "Bullinger teaches that there is a fundamental continuity between the law of nature in creation and the law of nature as expressed in the Mosaic law." Karlberg, *Covenant Theology in Reformed Perspective*, 21.

[12] T. David Gordon, "Van Til and Theonomic Ethics," in Howard Griffith and John R. Meuther, *Creator, Redeemer, Consummator: A Festschrift for Meredith G. Kline* (Greenville, S.C.: Reformed Academic Press, 2000), 275.

continues: "The theocracy is a 'model' of the perfect kingdom in glory; for Theonomists, theocracy is a 'model' for all other earthly governments."[13] The typological function of Israel is a major issue among Klinean theologians.[14]

The problem of varied ends. I can quickly dispose of Gordon's observation from Vos: Theonomists would not say that Israel's "chief end" was to teach political lessons. Bahnsen himself responds to a similar objection from Waltke, stating that he "nowhere 'alleges' that serving as a legislative model is a 'primary' purpose of the law" (NOS, 114 n6). Theoretically, we could even agree that Israel's "chief end" was typological of the perfected kingdom of God. But here is where Gordon stumbles: we must recognize that a "chief" end implies there are *other* ends; how could an end be "chief" if there were no other ends? Theonomists would say, based on biblical exegesis, that *an end* of Israel was to teach the world about the righteous standard of God for men and nations. After all, Moses himself says: "So keep and do them, for that is your wisdom and your understanding in the sight of the peoples who will hear all these statutes and say, 'Surely this great nation is a wise and understanding people'" (Deut. 4:6). And I have shown (as did Bahnsen) that the kings and prophets of Israel spoke God's law to the nations of the world (TCE, 16-19).

The problem of false antithesis. And why does Gordon treat the matter as if it is an either/or situation: "Was that theocracy a model for all civil government, or was it a type of the eschatological kingdom?" (CT, 38) He is presenting a false antithesis. Why would it be impossible for Israel to typologically model the perfect kingdom *while simultaneously*

---

[13] Gordon, "Van Til and Theonomic Ethics," 275.

[14] Interestingly, Karlberg deems the Mosaic code to be "pattern," though not a "standard" for the civil magistrate today. "all can agree that the Mosaic law serves as a 'pattern' for public policy. But what does one mean by that term? Is the Mosaic pattern a guide or a standard?" "The civil laws of Moses are considered by Calvin to be a guide, not a standard or norm, for national public policy in any given period and culture." "By the middle of the seventeenth century, English reformers favored viewing the Mosaic civil laws as a standard or norm, rather than as a guide, for present-day legislation." Karlberg, *Covenant Theology in Reformed Perspective*, 72 n. 29, 65, 66.

modeling righteous governmental standards for earthly governments? That would be like asking: "Was Christ the ultimate *revealer* of God to man, or was he the *redeemer* of sinners?" That is, was the chief end of his work primarily revelatory or redemptive? After all, was he not *both* a revealer and redeemer (see: John 1:18;Gal. 4:5; 1 Tim. 1:15 Heb. 1:1-3)?

Was not David preeminently a type of Christ (Matt. 22:42-45; Acts 2:29-34), while *simultaneously* ruling an earthly kingdom which operated among the community of nations (2 Sam. 5:12; 8:3)? In other words, did not King David operate *as* did kings of nations in history, *as well as* function as a type of Christ?

Is not marriage itself a type of the relationship of Christ to his church (Eph. 5:26-31; 2 Cor. 11:2)? Yet it also serves as a *common* moral relationship foundational to all human society (Gen. 2:24).

The problem of self-refutation. To make matters worse, Gordon criticizes Dabney for posing a similar false antithesis: "Dabney's disagreement was partially due to a misunderstanding. Dabney apparently believed that a covenant was *either* gracious *or* legal" (CT, 35). If a covenant can be *both* gracious *and* legal (on Gordon's Klinean assumptions), then cannot Israel's kingdom be *both* a forward looking *type* and an outwardly relevant *model?* Why cannot Israel handle both tasks: redemptive typology and moral model? Even Gordon admits this possibility later (though he makes one element "purely incidental"): "For Vos and Van Til, whatever civil instruction may be gained from the theocratic legislation is purely incidental to her primary purpose, which is to typify the glorious kingdom of God."[15]

Bahnsen well comments:

> From a logical standpoint, the error most readily committed
> by critics who appeal to Israel's theocratic uniqueness is that
> they demonstrate no ethical relevance between (or necessary
> connection between) the unique features of Israel and the
> moral validity of the law. Plenty of things were unique about
> Israel, but Scripture does not teach that God predicated the

---

[15] Gordon, "Van Til and Theonomic Ethics," 277.

justice or obligation of His commandments upon those features. Yes, Israel alone received the 'ceremonial law' for her
salvation. However, this redemptive blessing was not the reason (or only reason) that rape called for the death penalty and
theft called for restitution in Israel. (NOS, 115)

A little later Bahnsen directly engages Kline's argument that since
Israel's kingdom is typological, its socio-political laws are part of the
total system of kingdom typology, consequently we must not follow
them today:

One should now stop and remember that the laws given to
Israel to regulate sexual relations were also just as much a part
of the kingdom established by God — a "total system of
kingdom typology" — as the political or ceremonial laws
mentioned by Kline. Following his proposed pattern of reasoning, we should conclude that the sexual laws of the Mosaic code are not to be honored in this day of Messiah's
antitypical kingdom. Anyone who insists that bestiality is contrary to God's permanent and objective moral standards is —
in Kline's view — *ipso facto* denying the status of Israel as a
redemptive type and holy nation! But surely this is absurd and
morally unacceptable. (NOS, 119)

The problem of partial citation . In fact, Gordon only partially cites Vos,
leaving out additional material that will at least theoretically allow for a
theonomic use of the Mosaic legislation. On the same page (and the
following page) where Gordon quotes Vos as saying that "the chief
end" of Israel was not to teach "political economy," we read the following:

From the nature of the theocracy thus defined we may learn
what was the function of the law in which it received its pro-
visional embodiment. It is of the utmost importance carefully to distinguish between the purpose for which the law
was professedly given to Israel at the time, and the various
purposes it actually came to serve in the subsequent course

of history. These other ends lay, of course, from the outset in the mind of God.[16]

As noted previously, *Theonomy* provides abundant evidence that Israel's law code was applicable outside of Israel. I would cite again 1 Timothy 1:8-11, which sets forth *a function* of the law of God in the New Covenant era, serving as "sound teaching," and in accordance with the "gospel":

> But we know that the Law is good, if one uses it lawfully, realizing the fact that law is not made for a righteous man, but for those who are lawless and rebellious, for the ungodly and sinners, for the unholy and profane, for those who kill their fathers or mothers, for murderers and immoral men and homosexuals and kidnappers and liars and perjurers, and whatever else is contrary to sound teaching, according to the glorious gospel of the blessed God, with which I have been entrusted.

Gordon's typological approach cannot overthrow the exegetical evidence.

The problem of continuity. Theonomists recognize both a continuity and a discontinuity between Israel and the nations. Of the very real discontinuity, Bahnsen writes: "God made a unique covenant with Israel, ruled uniquely in Israel, made Israel a holy nation, and specially revealed Himself to it — all very true" (NOS, 114). "Israel's king and political laws were *unlike* those of other nations (e.g., the kings and laws of the other nations did not, except with rare exception, typify the coming kingdom of Christ; Yahweh was enthroned in Israel and over the nations)." (NOS, 120) He even allows the possibility of Kline's typology: "even if typological anticipations are appropriately found in God's 'positive' commands. . ." (TCE, 560).

But while Gordon argues that Bahnsen overlooks discontinuity (claiming Bahnsen is following Murray's lead, CT, 38), he himself overlooks the *continuity* subsisting between Israel and nations, choosing to

---

[16] Vos, *Biblical Theology*, 141-42.

take the typological approach in demonstrating only discontinuity. Bahnsen writes:

> There was discontinuity and continuity. It is the latter (continuity) that Theonomy takes up as a subject. Like all rulers and laws, Israel's kings and commandments addressed historical problems of government, performed common political functions, dealt with non-consummation issues of crime and punishment. God's law was not given exclusively as a foreshadow of consummation (remember, no explicit statement of Scripture speaks of the law in this way anyway); it also rendered impartial justice in pre-consummation situations. And common to all civil rulers is God's demand for justice in their proceedings. Indeed, all civil magistrates are to be 'ministers of God' who punish "evildoers." (NOS 121)

He continues:

> What we observe in Scripture, therefore, is that the unique topological value and holiness of Israel's kings and law did not cancel out the common standards of justice between Israel and the nations as expressed in the law. Contrary to Kline's pattern of ethical reasoning, elements of discontinuity did not wipe out all traces of moral continuity. As Paul says, both Jew and Gentile are found to be under the requirements of the law (Rom. 1:32; -2:12, 14-15, 17-23; 3:9, 19-20, 23). (NOS, 121)

The problem of typological confusion. The Theonomist also finds the typological approach confusing when pressed to logical conclusions. How is capital punishment for murder or rape or kidnaping a type of the redemptive work of Christ? How is restitution in criminal theft a type of redemption? And if the Mosaic criminal penalties serve *only* (remember Gordon's antithesis!) as foreshadows of the severity of Final Judgment, why are not all crimes and sins *capital* crimes in Israel? And if the typological law code of Israel were a feature of a temporary, typological system, and none of her laws are "abstractable," then why are not *all* her laws temporary, including laws against theft, rape, murder, and so forth?

The problem of covenantal dimension. Furthermore, does not Gordon himself recognize various "dimensions" in divine covenants? Gordon speaks of the "the widespread willingness [among covenant theologians] to concede a legal dimension to the Sinai administration" (CT, 34). Responding to Dabney, he writes: "What he appears to have misunderstood is that the legal dimension recognized by many at Sinai was only *one dimension.* That is, other orthodox theologians had not argued that the Sinai administration was exclusively, or even primarily, legal; they had argued that there was a legal dimension, related to the inheritance of the land of Canaan." (CT, 35)

I would also point out in this last quotation that he recognizes elements that are "exclusively" and "primarily" such, their requiring the removal of any *other* dimensions and realities. Bahnsen's Mosaic model for Israel can co-exist with Kline's typological eschatology. Though Theonomy accepts the typological character of Israel in certain respects, we do not believe that typological foreshadowing is the only function of Israel. Nor that it necessarily overthrows the case for God's law embodying universal, invariant, moral principles. In fact, we would rather *expect* that any righteous, non-redemptive social system set up in history by God would have a moral component rooted in God's eternal, righteous character.

Gentiles "Outside the Law"

Gordon offers a quick one sentence comment that, though undeveloped, supposedly guarantees him a good deal of mileage in the debate: "How could the Gentiles, described by the apostle Paul as 'outside of the law' (ἀνόμως) possibly be obliged to the law?" (CT, 40). Here he is obviously alluding to Romans 2:12: "For all who have sinned without [ἀνόμως] the Law will also perish without [ἀνόμως] the Law; and all who have sinned under the Law will be judged by the Law."[17]

The context, however, does not leave us with the notion that the law of God has no bearing upon or authority over the Gentiles. Paul is simply declaring that the Gentiles were not *given possession* of the law of God in *objective form* (i.e., on tables of stone or in revelatory scripture) — not that they have no obligation to the law.

---

[17] The Greek adverb ἀνόμως is used twice here in verse 12, but nowhere else in the New Testament.

First, Romans 2:12-13 speaks of the final judgment of all men. Then in verses 14 and 15 Paul points out that the Gentiles have "the work of *the law* written *in their hearts*," which will be their standard of judgment. Reformed theologians have generally agreed that this law on the heart is God's moral law, which is summarized and objectified in the Ten Commandments. The Westminster Larger Catechism, for instance, teaches that "the moral law is the declaration of the will of God to *mankind*, directing and binding *everyone*" (LC 93), and which "is summarily comprehended in the ten commandments" (LC 98; cp. WCF 19:2), and that Adam and Eve, the fountain of the human race were created "having the law of God written in their hearts" (LC 17; cp. WCF 19:1).

Second, in the very next verse Paul appears to parallel the thought of being "without law" with the declaration that the Gentiles do not "possess" the law: "For when Gentiles who *do not have theLaw* [μη´ νόμον ἔξοντα] do instinctively the things of the Law, these, not having the Law, are a law to themselves" (Rom. 2:14). Clearly, being "without law" (Rom. 2:13) corresponds with "do not have the law" (Rom. 2:14). The verb ἔξοντα speaks of possession, an issue which arises in a different form in Romans 3:2b ("they were entrusted with the oracles of God"). He seems also to underscore the notion of the objective revelation of God by mentioning the "hearing" (Rom. 2:13) of the law as over against a mere subjective sensing the law in the heart (Rom. 2:15). Hendrikson translated ἀνόμως as "ignorance of law."[18]

He further mentions that the Jews "know his will, and approve the things which are essential" (Rom. 2:18) and are a "light" to those in "darkness" (Rom. 2:19), "having in the Law the embodiment [μόρφωσιν[19]] of knowledge and truth" (Rom. 2:20). In fact, to Israel belonged the great advantage of "the giving [νομοθεσία] of the law" (Rom. 9:5; see discussion below; cp. Deut. 4:7-8; 33:3; Psa. 147:19). According to Moo, when Paul declares that the Gentiles do "the things of the law" [τα´ τοῦ νόμου] (Rom. 2:14), this is a "general way of

---

[18] William Hendrikson, Roman (NTC) (Grand Rapids: Baker, 1981), 96.

[19] In the only other instance it is used in the New Testament it speaks of "outward form" (2 Tim. 3:5). Thus, it appears to emphasize objectivity over subjectivity in Romans 2:20.

stating certain of those requirements of the Mosaic law that God has made universally applicable to human beings in their very constitution."[20]

Third, just a few verses later, Romans 2:21 and 22 expressly allude to at least two of the Ten Commandments. Paul complains regarding the Jews (who had the objective revelation of God's law): "You, therefore, who teach another, do you not teach yourself? You who preach that one should not steal, do you steal? You who say that one should not commit adultery, do you commit adultery?" (Rom. 2:21-22a). Though they had an "advantage" by possessing the objective "oracles of God" (Rom. 3:2), they failed to live in terms of their advantage: "You who boast in the Law, through your breaking the Law, do you dishonor God?" (Rom. 2:23).

Fourth, in Romans 2:25-27 circumcision is set over against "the law" (cp. 1 Cor. 7:19), showing that "the law" must refer to the moral rather than the ceremonial obligations. Paul's complaint exposes the Jewish tendency to boast in their ceremonial holiness *while breaching* the moral obligations in God's law (which is a major point in the Lord's teaching in Matt. 5:21-48, see earlier discussion). Paul even mentions "the letter" of the law, showing it is the objective revelation he has in mind (v. 27; 2 Cor. 3:6).

Fifth, Romans 3:20 speaks of the moral law's sin-defining characteristic: "through the Law comes the knowledge of sin" (cp. Rom. 4:15; 5:13, 20; 1 John 3:4). This sin-defining function of God's law is also found a few paragraphs later in Romans 7:7, which expressly mentions one of the Ten Commandments: "What shall we say then? Is the Law sin? May it never be! On the contrary, I would not have come to know sin except through the Law; for I would not have known about coveting if the Law had not said, 'You shall not covet'" (Rom. 7:7). Since Romans 3:20 defines sin in terms of the law, and since Romans 7:7 clearly cites one of the Ten Commandments, and since Romans 3:23 declares: "for all have sinned and fall short of the glory of God," Paul clearly deems all men under God's law, and not "without law" *in this sense.*

Sixth, Romans 3:21 even mentions "the Law and the Prophets." This is not some vague, general notion of "law," for this phrase com-

---

[20] Douglas J. Moo, *The Epistle to the Romans* (Grand Rapids: Eerdmans, 1996), 150.

monly designates the written Mosaic law in conjunction with the documents of the lawyers of God, the prophets (see earlier discussion of Matt. 5:17). And even if one were to broaden the meaning of this phrase to cover the entire Old Testament revelation, we are left with the same conclusion, for the Old Testament includes the Mosaic law of God.

Seventh, though he denounces circumcision as a matter of boasting before God (Rom. 2:25-29), in Romans 3:31 Paul insists that "we establish the Law" and in Romans 4:13-16 he continues his rebuke of Jewish self-righteousness in boastful law-keeping.

So then, Paul's comment about the Gentiles being "without law," does not teach us that the Gentiles have *no* relationship to the law of God. It means rather that they did not have the law in objective format. As Morris puts it: "He may not have the law, but his conduct shows that what the law requires is written in his heart."[21]

To the Israelites "Belong the Covenants and the Law"

Gordon also quickly mentions Romans 9:4 in piling on his biblical complaints against theonomic reasoning: "How could it possibly be meaningful for Paul to distinguish Jews from Gentiles because 'to them belong...the covenants, the giving of the law' (Rom 9:4), if the covenant and its laws oblige non-Jews equally with Jews?" (CT, 40). Here again Gordon is arguing that covenants have parties and that in the case of the Mosaic law we have the stipulations of a covenant specifically effected with Israel. Therefore, reasons Gordon, Gentiles cannot be brought under obligation to the moral and judicial laws of the Mosaic revelation.

I have already answered the fundamental argument embodied in this objection. However, I will briefly respond to Gordon's use of Romans 9:4 particularly in that he thinks it provides evidence against Theonomy.

Paul's full statement in this passage reads:

> For I could wish that I myself were accursed, separated from Christ for the sake of my brethren, my kinsmen according to the flesh, who are Israelites, to whom belongs the adoption as

---

[21] Morris, *Romans*, 121.

sons and the glory and the covenants and the giving of the
Law and the temple service and the promises, whose are the
fathers, and from whom is the Christ according to the flesh,
who is over all, God blessed forever. Amen. (Rom. 9:3-5)

All would agree that Paul is definitely focusing upon racial Israel as
the party to God's covenant through Moses. The whole context of
Romans 9-11 demands that. Here he mentions her racial identity ("my
brethren, my kinsmen according to the flesh"), her title of status ("Is-
raelites"[22]), her redemptive-covenantal relationship to God ("the adoption as sons and the glory and the covenants"[23] and "the promises,
whose are the fathers"[24]), her revealed worship form ("the giving of
the Law and the temple service"), and her genealogical relationship to
the Messiah ("from whom is the Christ according to the flesh").

Gordon's focus, of course, is on the phrase: "and the giving of the
Law," noting that this is part-and-parcel to Israel's distinct, privileged
covenantal relation to the Lord God. Though in English it appears as a
phrase, in Greek it really is one word (not counting the definite article),
and a hapax legomenon at that: ἡ νομοθεσία.

As he did earlier in Romans, Paul is here highlighting Israel's glorious privilege: the objective revelation of God in his holy law as over
against the non-objective, natural revelation known to the darkened,
blinded Gentiles (cp. Rom. 1:18-20; 2:14-19; see my preceding argument). His earlier conclusion in this regard focuses on the objective
revelation of God as a trust: "Then what advantage has the Jew? Or
what is the benefit of circumcision? Great in every respect. First of all,
that they were entrusted with the oracles of God' (Rom. 3:1-2). Murray

---

[22] Notice the status implication of "Israelite" not only here, but in Rom. 11:1 and
2 Cor. 11:22. See also the parallel privilege in the name "Jew" (Rom. 2:17, 28-29; 3:1-
2; Acts 21:39; 22:3). And note the divine blessings flow in history "to the Jew first"
(Rom. 1:16; 2:10). See Gen. 48:16 and Isa. 48:1 for the Old Testament backdrop.

[23] Note the plural "covenants." He is gathering together all of the Jewish covenants, including the Abrahamic, Mosaic, and Davidic. John Murray, *The Epistle to the
Romans* (Grand Rapids: Eerdmans, 1965), 2:5.

[24] See Exo. 4:22; 19:15; Hos. 11:1; Isa. 43:20. See Paul's description of the lack of
Gentile standing with God in Eph. 2:12: "remember that you were at that time sprarate
from Christ, excluded from the commonwealth of Israel, and *strangers to the covenants
of promise*, having no hope and without God in the world."

explains: "The attachment to Israel is not due merely to natural ties. It is accentuated by the place Israel occupied in the history of revelation."[25]

In Romans 9:4 he is simply reiterating that advantage of the Jew. And he does so by mentioning the actual, historical giving of the law at Sinai. Moo points out that νομοθεσία speaks of "the *act* of giving the law" in that "he wants to focus on the law *as given* to Israel by God."[26] Murray writes that it "refers to the Sinaitic promulgation."[27] Morris interprets Paul's statement as highlighting "both the fact that God gave the law and that the law remained as an abiding possession of God's people."[28] The point in all of this is: Israel had great privileges from God, privileges which came into history by direct, supernatural, objective, propositional, special revelation — as witness the Sinaitic giving of the law. Her failure is accentuated because she has stumbled despite the light God gave her.

So then, Paul's statement focuses on the historical act of objectively revealing God's law at Sinai. We must recall her history: "Indeed, ask now concerning the former days which were before you, since the day that God created man on the earth, and inquire from one end of the heavens to the other. Has anything been done like this great thing, or has anything been heard like it? Has any people heard the voice of God speaking from the midst of the fire, as you have heard it, and survived?" (Deut. 4:32-33). Paul's statement and the actual Jewish privilege *do not limit* the law of God as a moral directive to Israel alone; rather *highlight her privilege* in receiving it thus. In fact, the point of his ongoing argument is that the Gentiles sometimes perform better morally than the Jew despite lacking this objective revelation, a performance that is measured by the same moral standard (Rom. 2:12-15). My reader should recall all of the evidence heretofore for the world-scope of God's law.

Sin Was "In the World Before the Law"

Once again Gordon quickly mentions a text in an effort to show the law of God, summarized in the Ten Commandments was a temporary moral directive obligating old covenant Israel alone:

---

[25] Murray, *Romans*, 2:4.

[26] Moo, *Romans*, 564. Emphases mine.

[27] Murray, *Romans*, 6

[28] Morris, *Romans*, 349.

> This assertion then, if unchallenged, permits the decalogue to be perceived as a timeless, 'covenant-less' expression of God's moral will.
>
> This assertion is not only completely without any biblical evidence, but it is an assertion contrary to some of the evidence in Scripture, most notably Rom 5:13, 'sin was indeed in the world before the law.' Note that the assembly places the law 'in the garden'; Paul places it outside of the garden, after sin entered the world. (CT, 40)

He presents his approach to this passage as evidence over against the Westminster Standards. The assembly asserted that God gave the Ten Commandments (or the equivalent thereof, LC 93, 98) to Adam, and then gave the same law to Moses (LC 98).

In approaching this passage Gordon apparently endorses Kline's innovative approach as found in the *Journal of the Evangelical Theological Society*.[29] But as usual, he does not provide his reader with any exposition of the text (Matthew 5:17-19 being a notable exception to this tendency). Consequently, we will have to go with what we have, which is basically a brief assertion.

Gordon writes against the Assembly and Theonomy that Romans 5:13 teaches that "'sin was indeed in the world before the law,'" so that whereas "the assembly places the law 'in the garden' . . . ; Paul places it outside of the garden, after sin entered the world" (CT, 40). He is certainly correct about the Assembly's position, but not about Paul's. Actually, this very verse in Romans has been used by Bahnsen as positive support for the theonomic position (TCE, 198, 265). Let us see how this is so.

In the opening chapters of Romans Paul is arguing that *all* men are sinners, but that God has a plan of salvation for fallen sinners. He opens the book with his theme verse which declares the gospel is powerful unto salvation for *all men*, Jew and Gentile alike (Rom. 1:16). He points out that all men know God, whether they possess the law of God in their hands by means of special revelation (2:17-20) or only

---

[29] Meredith G. Kline, "Gospel Until the Law: Rom 5:13-14 and the Old Covenant," *Journal of the Evangelical Theological Society* 34/4 (December 1991): 433-446.

have it in their hearts through general revelation (Rom. 1:18-21; 2:14-15). All men, irrespective of national descent, are sinners (3:10-18, 23).

He is presenting the case for all men being morally responsible to God. And he uses the law of God to support the responsibility of all men. In 3:19 he clearly declares: "Now we know that whatever the Law says, it speaks to those who are under the Law, that every mouth may be closed, and all the world may become accountable to God." This shows all men are subject to God as he is revealed in his law.

And in the very context of Romans 3:19, indeed in the very next verse, he establishes a principle of sin that has a great bearing on our understanding of 5:13. He declares in 3:20 that "through the Law comes the knowledge of sin." The law as the transcript of the holy character of God (Rom. 7:12) objectively *defines* sin. In fact, he argues that law *must* exist if we speak of sin, for "where there is no law, neither is there violation" (Rom. 4:15). Paul himself even felt the power of the law's defining sin in his own life: "What shall we say then? Is the Law sin? May it never be! On the contrary, I would not have come to know sin except through the Law; for I would not have known about coveting if the Law had not said, 'You shall not covet'" (Rom. 7:7). As John writes elsewhere: "Sin is transgression of the law" (1 John 3:4).

With this (brief) overview of the development of an early theme in Romans, we can now see the function of Romans 5:13-14. As Dunn expresses it, "this paragraph (Rom. 5:12-21) is evidently intended as a conclusion to the whole opening section (1:18-5:21)."[30] It does not appear out of the blue, but in a flowing argument. The critical verses in this section state: "Until the Law sin was in the world; but sin is not imputed when there is no law. Nevertheless death reigned from Adam until Moses, even over those who had not sinned in the likeness of the offense of Adam, who is a type of Him who was to come."

The statement "until the Law" obviously means until the giving of the law to Moses (Rom. 9:4; cp. Rom. 3:2; 17-20; Gal. 3:19), for the next verse specifically mentions the period demarcated by "Adam until Moses" (5:14). So then, since it is true that "through the Law comes the

---

[30] James D. G. Dunn, *Romans 1-8* (*Word Biblical Commentary*) (Dallas: Word, 1988), 271. See also: Charles Hodge, *Commentary on the Epistle to the Romans* (Grand Rapids: Eerdmans, rep. [1886]), 144. Morris, *Romans*, 228.

knowledge of sin" (Rom. 3:20), and "where there is no law, neither is there violation" (4:15), and "I would not have come to know sin except through the Law" (7:7). . . . And since it is also true that "Jews and Greeks are *all* under sin" (Rom. 3:9), and "there is *none* righteous, not even one" (Rom. 3:10), and "*all* have sinned and fall short of the glory of God" (3:23) . . . . It follows, then, that the law must exist even *before* its *inscripturation* to Moses, "because *all* sinned" (Rom. 5:12). Therefore this passage asserts the relevance of God's law all the way back to Adam, even before Sinai.

The Question of Covenantal Discontinuity

Early in his consideration of Theonomy from a covenantal perspective, Gordon provides a brief history-of-doctrine survey of the development of covenantal theology. In that overview he states that Murray's attempted revision of covenant theology resulted in "acknowledging fewer areas of covenantal discontinuity than had been previously recognized within covenant theology" (CT, 38). He even calls Murray's tendency "mono-covenantal": "Murray's recasting, however, became effectively mono-covenantal, as he proposed a view which perceived all biblical covenants as essentially similar" (CT, 36). And since Bahnsen appreciates much in Murray's writings and follows after him in history, Gordon states that it is "without doubt that Theonomy's approach to biblical covenants tends toward mono-covenantalism. What is distinctive about Theonomy is its resistance to recognizing discontinuity in the legislation of the various covenants" (CT, 39).

Gordon continues:

> Theonomy's resistance to recognizing covenantal distinctions as they are represented in Scripture goes even so far as to change conventional Christian nomenclature. Throughout *Theonomy in Christian Ethics*, Bahnsen promotes the neologistic 'older covenant' and 'newer covenant.' Jeremiah was most assuredly not looking forward to a 'newer' edition of the 'older covenant'; he anticipated a 'new covenant...*not like* the covenant I made with their fathers' (Jer 31:31–32). Jesus, similarly, did not institute, by his sacrifice, merely a 'newer' covenant. He did not refer to the cup as a 'newer' covenant, but

as a 'new' covenant, and his apostles similarly considered themselves 'ministers of a new covenant' (2 Corinthians 3). The point is not merely terminological, but conceptual. The New Covenant is not merely different in comparative *degree* from the Sinai covenant; it is also different in qualitative *kind* from that covenant; it is, at least in some respects, 'not like' the covenant God made with the ancestors when he took them out of Egypt. (CT, 39)

As I respond to this objection I would call the reader to bear in mind previous arguments which touch on this theme. But here I need to provide additional, focused responses to Gordon's covenantal concerns.

The Implication of Scripture

Gordon correctly highlights a major point of contention between his Klinean commitments and Bahnsen's theonomic ones: the question of continuity v. discontinuity. Bahnsen's position is rooted in the presupposition that Scripture is the self-attesting word of God, which is not subject to dismissal by man. Gordon (and Kline) hold this too, of course. But Bahnsen builds on this foundational commitment, noting that the very nature of God's word as his authoritative revelation places the burden of proof on those who would call for *changes* in divine directives in God's word in the New Covenant era:

> The methodological point, then, is that we presume our obligation to obey any Old Testament commandment unless the New Testament indicates otherwise. We must assume continuity with the Old Testament rather than discontinuity. This is not to say that there are no changes from Old to New Testament. Indeed, there are important ones. However, the word of God must be the standard which defines precisely what those changes are for us; we cannot take it upon ourselves to assume such changes or read them into the New Testament. God's word, His direction to us, must be taken as continuing in its authority until God Himself reveals otherwise. This is, in a sense, the heart of 'covenant theology' over against a

dispensational understanding of the relation between Old and New Testaments. (BTS, 3)[31]

Careful critics note how this principle operates in Bahnsen. David Jones of Covenant Theological Seminary writes: "Greg Bahnsen, who is the movement's chief apologist, argues for the presumptive continuity of the Mosaic laws on the principle that laws continue in force until revoked. Discontinuity must assume the burden of proof."[32] Another critic, Westminster Seminary's Dennis Johnson, tries to dismiss the burden-of-proof argument, but is vigorously rebutted by Bahnsen, who effectively brings his skills as a logician to bear upon the matter.[33]

The theonomic position — so well articulated by Bahnsen — is that we are not left to wonder whether we should assume continuity or discontinuity as our basic exegetical principle. The Lord himself forthrightly declares to us: "truly I say to you, until heaven and earth pass away, not the smallest letter or stroke shall pass away from the Law, until all is accomplished" (Matt. 5:18). Paul concurs: "*all* Scripture is inspired by God and profitable for teaching, for reproof, for correction, for training in righteousness" (2 Tim. 3:16).

Divinely inspired speakers and writers in the New Testament often cite Old Testament passages as confirmation of their teaching. They are obviously assuming the Old Testament's continuing validity. Many New Testament references establish the operating principle of continuity, even though New Testament writers *can* and *do* speak for God *as*

---

[31] And too, we must remember that the burden-of-proof argument is not an argument from silence at all. As a matter of historical fact, God did rather noisily (Exo. 19:16, 19; 20:18-19; Heb. 12:19) give a law and included it in the canon of Scripture. By the very nature of the case, there could only be a divine repealing of that law in Scripture (Deut. 4:2; 12:32; Psa. 119:160; Prov. 30:5-6; Isa. 51:6; Matt. 4:4; John 10:35; 2 Tim. 3:16-17). But instead of repealing it, the New Testament confirms it (Matt. 5:17; Luke 16:17; Rom. 3:31; 1 Cor. 7:19; 9:21; 1 John 2:3-4; 5:3). This is because the law is not contrary to the promise of God (Gal. 3:21a). In other words, the argument that urges discontinuity in Scripture requires proof; not that which urges continuity (cf. John 10:35; 2 Tim. 3:16-17).

[32] David Clyde Jones, *Biblical Christian Ethics* (Grand Rapids: Baker, 1994), 113.

[33] See Bahnsen's response to Dennis Johnson's "burden of proof" argument in Gary North, ed. *Theonomy: An Informed Response* (Tyler, Tex.: Institute for Christian Economics, 1991), 118-122.

divinely inspired men in amending or repealing God's directives at particular points.[34] As Bahnsen puts it:

> Orthodox theology, with its dogma of the immutability of God, should recognize as an interpretative principle the unity and continuity of all God's inscripturated revelation; only the Author of Scripture can discontinue what He has said previously. We must presuppose unity in the word of God, which stands to all generations, and not discontinuity, for who among men can presume to alter the word of the living God? (TCE, 183-84)

> When we read through the New Testament we see that its writers presupposed continuity with the Older Testamental Scriptures (and not merely in matters of prophecy). The section on New Testament substantiation in a former portion of this treatise cited numerous Scriptures where a New Testament author appeals to, alludes to, or quotes the prescriptions of the Older Testament, and this is done with no apology or rationalization for violating a general policy of discontinuity with the Older Testament. (TCE, 305)

> Only God has the authority and prerogative to discontinue the binding force of anything He has revealed; man, therefore, must live by everything which proceeds from God's mouth (Matt. 4:4) without diminishing it (Deut. 4:2). Since the law is not against the promises (Gal. 3:21), we are not warranted to affirm discontinuity with the Older Testament except where expressly indicated otherwise; such a method

---

[34] Remember: global assertions in Scripture are subject to qualification by Scripture: In Mark 10:11 Jesus declares: "Whoever divorces his wife and marries another woman commits adultery against her." But in Matthew 19, this is qualified: "And I say to you, whoever divorces his wife, except for immorality, and marries another woman commits adultery" (Matt. 19:9). And, of course, we have the example of the fulfillment and putting-out-of-gear the ceremonial features of God's law mentioned previously in this book.

would be backwards. We must live by every Scripture, not just those which God has spoken twice (and in the right places). The Christian is not to wield an "unwritten Torah" in opposition to God's clearly revealed word. Continuity between the testaments, not discontinuity, must be presupposed. (TCE, 306)

Theonomy, then, states that our foundational hermeneutical assumption is continuity, when dealing with divine directives in God's word. Theonomists do not *resist* discontinuity; they allow it only on the basis of express New Testament revelation from God.

The History of Covenantalism

Bahnsen's biblical methodology of continuity also happens to be characteristic of covenant theology, serving effectively as a hallmark of Reformed theology. Covenantal theology really began to emerge in the German-Swiss Reformation, especially during Zwingli's debate with the Anabaptists.[35] The principle of continuity was essential for establishing the doctrine of infant baptism on a biblical basis: "Zwingli begins what would become the dominant concept for defending infant baptism, namely, the continuity of the covenants."[36] As Lillback observes: "The first of these two passages mentioned by Locher shows that Zwingli held to a concept of covenant continuity between the Old and New Testaments."[37] He even speaks of "Zwingli's declaration of the uninterrupted continuity between the age of the Old Testament prophets and the Gospel era."[38] Zwingli's influence was felt by Oecolampadius and Bullinger who "had a clear picture of covenant continuity."[39]

Interestingly, in a joint work written *against* Theonomy, Moisés Silva writes: "The Reformed tradition, in contrast, has been concerned to minimize the antithetical elements, to assert the coherence of God's

---

[35] Peter A. Lillback, *The Binding of God: Calvin's Role in the Development of Covenant Theology* (Grand Rapids: Baker, 2001), ch. 4.
[36] Lillback, *The Binding of God*, 93.
[37] Lillback, *The Binding of God*, 82.
[38] Lillback, *The Binding of God*, 83.
[39] Lillback, *The Binding of God*, 90.

gracious provisions in both dispensations, and to stress the continuing validity of God's law for the Christian."[40] The *Encyclopedia of the Reformed Faith* notes that "The continuity of the two covenants, Old and New, is portrayed by Paul through the figure of an olive tree. Some natural (Jewish) branches were broken off; Gentile branches were grafted in. . . . The new covenant, that is, the new form of the old covenant with Abraham, has been established with" the "Christian church."[41] In covenant theology we find an underlying unity of the covenants, as over against dispensationalism with its elemental discontinuity.

This principle has an important impact on the theonomic debate. For instance, early covenantal scholar Herman Witsius (1636-1708) wrote long ago:

> As the people of Israel constituted the church at that time, and as Jesus Christ the Son of God, and king of the church, prescribed the decalogue to them, it follows that the same law retains its force in the church, till it be abrogated again by the king of the church. We are not to think, that the church of the Old Testament, which consisted of Israelites, and that of the New, though for the greatest part made up of Gentiles, were a quite different people. They ought to be looked upon as one kingdom of Christ, who made *both one*, Eph. ii. 14. and who graffed us, when wild olives, into that fat olive, Rom. xi. 17. And consequently, the laws which were once given to the church by Christ the king, are always binding on the whole church, unless Christ shall declare, that he has abrogated them by some other institution. But it is absurd to imagine, that Christ abrogated the moral law, in so far, as he gave it by the mediation of Moses to the church of Israel, and directly confirmed the same law to the Christian church. For seeing it is the same law, of the same king, in one and the same kingdom,

---

[40] Moisés Silva, "Is the Law Against the Promises?," in Will S. Barker and W. Robert Godfrey, *Theonomy: A Reformed Critique* (Grand Rapids: Zondervan, 1990), 154.

[41] Donald K. McKim, ed., *Encyclopedia of the Reformed Faith* (Louisville: Westminster, 1997), 86.

though that kingdom is enriched with new accessions and new privileges; why should we suppose it abrogated and ratified again almost in the same breath? Nay, many considerations persuade us to believe, that the law of the decalogue was given to the church, in order to be a perpetual rule, from the manner in which it was given.[42]

Some covenant theologians express concerns regarding the peculiarities of Klinean covenantalism — as held by Gordon — that seem too strongly to emphasize discontinuity in the covenant. A Kline disciple Jeong Koo Jeon is put on the defensive in this regard: "As we proceed further in the discussion, we will interact with the accusation that Kline's hermeneutics shares some affinity with dispensational hermeneutics."[43] He cites comments by Reformed scholars Peter Lillback and Moisés Silva in evidence.

In 1988 an important work was published on the debate between Reformed and dispensational theologies. It highlighted the foundational principle distinguishing these contradictory systems. The book's title was: *Continuity and Discontinuity: Perspectives on the Relationship Between the Old and New Testaments*.[44] The editor, John Feinberg, noted this tendency: "Generally, systems that move toward absolute continuity fit more in the mold of Reformed or covenantal theologies. Systems that move toward absolute discontinuity fit more in the mold of dispensational theologies."[45]

Consequently, Bahnsen's tendency to continuity is rooted in a fundamental principle of historic covenantal, Reformed theology.

The Position of Bahnsen
Gordon complains of "Theonomy's resistance to recognizing covenantal distinctions as they are represented in Scripture," noting that

---

[42] Herman Witsius, *Economy of the Covenants Between God and Man: Comprehending a Complete Body of Divinity* (Phillipsburg, N.J. : P & R, rep. 1990 [1822]), 177.

[43] Jeong Koo Jeon, *Covenant Theology: John Murray's and Meredith G. Kline's Response to the Historical Development of Federal Theology in Reformed Thought* (Lanham, Md.: University Press of America, 2004), 193.

[44] John S. Feinberg, ed., *Continuity and Discontinuity: Perspectives on the Relationship Between the Old and New Testaments* (Westchester, Ill.: Crossway, 1988).

[45] Feinberg, *Continuity and Discontinuity*, 64.

what is "distinctive about Theonomy is its resistance to recognizing discontinuity in the legislation of the various covenants" (CT, 39). As I have been arguing, it certainly is true that Bahnsen emphasizes the continuity of the covenants. This is consistent with the biblical revelation which speaks of "the covenants of *the* promise" (Eph. 2:12) and historic covenant theology which emphasizes continuity in defense of its doctrine of infant baptism, the unity of the church in all ages, the unity of the covenant of grace, and more. Nevertheless, it is not true that Bahnsen exercises a "resistance" against discontinuity. He simply recognizes the priority of continuity.

As a covenant theologian, Bahnsen *begins* with the biblical and historical foundation of the *unity of the covenants*. Regarding the covenant theology of Scripture, continuity is Bahnsen's *operative principle,* but it is not his *sole observation*. He clearly allows for *exegetically derived* discontinuities. For instance, in *By This Standard*, chapter 16 is titled: "Discontinuity Between the Covenants of the Law." What Gordon is criticizing, then, is Bahnsen's covenantal *reflex*, not his total *system*.

One critic of Theonomy complains that Theonomy overlooks an obvious discontinuity between the Old and New Testaments. Bahnsen's response (in part) shows he does recognize covenantal discontinuities (after all he is not Jewish!):

> But if this discontinuity is taught in the Bible, then Theonomists have no difficulty with it at all; it would simply be the result of studying every jot and tittle of the Lord's revealed word, which Theonomy calls upon us to do. Theonomic ethics does not maintain a priori and necessarily that there simply cannot be alterations in the application of the law introduced by the law-giver Himself e.g., animal sacrifices, dietary laws, etc.). But apart from such a word from the Lord, we ourselves do not have the prerogative to introduce such changes. (NOS, 148)

Notice how a discontinuity (if it exists) would be rooted in exegesis, not in a predisposition toward discontinuity. Bahnsen is very clear in this regard: "Theonomic ethics certainly permits changes from the Old to New Covenants as long as those changes are exegetically controlled." (NOS, 85)

Bahnsen ties his covenantal thinking to the Lord's direct teaching:

> Did Jesus assume basic continuity or basic discontinuity be-
> tween His ethic and that of Moses? In asking whether we
> should presume that the old covenant law is binding or abro-
> gated today, one relevant and important passage which can-
> not be avoided is Matthew 5:17-19. Thus it was given detailed
> attention in my book *Theonomy in Christian Ethics*, even though
> it is not the only text which could be used to substantiate the
> theonomic operating premise. The absolutistic character of
> Christ's words in Matthew 5:17-19 certainly supports the op-
> erating assumption of basic continuity. (NOS, 273)

In his Preface to his second edition of *Theonomy*, Bahnsen expresses
dismay with those who misread him in this matter:

> These false depictions cannot be justified from a careful read-
> ing of the book. There are no fewer than seventy pages that
> refer to the progress of revelation and redemptive history,
> God's right to change the law, exceptions to general continu-
> ity, laws which are laid aside, or advances over the Old Cov-
> enant. I mentioned "radical differences," "legitimate and note-
> worthy discontinuities," and laws which have "become obso-
> lete." What is championed is "the presumption" of moral
> continuity between the Testaments. It was clearly spelled out
> that "if we are to submit to God's law, then we must submit
> to every bit of it (as well as its own qualifications)." Because
> "only God has the authority and prerogative to discontinue
> the binding force of anything He has revealed," we should
> live by the Old Testament law except where expressly indi-
> cated otherwise. (TCE, xxiv)

Regarding Gordon's history-of-doctrine analysis, though Bahnsen
does appreciate Murray we must not presume, as Gordon seems to,
that Bahnsen follows lock-step with Murray. Contrary to Bahnsen,
Murray denied a covenant of works, preferring instead an "Adamic

administration."[46] He even criticizes Murray for inconsistency within his covenantal principle:

> Quite obviously one cannot have it both ways: assuming a principle of continuity with the Older Testament unless explicitly rescinded, but assuming a principle of discontinuity with the Older Testament unless explicitly repeated. Matthew 5:17-19 shows us which general principle is to be followed (viz., continuity) when the New Testament is silent on something. Murray's argument against the penal sanctions of the Older Testament as being binding today then must be rejected. (TCE, 445).

In light of all of this, we must not suppose that Bahnsen's theonomic argument resists the fact of discontinuity in the covenants. He does allow for such, but only on exegetical grounds.

The Continuity of Morality

Since the debate between Theonomists and Gordon and the Intrusionists is over the role of God's law in the New Covenant era, a major implication of the debate over continuity is whether a *continuity of morality* exists between the covenants. As Gordon puts it: "If there is a hermeneutical commitment evident in Theonomy (despite the genuine differences on many particular exegetical points within Theonomy) it is the belief that the Sinai legislation, even in its judicial dimensions, is legislation which is well-suited for, and intended to be observed by, all nations and peoples" (CT, 39). He then complains: "Now plainly, the duties of a given covenant are only obligatory on those who are parties to the covenant" (CT, 39).

In a later section ("The Focus of Discontinuity") I will highlight genuine, covenantally-unique, redemptively-controlled discontinuities that exist between Israel and the New Covenant church and the world, which all orthodox Christians hold — including Bahnsen *as a Theonomist*. Those unquestionable discontinuities relate to *redemptive realities* which are embodied in *ceremonial-ritual legislation*. But for now the question is:

---

[46] See Jeon, *Covenant Theology*, 105-115. See: John Murray, *Collected Writings of John Murray* (Edinburgh: Banner of Truth, 1982), 2:49.

Do the standing *moral* directives of the Old Testament — for both the individual and the state — remain obligatory upon all men? Christian historians have long held to the three-fold division of the law, distinguishing ceremonial obligations from moral and judicial ones (cp. WCF 19:1-5).

Bahnsen provides a full chapter on just this question in *By This Standard* : "The Covenant's Uniform Standard of Right and Wrong" (ch. 5). That chapter opens with these words:

> If something was sinful in the Old Testament, it is likewise sinful in the age of the New Testament. Moral standards, unlike the price of gasoline or the changing artistic tastes of a culture, do not fluctuate. In the United States, there was a time when driving your car at 65 miles per hours was permissible; now any speed above 55 is illegal. But God's laws are not like that: just today, unjust tomorrow. When the Lord makes a moral judgment, He is not unsure of Himself, or tentative, or fickle. Unlike human lawmakers, God does not change His mind or alter His standards of righteousness: "My covenant I will not violate, nor will I alter the utterance of My lips" (Ps. 89:34). When the Lord speaks, His word stands firm forever. His standards of right and wrong do not change from age to age: "All His precepts are trustworthy. They are established forever and ever, to be performed with faithfulness and uprightness" (Ps. 111:7-8). (BTS, 37)

We must remember (as noted previously) that the New Testament itself teaches that the law of God reflects the very character of God, it is a transcript of his holiness: "So then, the Law is holy, and the commandment is holy and righteous and good" (Rom. 7:12). This is why Paul can state that the law of God, even in its public judicial response to criminal behavior, is "good" and is "sound teaching" that comports with "the glorious gospel":

> But we know that the Law is good, if one uses it lawfully, realizing the fact that law is not made for a righteous man, but for those who are lawless and rebellious, for the ungodly and

sinners, for the unholy and profane, for those who kill their
fathers or mothers, for murderers and immoral men and homosexuals and kidnappers and liars and perjurers, and whatever else is contrary to sound teaching, according to the glorious gospel of the blessed God, with which I have been entrusted. (1 Tim. 1:8-11)

Thus, the New Testament even evaluates the penal sanctions of the
Mosaic law as morally right and good: "For if the word spoken through
angels proved unalterable, and every transgression and disobedience
received a *just recompense*" (Heb. 2:2).

Even Jesus can state to the anti-theonomists' dismay:

Do not think that I came to abolish the Law or the Prophets;
I did not come to abolish, but to fulfill. For truly I say to you,
until heaven and earth pass away, not the smallest letter or
stroke shall pass away from the Law, until all is accomplished.
Whoever then annuls one of the least of these commandments, and so teaches others, shall be called least in the kingdom of heaven; but whoever keeps and teaches them, he shall
be called great in the kingdom of heaven. (Matt. 5:17-19)

Moral law is obviously "moral." But we must understand that by
the very nature of the case, judicial law is a species of moral law. After
all, it gives fallen sinners the authorization to take the lives of certain
criminals (by capital punishment) or confiscate their wealth (through
fines). If morality does not govern the state power in these matters,
then morality is just a relativistic personal preference issue.

Bahnsen criticizes Kline's (and by implication, Gordon's) discontinuity principle which disavows the Mosaic law in the modern context.
Kline argues that the redemptive peculiarity of Israel establishes her
discontinuity from the nations, thereby forbidding the application of
her specially revealed moral and judicial legislation to those nations.
Bahnsen responds that despite her redemptive status, nevertheless:

a continuity [is] to be found between Israel and the nations,
Israel and the New Testament kingdom – namely, a continuity of moral standards, private and public. The fact that two

things have one or more things in common does not imply that they have all things in common, just as the presence of one or more differences between them does not imply that they are completely different. A combination of continuities and discontinuities can characterize the relationship between two things. Kline is guilty of hasty generalization. (NOS, 119)

In *Theonomy* itself Bahnsen complains about Kline's argument against Theonomy:

Kline barely touched the actual theonomic position anywhere—and not at all when speaking of its 'radical fault.' He seemed to reason fallaciously that some discontinuity between Old Covenant Israel and modern nations proves complete discontinuity and that any typological value in Israel's civil policy meant it was merely typological (and not also definitive of justice). Kline's major conceptual error is to speak as though civil 'justice' in the same kind of case can be completely different in two cultures ('cultural relativism'). The critical arguments he advanced against theonomic ethics had already been answered in the book, and he attempted no biblical demonstration of anything contradictory to the book's conclusions anyway.(TCE, xxxiii)

Theonomy argues that though Israel was distinct from the nations in terms of her redemptive status, and though she received particular laws setting her off from the nations, nevertheless she also was a people living in God's world and operating as a nation needing moral foundations for her criminal code. Israel differs from the nations redemptively, but not morally because morality is absolute, being rooted in the very being and character of God.

The Revelation of the New Covenant

Gordon faults Theonomy for failing to understand the newness of the New Covenant:

What's in a word? Well, in this case, plenty. Theonomy's resistance to recognizing covenantal distinctions as they are

represented in Scripture goes even so far as to change conventional Christian nomenclature. Throughout *Theonomy in
Christian Ethics*, Bahnsen promotes the neologistic "older covenant" and "newer covenant." Jeremiah was most assuredly
not looking forward to a "newer" edition of the "older covenant"; he anticipated a "new covenant . . . *not like* the covenant I made with their fathers" (Jer 31:31–32). Jesus, similarly, did not institute, by his sacrifice, merely a "newer" covenant. He did not refer to the cup as a "newer" covenant, but
as a "new" covenant, and his apostles similarly considered
themselves "ministers of a new covenant" (2 Corinthians 3).
The point is not merely terminological, but conceptual. The
new covenant is not merely different in comparative *degree* from
the Sinai covenant; it is also different in qualitative *kind* from
that covenant; it is, at least in some respects, "not like" the
covenant God made with the ancestors when he took them
out of Egypt. (CT, 39)

The New Covenant, in Gordon's view, is *unlike* the old covenant, the
Mosaic covenant, and therefore is contra-theonomic in not continuing
to promote God's law as revealed to Moses.

I would point out just quickly that Bahnsen's "neologistic" phraseology was simply a rhetorical device to highlight the biblical principle
of covenantal continuity. He does not use this phraseology in any of
his other books when he discusses Theonomic Ethics. See: *By This Standard: The Authority of God's Law Today*; *No Other Standard: Theonomy and Its
Critics*; his chapters in Gary North, *Theonomy: An Informed Response*. In
fact, he does not even employ this rhetorical tool in his Preface to the
second edition of *Theonomy* itself. But as Gordon notes, the real question is what lay behind Bahnsen's rhetorical expression.

Bahnsen deals with this "New Covenant" objection in *By This Standard* (and elsewhere):

When we inquire as to what is new about the New Covenant
under which Christians now live, we must allow the Lord to
define the proper answer. We cannot read into the idea of a
"New Covenant" just anything we wish or can imagine. The

revealed terms of the New Covenant are given to us in both Jeremiah 31:33-34 and Hebrews 8:8-12, and when we look at them we find that the New Covenant is far from suppressing or changing the law or moral standard by which God's people are to live! Just the opposite is true. Contrary to those who think that the Mosaic law is not applicable to the New Testament believer, Scripture teaches us: 'This is the covenant that I will make with the house of Israel after those days, says the Lord: I will put my laws into their minds and I will write them upon their hearts' (Heb. 8:10). (BTS, 42-43)

Gordon's argument from Jeremiah's revelation of the coming New Covenant cannot be employed against Theonomic Ethics. As noted by Bahnsen, Jeremiah 31 actually serves as positive evidence supporting it. We must consider the actual wording of this prophecy:

"Behold, days are coming," declares the Lord, "when I will make a new covenant with the house of Israel and with the house of Judah, not like the covenant which I made with their fathers in the day I took them by the hand to bring them out of the land of Egypt, My covenant which they broke, although I was a husband to them," declares the Lord. "But this is the covenant which I will make with the house of Israel after those days," declares the Lord, "I will put My law within them, and on their heart I will write it; and I will be their God, and they shall be My people." (Jer. 31:31-33)

Note carefully in this regard:

First, it is true that Jeremiah expressly states the New Covenant is "not like" the old covenant. But the question arises as to *how* it is "not like the covenant which I made with their fathers." The prophecy itself casts light on the fundamental unlikeness: it points out that Israel easily "broke" the old covenant (v. 32), whereas the New Covenant will be empowered in the "heart" (v. 33). This glorious "unlikeness" of the New Covenant is repeated by God to Ezekiel: "Moreover, I will give you a new heart and put a new spirit within you; and I will remove the heart of stone from your flesh and give you a heart of flesh. And I will put My Spirit within you and cause you to walk in My statutes, and you will be careful to observe My ordinances" (Eze. 26:26-27).

The superiority of the New Covenant in this regard is precisely the point Paul makes in Romans 8: "For what the Law could not do, weak as it was through the flesh, God did: sending His own Son in the likeness of sinful flesh and as an offering for sin, He condemned sin in the flesh, in order that the requirement of the Law might be fulfilled in us, who do not walk according to the flesh, but according to the Spirit" (Rom. 8:3-4). Paul writes similarly of the law's inability in Galatians 3:21: "Is the Law then contrary to the promises of God? May it never be! For if a law had been given which was able to impart life, then righteousness would indeed have been based on law."

As Vos expresses it: "According to Romans 8:3 there is an ἀδύνατον τοῦ νόμου, an inability of the law to effect what must be accomplished if the religious ideal is to be realized. Galatians 3:21 implies that the law which has been given cannot make alive. . . . In II Corinthians 3:6 likewise it is said that the law, because it is γράμμα, i.e., an external instrument without power to project itself into the heart of man, fails to impart life as the Spirit does."[47]

Vos writes of the newness of the New Covenant as over against the old: "In this prophecy, besides the name 'New Berith', the two most distinctive features of the new order of affairs are described. The one is: Jehovah will create obedience to the law through writing it in the heart. The other is: there will be complete forgiveness of sin. And, what most closely concerns our present purpose the 'newness' is applied not merely in a general way to religious status, but is most specifically extended to the sphere of revelation and of knowledge of God: 'They shall all know me, from the least of them to the greatest of them.'"[48]

Consequently, that which makes the New Covenant "not like" the Mosaic covenant is its *spiritual empowerment* and complete forgiveness of

---

[47] Geerhardus Vos, "'Legalism' in Paul's Doctrine of Justification," in *Redemptive History and Biblical Interpretation: The Shorter Writings of Geerhardus Vos*, ed. by Richard B. Gaffin, Jr., (Phillipsburg, N. J.: Presbyterian and Reformed, 1980), 388.

[48] Vos, *Biblical Theology*, 322. Vos comments on the law under the ministry of the New Covenant in 2 Cor. 3: "The same is implied where Paul speaks of the law as bringing man under the curse. This again is an effect due entirely to the collision of

sin. The old covenant was on lifeless tables of stone and established an ongoing remembrance of sin (Heb. 7:11–12, 18-19-22, 26-28; 8:1-6; 9:8-15; 10:1-14). Whereas the New Covenant is in "a heart of flesh" empowered by "My Spirit within you" who will "cause you to walk in My statutes" and in the finality of redemption (Heb. 1:3; 10:10-18).

Second, clearly the "unlikeness" of the New Covenant is *not* due to God's law being abrogated. The New Covenant revelation specifically declares that that which directs the heart is God's law: "'But this is the covenant which I will make with the house of Israel after those days,' declares the Lord, 'I will put *My law* within them, and on their heart I will write it; and I will be their God, and they shall be My people'" (Jer. 31:33). "Moreover, I will give you a new heart and put a new spirit within you; and I will remove the heart of stone from your flesh and give you a heart of flesh. And I will put My Spirit within you and cause you to walk in *My statutes*, and you will be careful to observe *My ordinances*" (Eze. 26:26-27).

When we look through the Old Testament, we discover that when God refers to "My law" or when Old Testament speakers or writers are commenting on "His law," they are speaking of the Mosaic law: Deuteronomy 30:10; Joshua 24:26; 2 Kings 10:31; 17:13; 21:8; 1 Chronicles 22:12; 2 Chronicles 6:16; 31:21; Ezra 7:6, 12, 14, 21; Nehemiah 8:8, 18; 9:3; 10:28, 29; Psalm 78:1; 81:4; 89:30; 119:34, 77, 92, 97, 109, 174; Isaiah 1:10; Jeremiah 6:19; 9:13; 16:11; 26:4; 31:33; 44:10; 22:26; Daniel 6:5; Hosea 4:6; 8:1.

In addition, Reformed theology has generally noted that though the terms of the New Covenant were expressly framed "with the house of Israel and with the house of Judah," they nevertheless have been given to the church of Jesus Christ in the New Testament. The *Encyclopedia of the Reformed Faith* points out that "In Jer. 31:31-34 God prom-

---

the law and sin. In II Corinthians 3:6 the figure of the γράμμα comprises the two elements of the inefficacy and the condemnatory function of the law; for, because it is γράμμα, the law is affirmed not merely to fail of giving life but also to kill positively; the γράμμα, therefore, is in opposition to the spirit a 'letter' in the sense of something external, and in addition to this, a 'letter' in the sense of a writ of condemnation. Inasmuch as condemnation presupposes sin, no reflection is cast on the law itself or the forensic relationship between God and man regulated by it." Vos, "'Legalism' in Paul's doctrine of Justification," 389.

ises a New Covenant with God's ancient people. In Hebrews 8, that passage is quoted to teach that the covenant promised to Israel has been given to the church."[49] This is one reason why Reformed theology has generally recognized the continuing validity of God's law in the New Covenant age.

Bahnsen's comments on the New Covenant should help dispel false conceptions regarding the newness of the New Covenant:

> The New Covenant does not bring a new law which replaces and abrogates the old. Instead new depth and wealth is given to the covenant promise, "I will be to them a God, they shall be to me a people." This is seen in three main provisions: internalization and ability to keep the law of God, the overwhelming prosperity of gospel preaching, and the actual accomplishment of redemption for God's elect. (TCE, 190)

Bahnsen develops this point by highlighting features of Jeremiah's New Covenant promise: (1) In the New Covenant God promises "I will put my law within them, and on their heart I will write it" (Jer. 31:33). (2) He reminds Israel that the law "did not confer and justify even one sinner" whereas "the power of the New Covenant is manifest in the fact that everyone will know the Lord (Heb. 8:11; Jer. 31:34)" through overwhelming gospel prosperity (TCE, 191). (3) Jeremiah's explanatory "for" notes that "God will make a full satisfaction for sin (Heb. 8:12; Jer. 31:34)" (TCE, 192). Bahnsen concludes this three-fold observation: "The Older Covenant did not have promises like these three!" (TCE, 192).

In fact, Bahnsen posits as one of Theonomy's ten foundational principles: "In regard to the Old Testament law, the New Covenant surpasses the Old Covenant in glory, power, and finality (thus reinforcing former duties). The New Covenant also supercedes the Old Covenant shadows, thereby changing the application of sacrificial, purity, and 'separation' principles, redefining the people of God, and altering the significance of the promised land." (TCE, xxvi)

Bahnsen's theonomic ethic fits perfectly with the New Testament revelation in the New Covenant era. Jesus affirms the law of God in

---

[49] *Encyclopedia of the Reformed Faith*, 86.

the New Covenant / kingdom of heaven in Matthew 5:17-20. Paul, the "Apostle to the Gentiles," presses the law of God in this era (e.g., Rom. 3:19, 31; 7:12; 13:8-10; 1 Tim. 1:8-11).

The Question of Legalistic Element

In his section on "historical-theological considerations," Gordon sets before his reader the controversy over the legalistic element in the Sinaitic administration:

> As early as the seventeenth century, the Sinai covenant was considered to be perhaps the most difficult covenant administration for covenant theologians to come to terms with. According to Bolton, the difficulty was due to the way that covenant theology attempted to distinguish the covenants made with the two Adams from all other covenants. Having correctly determined that these covenants, made with two representative individuals who were sinless at the time of the administration, were necessarily different from other covenants, covenant theology then went on to distinguish these from other covenants, ordinarily by applying the label "covenant of works" to the Adamic covenants, and "covenant of grace" to the others. In and of itself, this was not too great a problem, but it became a problem when discussing the Sinai administration, which apparently all conceded had both legal and gracious aspects. (CT, 33-34)

He then notes that "the tension was caused by the Sinai covenant's having similarities both to the covenant of works/nature and to the covenant of promise/grace" (CT, 34).

As a committed Klinean, Gordon insists that the Sinaitic covenant "continued the covenant of grace while also retaining (for typological reasons) a 'legal' element" (CT, 34). He reiterates this later: "Paul, by contrast, describes covenants in terms of their administration and their stipulations or requirements, and thus contrasts the promissory character of the Abrahamic and the 'works' character of the Sinai covenant in e.g., Galatians 3. The earliest covenant theologians of the sixteenth and seventeenth centuries appear to have employed the term 'covenant' more as Paul did, including both the stipulations and the effects of varying covenants, and this is why for them (more than for Murray) the Sinai administration could be perceived as having a genuinely legal/works dimension, although not with regard to salvation but with regard to inheriting and prospering in Canaan" (CT, 38, n21). In arguing thus, he is following his mentor Kline and fellow Klinean theologian, Mark Karlberg.[50]

Thus, according to Gordon's Klinean reasoning, the Sinaitic covenant involves a strongly legalistic character which is part-and-parcel to the Mosaic law code. This legalism (which is typological, not redemptive) is inappropriate to our New Covenant age thereby rendering the contemporary application of the law out of keeping with the overarching covenant of grace. But Theonomists remain unimpressed with this analysis for a variety of reasons.

Gordon's Conclusions are Controversial. In Gordon's history-of-doctrine introduction to his covenantal analysis of Theonomy, his opening words are: "Not surprisingly, there has not been complete unanimity in understanding the relations among the various covenantal administrations in the Bible, even among those who consider themselves 'covenant theologians'" (CT, 33). He uses Samuel Bolton as his guide to the seventeenth century era debate, noting: "Bolton described four approaches to dealing with this situation" (CT, 34). He observes that the tension between the viewpoints has not abated into the modern era.

We must recall that on Gordon's own admission his theonomic critique differs from standard covenantal approaches in the debate over God's law. As noted previously he deems the "failure" of covenant theologians to follow a covenantal line of critique such as he does "one of the most profound ironies" (CT, 40). What is a "profound irony" to Gordon appears to be simply the normal covenantal understanding of mainstream Reformed theologians and not a mere oversight. As I also observe above, Kline (a powerful influence over Gordon's theological methodology) is well-known for several of his innovative views, even

---

[50] For fuller discussions of the Klinean approach, see: Meredith G. Kline, *Kingdom Prologue: Genesis Foundations for a Covenantal Worldview* (Overland Park, Kan.: Two Age, 2000); Karlberg, *Covenant Theology in Reformed Perspective* ; Jeon, *Covenant Theology.*

by his disciples and publishers, as well as his critics. I even noted that some of his disciples have been moved to defend him against fellow Reformed critics (e.g., Jeon, Blocher). Simply put, the controversial nature of Gordon's position (built on Klinean foundations) makes it difficult for him to write off Theonomy as out of the mainstream.

By "controversial" I am not implying that Klinean theology is heretical. Some features of his theological method as well as their theological conclusions, however, are cause for concern to a number of Reformed scholars. And why not? As Karlberg observes, the "adoption of Kline's interpretations leads inevitably to a number of significant modifications of traditional dogmatic exposition." This is true, for example, in his views on creation. Since "the theme on which many of Kline's writings have centered is the covenantal nature of divine revelation,"[51] Karlberg explains that Kline's distinctive approach is rooted in his covenantal views: "the opening chapters of the Book of Genesis, [which] is part of the historical prologue to God's covenant with Israel, set forth an account of the creation of the heavens and the earth."[52] Reformed theologian Douglas Kelly critiques Kline's defense of the framework hypothesis, noting that Kline and other framework advocates "have introduced a potentially disastrous dichotomy between literary form and historical chronological viability in interpreting biblical texts."[53] Likewise Reformed theologians J. Ligon Duncan and David W. Hall express concern over Kline's framework methodology: "This view is curiously selective, and we wonder whether the Church actually can draw the line there were it to adopt fully the hermeneutic that framework advocates employ. What, for example, would be the exegetical consequences for the rest of the Genesis protology? What elements of Genesis 1-11 — which, historically, have been taken literally — must we now reinterpret? What about the rest of Scripture?"[54]

Directing our attention briefly to the issue at hand — Christian ethics within a covenantal framework — we should note that the typological-legalistic interpretation of the Sinaitic administration is known

---

[51] Karlberg, *Covenant Theology*, 357.

[52] Karlberg, *Covenant Theology*, 363.

[53] Douglas F. Kelly, *Creation and Change* (Rossshire, Great Britain: Mentor, 1997), 115.

[54] J. Ligon Duncan III and David W. Hall in *The Genesis Debate*, 257-58.

in Klinean circles as "Intrusion Ethics."[55] This interpretive approach deems the Sinaitic administration to be a temporary "intrusion" of the eternal order into history. As Kline expresses and applies it, the Mosaic ethic is "an anticipatory exercise of the ethics of the world to come. Ignorance of this is fraught with danger for the formulator of Christian ethics, for he will be likely to found matters of present Christian duty upon cases of Intrusion ethics."[56] The law code structuring typological Israel embodies, then, the typological intrusion of the consummate order ethic into the national life of Israel. Needless to say, Theonomists marvel that the Church has had to wait almost 2000 years before it had the hermeneutical construct necessary to properly formulate Christian ethics, which lack was "fraught with danger." Though Gordon speaks of Theonomy as on the extreme end of the covenantal spectrum (CT, 42), his own Klinean distinctives appear more extreme.

Gordon's Position is Non-confessional

Gordon insists that the Sinaitic covenant "continued the covenant of grace while also retaining (for typological reasons) a 'legal' element" reflecting the covenant of works (CT, 34). He believes that this works-inheritance principle would agree with some older Reformed theologians that "had argued that there was a legal dimension, related to the inheritance of the land of Canaan" (CT, 35). And thus "the Sinai administration could be perceived as having a genuinely legal/works dimension, although not with regard to salvation but with regard to inheriting and prospering in Canaan" (CT, 38).

This inheritance-principle as legal-element reflecting the covenant of works is significant for Klinean Intrusion Ethics which seems clearly to be the unannounced presupposition of Gordon's line of reasoning. Accordingly, Gordon, Karlberg, and Kline hold that the threats of curse (including the penal sanctions) in God's law indicate the operation of a works-inheritance principle. Karlberg cites Kline regarding the Mosaic Covenant: "What we have found then is that once the typological kingdom was inaugurated under the Mosaic Covenant, Israel's retention of it was governed by a principle of works applied on a national scale." He

---

[55] See: Kline, *The Structure of Biblical Authority*, ch. 3 "The Intrusion and the Decalogue," 154-171.

[56] Kline, *Structure of Biblical Authority*, 157.

continues: "The standard of judgment in this national probation was one of typological legibility, that is, the message must remain reasonably readable that enjoyment of the felicity of God's holy kingdom goes hand in hand with righteousness."[57]

This position is clearly contrary to the view established in the Westminster Confession of Faith (19:6-7). The Confession does not view the threats of curse in God's law as indicative of a works-inheritance principle out of step with the New Covenant, rather such threats do "sweetly comply" with the "grace of the gospel":

Although true believers be not under the law, as a covenant of works, to be thereby justified, or condemned; yet is it of great use to them, as well as to others; in that, as a rule of life informing them of the will of God, and their duty, it directs and binds them to walk accordingly; discovering also the sinful pollutions of their nature, hearts and lives; so as, examining themselves thereby, they may come to further conviction of, humiliation for, and hatred against sin, together with a clearer sight of the need they have of Christ, and the perfection of His obedience. It is likewise of use to the regenerate, to restrain their corruptions, in that it forbids sin: and the threatenings of it serve to show what even their sins deserve; and what afflictions, in this life, they may expect for them, although freed from the curse thereof threatened in the law. The promises of it, in like manner, show them God's approbation of obedience, and what blessings they may expect upon the performance thereof: although not as due to them by the law as a covenant of works. So as, a man's doing good, and refraining from evil, because the law encourages to the one and deters from the other, is no evidence of his being under the law: and not under grace.

Neither are the forementioned uses of the law contrary to the grace of the Gospel, but do sweetly comply with it; the Spirit of Christ subduing and enabling the will of man to do that

---

[57] Karlberg, *Covenant Theology*, 365.

191

freely, and cheerfully, which the will of God, revealed in the law, requires to be done.

The minutes of Session 699 of the Westminster Assembly record the following adopted resolution: "Neither is it an evidence that a man is under law, and not under grace, when he refrains from evil and doeth good, because the law encourageth to the one, and deters from the other, but rather a sign of the power of God's grace in him, when his heart is subdued conscientiously to live according to the Rule, though in things contrary to the dictate of corrupt nature, from the consideration of God's goodness in rewarding freely those that do well, and of his justice in punishing them that do ill."[58]

These confessional observations fit with a Theonomic Ethic, but are contradictory to Gordon's (and Kline's) approach. In fact, according to the Confession the New Covenant church herself must fear the discipline of the Lord when she breaches his standards:

Church censures are necessary, for the reclaiming and gaining of offending brethren, for deterring of others from the like offenses, for purging out of that leaven which might infect the whole lump, for vindicating the honor of Christ, and the holy profession of the Gospel, and for preventing the wrath of God, which might justly fall upon the Church, if they should suffer His covenant, and the seals thereof, to be profaned by notorious and obstinate offenders. (WCF 30:3)

God does continue to forgive the sins of those that are justified; and although they can never fall from the sate of justification, yet they may, by their sins, fall under God's fatherly displeasure, and not have the light of His countenance restored unto them, until they humble themselves, confess their sins, beg pardon, and renew their faith and repentance. (WCF 11:5)

---

[58] Alexander F. Mitchell, and John Struthers, eds., *Minutes of the Sessions of the Westminster Assembly of Divines* (Edinburgh: William Blackwood, 1874), 274. Session 699, September 4, 1646.

Nevertheless, they may, through the temptations of Satan and of the world, the prevalency of corruption remaining in them, and the neglect of the means of their preservation, fall into grievous sins; and, for a time, continue therein: whereby they incur God's displeasure, and grieve His Holy Spirit, come to be deprived of some measure of their graces and comforts, have their hearts hardened, and their consciences wounded; hurt and scandalize others, and bring temporal judgments upon themselves. (WCF 17:3)

So then, according to Gordon the Westminster Confession of Faith — the first fully covenantal creed — developed a covenantal system "without any biblical evidence" and "contrary to some of the evidence in Scripture" (CT, 40). In the next major section, I will return to the Confession of Faith in defending Theonomy. But for now I am simply pointing out the conflict between confessional theology and Intrusion Ethics, a conflict that does not occur with the Theonomic Ethic.

Gordon's Position is Theonomically Compatible

As it turns out, Theonomists do not necessarily have to engage the complexities of the Klinean construct or rebut their typological understanding of Israel's role in history. We could very well accept the basic interpretation of the legalistic character of Israel's typological covenant. This is because adopting the typological orientation of Israel's experience does *not necessarily* require the theological conclusions of Kline's Intrusionist system. In other words, we could grant Gordon's history-of-doctrine analysis of the seventeenth century debate over the typological-legalistic character of the Sinaitic administration, while nevertheless adopting the ethical conclusions of both the general historic Reformed understanding of the law, the express teaching of the Westminster Standards, and Theonomic Ethics. Consider our possible responses.

Our multi-dimensional response. We must remember that Gordon himself admits various "dimensions" to the Mosaic legislation. He criticizes Dabney, noting that "what he appears to have misunderstood is that the legal dimension recognized by many at Sinai was only *one dimension*" (CT, 35; emphasis his). He even speaks of "the Sinai administration, which apparently all conceded had both legal and gracious aspects" (CT, 33-34).

Consequently, Theonomists could accept a legalistic dimension in God's law (for typological purposes and confined to the old covenant economy), while recognizing that the ethical directives of God's law *also* have a *non*-legalistic dimension — as do the Confession of Faith and historic Reformed orthodoxy. This would allow a New Covenant usefulness and application of God's law. Even Klineans agree that the Sinaitic covenant was given under the overarching covenant of grace (CT, 34). After all, it is one of the "covenants" (plural) of "the promise" (singular). Paul's rhetorical question to the Galatians shows that the law is not contrary to God's gracious promises: "Is the Law then contrary to the promises of God? May it never be!" (Gal. 3:21a). Indeed, the revelation of the New Covenant itself endorses God's law (as we have argued above), according to Jeremiah 31:31-34. As Vos himself observes: "in the covenant of grace, too, the participants are exempt from the demand of the law as the condition for eternal blessedness, but not from its demand as being normative for their moral life."[59]

As a matter of fact, we should *expect* that God's law would embody universal, invariant, ethical principles in that it reflects his own perfect, eternal moral character. The moral directives in God's law — both on the personal and the social levels — *could* have been applied in a *legalistic manner* for old covenant typological purposes, while simultaneously applying in a non-legalistic manner for New Covenant moral direction.

Reformed scholars have historically agreed that the Decalogue (at least) reflects the universal moral law of God, even though it was expressly embodied in the revelation to Israel on tables of stone in summary of her covenant. That being so, though Israel's covenant was for a "peculiar people" under the "old covenant," why may we not accept simultaneously the obligations of the moral dimension of God's law upon all men? May not the *moral substance* remain even when the *typological function* is removed? As Moisés Silva asks: "What is the relationship between the old and the new covenant? Does the newness of the gospel suggest a breach between it and the Sinaitic covenant? Or to use Paul's provocative language in Galatians, 'Is the law opposed to the

---

[59] Geerhardus Vos, *Redemptive History and Biblical Interpretation: The Shorter Writings of Geerhardus Vos*, ed. by Richard B. Gaffin, Jr., (Phillipsburg, N.J.: Presbyterian and Reformed, 1980), 244.

promises?'"[60] He observes further that "the Reformed tradition . . . has been concerned to minimize the antithetical elements, to assert the coherence of God's gracious provisions in both dispensations, and to stress the continuing validity of God's law for the Christian."[61]

Our symbolic-ceremonial response. Though Theonomists emphasize Jesus' own words that "not the smallest letter or stroke shall pass from the law until is accomplished" (Matt. 5:18), we recognize that *God himself* can make specific alterations to his law (see previous discussion). We hold that the redemptively distinct elements of the law are *not* the moral directives (including the judicial response to criminal deeds), but the ceremonial overlays in the law. Bahnsen deals with the matter of the ceremonial laws per se at length in *Theonomy* (ch. 9); *No Other Standard* (ch. 6), and *By This Standard* (ch. 14, 16).

We would argue that the moral obligations incumbent upon the civil magistrate as the "minister of God" (Rom. 13:4) remain, while the particular symbolic-ceremonial structure of those judicial laws were typologically designed for old covenant Israel alone. For instance, we believe that capital punishment obligations continue for the set crimes in God's law, but that the *manner* in which capital sanctions are imposed do not oblige nations outside of Israel, being tied in with the system of old covenant symbolism. I will mention just three symbolic aspects of the application of capital punishment for illustrative purposes.

In old covenant Israel judicial decisions demanding capital punishment were rendered at the gates of the city (Deut. 21:19; 22:15), the capital sanction administered outside the walls of the city (Lev. 24:14, 23; Num. 15:35-36; Deut. 17:15; 22:24; 1 Kgs. 21:13; Acts 7:58), and the capital punishment was accomplished by means of stoning (Num. 24:8, 17; Luke 20:18). That is, the judicial determination was made at the entry way into the city in order to portray the righteous requirements demanded for entering the kingdom of God (Mark 10:17-19; Heb. 12:14). The capital sanction was administered outside the city,

---

[60] Moisés Silva, "Is the Law Against the Promises?," 153.

[61] Silva, "Is the Law Against the Promises?," 154. His discussion of the controversial passage in Leviticus 18:5 is helpful. He is convinced that Paul "would have affirmed the truth expressed in Leviticus 18:5," but that he would have "vigorously denied that the law could be the source of righteousness and life" (Silva, 165).

demonstrating that death and judgment lie outside the city of God (Matt. 8:12; Rev. 22:14-17). Stoning was chosen not only for its death-dealing power, but as symbolizing the crushing wrath of God from heaven (Isa. 8:13-15; Dan. 2:34-35). These features of the *method* of criminal sanctions were symbolically-determined. But the punishment of death (the capital sanction) remains as a moral directive.

Our New Testament response. Theonomists note that while the New Testament specifically removes the ceremonial law by direct revelation (e.g., Acts 11:8-9; 15:10, 19-29; 1 Cor. 7:19; Gal. 5:6; Heb. 9:8-12), it never removes the moral law, including its criminal sanctions. We invariably discover the New Testament dismantling *only* ceremonial-ritual, redemption-defining laws, not moral or judicial laws.[62]

In the New Covenant era the very law of God is written on the heart (Jer. 31:33; Heb. 8:8-10; 10:16). Thus, in the New Testament itself, law obedience expresses the Golden Rule of social conduct (Matt. 7:12), defines the behavior of love (Matt. 22:40; Rom. 13:10; Gal. 5:14; Jms. 2:8), promotes spirituality (Rom. 7:14; 8:3-4; Heb. 8:10), and evidences holiness, justice, and goodness (Rom. 2:13; 7:12, 16; 1 Tim. 1:8). The law convicts of sin (Matt. 19:16-24; John 7:19; Acts 7:53; Rom. 7:7; Jms. 2:9-11; 1 John 3:4) and restrains the sinner through its criminal sanctions (1 Tim. 1:8-10), which effect a "just recompense" (Heb. 2:2) because it is the standard of God's judgment (Rom. 2:13-15; cf. Matt. 7:23; 13:41; Jms. 2:10-12). Consequently, he who is not subject to the law of God in the New Covenant era is at enmity with God (Matt. 5:19; Rom. 8:7; 1 John 2:3-4).

It is true, of course, that the author of Hebrews draws Mosaic penal sanctions into a discussion of the ultimate repercussions of spiritual apostasy from the Christian faith. But his *a fortiori* argument does not dismantle the civil utility of the penal sanctions. By parity of reasoning, consider that in Matthew 5 Jesus applies the prohibition against murder to the root cause of murder: hatred. And though he references the fact of the capital sanction against murder, his urging the deepest spiritual meaning of the law does not render its capital punishment inoperative. In Hebrews 10, the writer applies the prohibition against

---

[62] For the question of Jesus' forgiving the woman caught in adultery, see: *Theonomy*, 228-29.

idolatrous apostasy to its root effect, unbelief.[63] And though he references the fact of the capital sanction against idolatrous apostasy, his urging the deepest spiritual meaning of the law does not render its capital punishment inoperative. That is, there may be temporal capital sanctions against physical acts administered by the civil magistrate, while at the same time there exists the threat of eternal judgmental sanctions against related spiritual acts, administered by the Lord of glory. In fact, who believes that in the old covenant capital punishment of criminals did not lead to eternal punishment of the unrepentant criminal?

Our failed implication response

Gordon's article does not mention Intrusion Ethics per se. Nevertheless, his high appreciation for Kline and Kline's theology do suggest that something akin, at least, to an Intrusionist approach lurks in the background. We can assuredly state that Kline himself has long argued for an Intrusionist ethic based on the typological character of Israel's redemptive history (which typological thrust is emphasized by Gordon, CT, 38).

As usual, Kline's position is unique, as he admits in his introduction to the chapter "The Intrusion and the Decalogue" in *The Structure of Biblical Authority*. Speaking of himself in the third person he states of one who would investigate Old Testament ethics: "So will he give himself again to the exegesis of the Word in the conviction that the solution of the ethical problem must be one and the same as its accurate and adequate formulation. The attempt is, therefore, made here to seek a solution in terms of a *somewhat fresh formulation* of certain distinctive elements in the religion of the Old Testament."[64] In the very Preface to this book he writes: "The initial concern with the canonical aspect of Scripture led inevitably to reexamination of the formal character of Scripture as such. 'What is the Bible?' became a central question, and it receives here a *somewhat distinctive answer*, in line with the *new direction* taken in the formulation of biblical canonicity."[65]

---

[63] For a theonomic understanding of the apostasy legislation, see Appendix 2: "Apostasy Legislation."

[64] Meredith G. Kline, *The Structure of Biblical Authority* (Grand Rapids: Eerdmans, 1972), 154. Emphasis mine.

[65] Kline, *Structure of Biblical Authority*, 7. Emphasis mine.

Kline explains Intrusion Ethics (from here on I will abbreviate *The Structure of Biblical Authority* by: SBA):

> When we survey the Old Testament, a divinely sanctioned pattern of action emerges which is not consonant with the customary application of the law of God according to the principle of common grace. It will be our purpose to show that this ethical pattern is congenial to biblical religion by relating it to the Intrusion phenomenon which we have found to be an integral element in the Old Testament. (SBA, 158)
>
> Now it appears that there was introduced in the Old Testament age a pattern of conduct akin to that found in the prophetic portrayals of the kingdom of God beyond the present age of common grace. Our thesis is that this Old Testament ethical pattern is an aspect of the Intrusion. Included in it are both anticipations of God's judgment curse on the reprobate and of his saving grace in blessing his elect. (SBA 160)

Overlooking some elements of Intrusion Ethics that do not concern us (the conquest of Canaan and the imprecatory psalms), we should consider Kline's observations that:

> Ethical anticipations of the judgment of the reprobate are found in cases involving all the rest of commandments five through ten, excepting the seventh for the reason that 'every sin that a man doeth is without the body; but he that committeth fornication sinneth against his own body' (1 Cor. 6:18). (SBA, 164)
>
> In the area of penal sanctions against offending covenant members, the Intrusion principle again manifests itself. It is especially significant that among the offenses for which the death penalty was prescribed are violations of the first four laws of the Decalogue. . . . In the present age such violations are subject to ecclesiastical discipline, but the sword may not be wielded by either church or state in punishment of such offenders, according to the principle of common grace. In the consummation, however, the portion of those who do

not obey these laws from the heart will be the 'the second death.' It is then consummation justice that was introduced when death was prescribed for religious offenses in Israel, the kingdom where the consummation was typically anticipated. (SBA 166-67)

Theonomists (along with many Reformed scholars) find Kline's unique Intrusion formulation wholly unacceptable for a number of reasons, a few of which I will mention. Bahnsen presented some of the following objections in his original edition of *Theonomy in Christian Ethics*. They need reiteration because they still stand as potent objections.

First, the New Testament evidence counters Kline. The New Testament does not deem the Old Testament moral order passe. Nowhere does the New Covenant revelation suggest the moral directives of the Mosaic law have only temporary validity (TCE, 560). In fact, it frequently and clearly *establishes* the Mosaic law — even quoting it precisely — as a continuing obligation in the New Covenant order and (where relevant) upon the nations (see previous discussions and abundant argumentation by Bahnsen, TCE, chs. 2, 10, 12, 13, 16-19, 21). As Bahnsen states it: "the commands of Scripture reveal abidingly proper ethical relationships" (TCE, 560). How could the civil magistrate be a "minister of God" (Rom. 3:4) and not be subject to the moral standard of God revealed in his law?

We should recall particularly the following two references as examples of the theonomic position:

Now we know that whatever the Law says, it speaks to those who are under the Law, that every mouth may be closed, and all the world may become accountable to God (Rom. 3:19).

But we know that the Law is good, if one uses it lawfully, realizing the fact that law is not made for a righteous man, but for those who are lawless and rebellious, for the ungodly and sinners, for the unholy and profane, for those who kill their fathers or mothers, for murderers and immoral men and homosexuals and kidnappers and liars and perjurers, and whatever else is contrary to sound teaching (1 Tim. 1:8-10).

Second, the Old Testament even contradicts Kline. We have briefly noted numerous Old Testament passages that speak of God's law as the moral obligation of the nations. Even in the early giving of the law Moses states:

> So keep and do them, for that is your wisdom and your understanding in the sight of the peoples who will hear all these statutes and say, 'Surely this great nation is a wise and understanding people.' For what great nation is there that has a god so near to it as is the Lord our God whenever we call on Him? Or what great nation is there that has statutes and judgments as righteous as this whole law which I am setting before you today? (Deut. 4:6-8)

And though Kline attempts to make a special case for the extermination of the Canaanites on the Intrusion principle (SBA, 162-64), we see the same mass judgment upon Sodom and Gomorrah long before the conquest of the Promised Land (Gen. 19:28; 2 Peter 2:6). In the prophets we find numerous denunciations of foreign peoples on the basis of God's moral law (but never the ceremonial law). (*Theonomy*, chapter 18). In fact, we find God's law commended to the nations: "Pay attention to Me, O My people; and give ear to Me, O My nation; for a law will go forth from Me, and I will set My justice for a light of the peoples" (Isa. 51:4).

Third, Kline contradicts himself in his argumentation. While presenting the case for his Intrusion Ethics, he asserts that the old covenant penal sanctions are examples of divine intrusion which cannot be applied today in the New Covenant era: "In the present age such violations are subject to ecclesiastical discipline, but the sword may not be wielded by either church or state in punishment of such offenders" (SBA, 166). But he then allows that "an analogy exists between the state's judicial use of the sword and Israel's conquest of Canaan" (SBA, 165ff). These two assertions are mutually incompatible in themselves. But what is worse, the command to destroy the Canaanites does not serve — even by analogy — to guide the state in the judicial use of the sword. That legislation was positive law designed for limited application, and therefore unrepeatable elsewhere, even causing the deaths of many who were not formally criminals (Deut. 7).

Fourth, Kline uses language in unusual ways. The demands of Kline's typological system and interpretive methodology force him to use language in unnatural ways. In one place he writes: "just because the grand principle . . . . is immutable, the application . . . must be changed" (SBA, 160). Immutability and change are mutually antithetical concepts. If it is immutably the case that murderers must die for their crimes, then to change the application so that murders do *not* die, would undermine the immutability principle.

Earlier he had stated that the conquest of Canaan was an example of the "meek inheriting the earth" (SBA, 163). How can meekness describe the following: "when the Lord your God shall deliver them before you, and you shall defeat them, then you shall utterly destroy them . . . You shall consume all the peoples whom the Lord your God will deliver to you; your eye shall not pity them" (Deut. 7:2, 16). Of Jericho we read: "And they utterly destroyed everything in the city, both man and woman, young and old, and ox and sheep and donkey, with the edge of the sword" (Josh. 6:21). God's directive to Israel is morally repulsive to the liberal, shocking to even Christian sensibilities, and can in no way speak of meekness.

Fifth, Intrusion Ethics cannot explain disparate punishments. If the capital sanctions of the Mosaic law are "ethical anticipations of the judgment of the reprobate" (SBA, 164), we must ask why are not *all* sins not punished by death? The Scripture teaches that *all* sin deserves the eternal wrath of God (Matt. 12:36; Gal. 3:10; Jms. 2:10). We should also wonder why some crimes are punished by fines, in that fines do not reflect "the judgment of the reprobate" at the last day.

These and various other arguments render Kline's Intrusion Ethic null and void. Gordon's larger legalistic argument collapses under its own weight.

The Question of Decalogue Abstraction

As I noted in another context above, Gordon argues that even the Ten Commandments themselves are relevant and applicable *only* in their Mosaic environment, that is, in the land of Israel, during the Mosaic economy, and among the Jews. They are, therefore, the unabstractable heart of the Sinaitic covenant which is inapplicable both to Christians in the New Covenant era and to non-Christians in the world at large.

I have already responded to much of his argument in previous contexts. I will, however, focus a little more on this point in that Gordon brings in the Confession of Faith at this juncture, criticizing its (allegedly) deficient understanding of the covenant, rebutting its theology and ethics, and misinterpreting its statements on the law of God.

The Confessional error of abstraction

Gordon traces the theonomic error back to the Westminster divines: "Theonomists are not the first to abstract legislation from the Sinai covenant. The Westminster Assembly appears to have done it beforehand, though on a much smaller scale and in a more ambiguous manner. The divines at Westminster appear to have abstracted the decalogue from the Sinai covenant, and to have understood the ten words as timeless and, if you will, 'covenant-less'" (CT, 40).

He rebuts the Confession on this matter as being wholly unbiblical and deserving of criticism: "The assembly asserted that God gave the Ten Commandments (or the equivalent thereof) to Adam, and then gave the same law to Moses. This assertion then, if unchallenged, permits the decalogue to be perceived as a timeless, 'covenant-less' expression of God's moral will. This assertion is not only completely without any biblical evidence, but it is an assertion contrary to some of the evidence in Scripture." (CT, 40)

The Confession is historically Reformed

But Gordon's rebuttal of the Confession of Faith itself needs to be challenged. His criticism is based on his peculiar Klinean Intrusion commitments, rather than on more broadly based Reformed theological reflection. Traditionally, Reformed theology has adopted the Ten Commandments as the ethical core of the Christian life and the foundational principle of morality in the world. For instance, *The Dictionary of the Presbyterian & Reformed Tradition in America* notes of the Heidelberg Catechism: "It acknowledges good works as the fruits of saving faith [and] views the Ten Commandments as a summary of the ethical Christian life."[66]

---

[66] D. G. Hart, ed., *Dictionary of the Presbyterian & Reformed Tradition in America* (Downers Grove, Ill: InterVarsity, 1999), 118-19.

R. B. Kuiper laments the decline of the Reformed faith in his denomination, even writing a book titled *To Be or Not to Be Reformed*, wherein he states: "And what right have we to stress some of the ten commandments less than others? . . . We are in great danger of substituting our *mores* for the moral law of God."[67] He notes of the Christian Reformed Church in the first half of the twentieth century: "It would not be difficult to draw up a long list of such traditions, prevalent in the Christian Reformed Church. To name a few, it is customary in our churches to read the law of the ten commandments, together with its Scriptural summary, in the Sunday morning service of worship . . . ."[68]

Beeke and Ferguson commend the Confession of Faith's endorsing God's law: "Careful attention is given to the exposition of the Decalogue (questions 41-81). Far from being an indication of actual or incipient legalism, the Westminster divines themselves regard this as an essential lesson in Christian living."[69]

The reader should recall the evidence from Calvin and other Reformed scholars regarding the role of the Ten Commandments in the Christian life. Klinean theologian Mark Karlberg admits that "it has been *commonplace* in Reformed theology *from the beginning* to speak of the law as a 'rule' for life both in creation and redemption."[70] Vos wrote of the Ten Commandments: "The primary application to Israel in no wise interferes with a world-wide application in all ethical relationships. . . . Certain features at first sight would seem applicable to Israel alone, for instance what is said of the deliverance from the Egyptian bondage. . . . The historical adjustment does not detract from the universal application, but subserves it."[71]

And even of the controversial fourth commandment Vos writes: "The fourth word has reference to the hallowing of the seventh day of the week. This duty is based in Exodus (but cpr. Deuteronomy) not on something done to Israel in particular, but on something done in the creation of the world. This is important, because with it stands or falls

---

[67] R. B. Kuiper, *To Be or Not to Be Reformed* (Grand Rapids: Zondervan, 1959), 56.

[68] Kuiper, *To Be or Not to Be Reformed*, 52.

[69] Joel R. Beeke and Sinclair B. Ferguson, *Reformed Confessions Harmonized with An Annotated Bibliography of Reformed Doctrinal Works* (Grand Rapids: Baker, 1999), xiii.

[70] Karlberg, *Covenant Theology in Reformed Perspective*, 39. Emphasis mine.

[71] Vos, *Biblical Theology*, 147.

the general validity of the commandment for all mankind."[72] He continues:

> The Sabbath brings this principle of the eschatological structure of history to bear upon the mind of man after a symbolical and typical fashion. . . . Man is reminded in this way that life is not an aimless existence, that a goal lies beyond. This was true before, and apart from, redemption.

And after considering an objection to the Sabbath, he writes:

> Of such a view it might be maintained that for one sufficiently at leisure to give all his time to the cultivation of religion the keeping of the Sabbath would be no longer obligatory. Some of the continental Reformers, out of reaction to the Romish system of holy days, reasoned after this fashion. But they reasoned wrongly. . . . The universal Sabbath law received a modified significance under the Covenant of Grace.[73]

And what is more, the Westminster Confession against which Gordon objects is not simply an historical specimen of Reformed theology, but both Bahnsen and Gordon took ordination vows adopting the Confession of Faith as their own. So then, whereas Bahnsen affirmed the Confession's view of the law (as I will show below), Gordon rejects it.

The Confession is eminently biblical

Sadly, Gordon's objection does not simply disagree with the divines' conclusions. He rejects Westminster's approach to the law of God as "*completely* without *any* biblical evidence," even being "an assertion *contrary* to some of the evidence in Scripture" (CT, 40; emphasis mine). This is an incredible criticism against this venerable Reformed creed. After all, the divines supplied ample proof-texts throughout the

---

[72] Vos, *Biblical Theology*, 155.
[73] Vos, *Biblical Theology*, 157.

Confession. The (post-Westminster) Reformed tradition has a much higher view of the work of the divines. And it certainly has never denounced this issue of the law (or any other!) as "completely without any biblical evidence."

Warfield speaks of the Confession's "preeminence among Reformed Confessions, not only in fulness but also in exactitude and richness of statement," being "the ripest fruit of Reformed creed-making," representing "Reformed theology at its best."[74] He views the Confession as "the culminating Reformed Confession of Faith, and a Catechism preeminent for the exactness of its definitions of faith and the faithfulness of its ethical precepts."[75] He praises the Confession for its "peculiar comprehensiveness, while yet it permits to its statements of the generic doctrine of the Reformed Churches a directness, a definiteness, a crisp precision, and an unambiguous clarity which are attained by few Confessional documents of any age or creed."[76]

William Hetherington wrote in his important history of the Assembly: "The first thing which must strike any thoughtful reader, after having carefully and studiously perused the Westminster Assembly's Confession of Faith, is the remarkable comprehensiveness and accuracy of its character, viewed as a systematic exhibition of divine truth, or what is termed system of theology. In this respect it may be regarded as almost perfect, both in its arrangement and in its completeness."[77] He speaks of its "astonishing precision of thought and language."[78]

McClintock and Strong note that it "ranks as one of the best Calvinistic symbols."[79] The *Encyclopedia of the Reformed Faith* speaks of its "high technical competence" and "its success in embodying a consensus

---

[74] Benjamin B. Warfield, *The Westminster Assembly and Its Work* (Cherry Hill, N. J.: Mack, rep. 1972 [n.d.]), 58-59.

[75] Warfield, *The Westminster Assembly and its Work*, 72.

[76] Warfield, *The Westminster Assembly and Its Work*, 56.

[77] William Hetherington, *History of the Westminster Assembly of Divines* (Edmonton: Still Waters Revival, rep. 1991 [1856]), 350.

[78] Hetherington, *History of the Westminster Assembly*, 352.

[79] John McClintock and James Strong, *Cyclopedia of Biblical, Theological, and Ecclesiastical Literature* (New York: Harper and Bros, 1867-87; rep. Grand Rapids: Baker, 1981), 10:965.

of Reformed theology."[80] Beeke and Ferguson write: "The Confession of Faith produced by the Westminster divines has undoubtedly been one of the most influential documents of the post-Reformation period of the Christian church. A carefully worded exposition of the seventeenth-century Reformed theology, the calmness of its sentences largely hides the tempestuousness of the political backcloth against which it was written."[81] "It is the outstanding expression of classical Reformed theology framed for the needs of the people of God."[82]

Gordon sympathizer Karlberg highly commends the Confession: "The most definitive creedal statement to come out of the period of the Reformation is the *Westminster Confession of Faith.*" He observes that it "is unsurpassed both in its definition and comprehensiveness, and continues to be the creedal standard for a great many within the Reformed orthodox church today."[83]

Contrary to Gordon's lament that the Confession is "completely without any biblical evidence" on the matter of the Decalogue, Erik Routley highly commends the Confession and its *biblically-based* presentation: "Its ample language and combination of lucid theological statement with scriptural precision place it, as a statement of Reformed theology, far above any of the other Confessions in any language. It stands almost at the end of the period of classic Confession, and forms a worthy climax to them."[84] McClintock and Strong concur: "it is clear, incisive, compressed, and provided throughout with Scripture proofs."[85] And, of course, the Reformed theological community would never have so highly praised the Confession if it tended to act "completely without any biblical evidence."

The formal publication of the Westminster Standards was prefaced with an "Epistle to the Christian Reader, especially Heads of Families," which declared their desire to secure the doctrines in Scripture:

---

[80] McKim, *Encyclopedia of the Reformed Faith*, 393.

[81] Beeke and Ferguson, *Reformed Confessions Harmonized*, xii.

[82] Beeke and Ferguson, *Reformed Confessions Harmonized*, xii.

[83] Karlberg, *Covenant Theology*, 38

[84] Erik Routley, *Creeds and Confessions: From the Reformation to the Modern Church* (Philadelphia: Westminster, 1962), 118-19.

[85] McClintock and Strong, *Cyclopedia of Biblical, Theological, and Ecclesiastical Literature*, 10:965.

If the reverend and learned composers of these ensuing treatises were willing to take the pains in annexing scripture proofs to every truth, that the faith of people might not be built upon the dictates of men, but the authority of God, so some considerable pains hath now been further taken in transcribing those scriptures; partly to prevent the grand inconvenience, (which all former impressions, except the Latin, have abounded with, to the great perplexing and disheartening of the reader,) the misquotation of scripture, the meanest reader being able, by having the words at large, to rectify whatever mistake may be in the printer in citing the particular place; partly, to prevent the trouble of turning to every proof, which could not but be very great; partly, to help the memories of such who are willing to take the pains of turning to every proof, but are unable to retain what they read; and partly, that this may serve as a bible commonplace, the several passages of scripture, which are scattered up and down in the word, being in this book reduced to their proper head, and thereby giving light each to other. The advantages, you see, in this design, are many and great; the way to spiritual knowledge is hereby made more easy, and the ignorance of this age more inexcusable.[86]

The Confession is self-consciously covenantal

Though Gordon's understanding of covenant theology serves as his foundational criticism of the Confession, the Confession is self-consciously and thoroughly covenantal. The *Encyclopedia of the Reformed Faith* notes the prominent place the Confession has in the history of covenant theology: "By the mid-seventeenth century, the double covenant was a commonplace of Reformed theology. It appeared in the WCF (1646) and became the central organizing principle in the writings of Hermann Witsius and Johannes Cocceius in the Netherlands."[87]

Even further, Routley notes of the Confession's covenantal emphasis: "it differs from most other confessions especially in the space it gives to . . . the Covenant between God and man."[88] The *Evangelical*

---

[86] *Westminster Confession of Faith* (Glasgow: Free Presbyterian Publications, 1994), 8.

[87] McKim, *Encyclopedia of the Reformed Faith*, 137.

[88] Routley, *Creeds and Confessions*, 119.

Dictionary of Theology traces the history of covenant theology, finally noting its first affirmation in creedal form: "it was taken up into the Westminster Confession."[89] Beeke and Ferguson concur: "The Westminster Confession of Faith represents a high point in the development of federal theology, and its inner dynamic is powerfully covenantal."[90] J. I. Packer writes: "Historically, covenant theology is a Reformed development, . . . the Westminster Confession and Catechisms gave it confessional status."[91]

Vos agrees: "The Westminster Confession is the first Reformed confession in which the doctrine of the covenant is not merely brought in from the side, but is placed in the foreground and has been able to permeate at almost every point."[92] Even Karlberg notes regarding the development of covenant theology: "It is not until the time of the Reformation, considered in its widest range from the second decade of the sixteenth century to the writing of the Westminster Standards (1648), that the doctrine of the covenant comes fully into its own."[93] He observes of the place of covenant theology in the Confession that : "The federal structure of the *Confession* is by no means idiosyncratic, but rather is reflective of Reformed catholic doctrine in its deepest and most characteristic insight into biblical truth. Indeed, it is the architectonic principle of the *Westminster Confession.*"[94]

Karlberg evidently followed Warfield in respecting the Confession's place and role in the matter of creedalizing covenant theology, for Warfield comments: "The architectonic principle of the Westminster Confession is supplied by the schematization of the Federal theology, which had obtained by this time in Britain, as on the Continent, a dominant position as the most commodious mode of presenting the *corpus* of Reformed doctrine."[95]

---

[89] Walter A. Elwell, ed., *Evangelical Dictionary of Biblical Theology* (Grand Rapids: Baker, 1984), 279.

[90] Beeke and Ferguson, *Reformed Confessions Harmonized*, xii.

[91] J. I. Packer, "Introduction" to *Witsius, Economy of the Covenants Between God and Man*, 1: xvii:

[92] Vos, *Redemptive History and Biblical Interpretation*, 239.

[93] Karlberg, *Covenant Theology*, 17.

[94] Karlberg, *Covenant Theology*, 38.

[95] Warfield, *The Westminster Assembly and Its Work*, 56.

So then, despite such widespread Reformed acclamation of the Confession of Faith, and despite the Confession's pre-eminent role in creedalizing covenant theology, Gordon criticizes its approach to God's law as involving an "a-covenantal hermeneutic" (CT, 42) and laments its "misunderstanding of the covenantal role of the decalogue" (CT, 41). Theonomists, however, praise the Confession in concert with traditional Reformed tendencies which deem the creed to be the "high point in the development of federal theology."[96] Gordon criticizes it even in one of its most distinctive characteristics, its covenantal emphasis.

The Confession is intensely theological. Gordon does attempt to rescue the divines from their confusion by noting they were merely attempting to be catechetical, and were not carefully engaging in biblical-theological expression: "Although the assembly appears to have contributed to misunderstandings of the decalogue in subsequent generations, it must be remembered that their purpose was catechetical, not biblical-theological. Their desire to find some location in which the moral will of God was 'summarily comprehended' was catechetically proper, despite the misunderstanding of the covenantal role of the decalogue which may have resulted therefrom." (CT, 41)

This fails to convince Theonomists for several reasons. In the first place, catechisms are generated out of a theological outlook. The Westminster Standards *summarize* doctrinal truth in order to secure that truth in the minds and hearts of the faithful, protecting the system of truth from erosion. If a catechism is a *summary* of theological truth, the theological truth that lies behind it exists in fuller form. That which is catechetically summarized therein reflects the underlying theological commitment of those formulating the catechism. As an early edition of the Standards state:

> Never did any age of the Church enjoy such choice helps as this of ours. Every age of the gospel hath had its Creeds, Confessions, Catechisms, and such breviaries and models of divinity as have been singularly useful. Such forms of sound words (however in these days decried) have been in use in the

---

[96] Beeke and Ferguson, *Reformed Confessions Harmonized*, xii.

Church ever since God himself wrote the Decalogue, as a summary of things to be done; and Christ taught us that prayer of his, as a directory what to ask.[97]

Secondly, surely Gordon is not accusing the divines of catechizing *against* their own theology, is he? By the very nature of the case, a catechism seeks to promote the truth held by those writing the catechism, not altering or overlooking it. In fact, the Greek word κατεχέω, according to the famed Reformed catechist Zacharias Ursinus, "signifies to teach the first principles and rudiments of some particular doctrine."[98] A catechism does not *bypass* theology, but summarizes it.

Thirdly, the universal Reformed tradition agrees with the Confession's view of the law over against Gordon's peculiar views. We have seen this in a sampling of a number of significant works by various authors. I would remind the reader of just one sample: the Heidelberg Catechism (Questions 92-115).

The Confessional consistency with Theonomy

Gordon suggests that despite the error of the divines, they at least limited the damage done to theological reasoning by qualifying themselves: "Further, it must be noted that the assembly 'limited' the damage done, by abstracting *only* the decalogue. In *WCF* 19.3-4, the assembly indicated that there were other aspects of the Sinai legislation (which they called 'ceremonial' and 'judicial') that were covenantally conditioned." (CT, 41) Yet Theonomy, Gordon insists, rejects the Confession's qualifications, exacerbating the error of "a-covenantalism" committed in the Confession:

> Theonomy follows the a-covenantal hermeneutic of the Westminster Assembly, yet without the qualifications or limitations of *WCF* 19:4: 'To them also, as a body politic, he gave sundry judicial laws, which expired together with the state of

---

[97] *The Westminster Confession of Faith*, 7.

[98] Zacharias Ursinus, *Commentary of Dr. Zacharias Ursinus on the Heidelberg Catechism*, trans. by G. W. Willard (2d ed.: Phillipsburg, N.J.: Presbyterian and Reformed, rep. n.d. [1852]), 10-11.

that people; not obliging any other now, further than the general equity thereof may require.' Theonomy tends to abstract *all* of the Sinai legislation from its covenantal setting. While some Theonomists borrow the confessional language of 'general equity,' they rarely employ it with the four confessional qualifications, namely, the recognition that those in covenant with God at Sinai were a 'body politic' (unlike the New Covenant community); that those laws 'expired together with the state of that people'; that such are 'not obliging any other now'; and that the general equity only *may* require that some of that body of legislation would be equitable generally to other nations. (CT, 42)

By way of quick response, we must ask if Paul the Apostle makes the same mistake as the divines in "abstracting" the Ten Commandments from their covenantally-limited setting. After all, he directs the Ephesian Christians: "Children, obey your parents in the Lord, for this is right. Honor your father and mother (which is the first commandment with a promise), that it may be well with you, and that you may live long on the earth" (Eph. 6:1-3). We should note that he even mentions it "is the first commandment with a promise" (therefore it is a "commandment") and states that promise which appears to limit its application to Israel: "that it may be well with you, and that you may live long on the earth" (for it picks up on Gordon-Karlberg-Kline's "inheritance principle").

Paul makes the same a-covenantal mistake when he writes to the Roman Christians: "Owe nothing to anyone except to love one another; for he who loves his neighbor has fulfilled the law. For this, 'You shall not commit adultery, You shall not murder, You shall not steal, You shall not covet,' and if there is any other commandment, it is summed up in this saying, 'You shall love your neighbor as yourself.' Love does no wrong to a neighbor; love therefore is the fulfillment of the law" (Rom. 13:8-10).

But let us dig a little deeper. I will consider WCF 19:4 specifically. What are we to make of the Confession's express statements regarding the judicial laws? What do the divines mean when they state: "To them [the Jews] also, as a body politic, He gave sundry judicial laws, which expired together with the State of that people; not obliging any other now, further than the general equity thereof may require" (19:4)?

Ceremonial abrogation

We should begin by noting that the divines treat the judicial laws in a fundamentally different way than the ceremonial laws. This observation, though not conclusive, will put us on the right track for arriving at their intent.

When we compare the statement in 19:3 on the ceremonial law with 19:4 on the judicial law, we discover a much stronger word used in removing our obligation to the ceremonial: "All which ceremonial laws are now abrogated, under the New Testament." According to the *Oxford English Dictionary*, the word "abrogated" means "abolished by authority, annulled." Indeed, the word "abrogate" is derived from Latin legal language, being a compound of *ab* ("away") and *rogare* ("to propose a law"). Thus, our Confession states that "all" of these ceremonial laws are positively "abrogated," as by decree, i.e., the revelation of "the New Testament." The statement on the judicial law, to which I will return shortly, is milder: "He gave sundry judicial laws, which expired." Neither is it attached to the arrival of the "New Testament."

In WCF 7:5 we read of the nature of the Old Testament economy which is now defunct:

> This covenant was differently administered in the time of the law, and in the time of the Gospel: under the law it was administered by promises, prophecies, sacrifices, circumcision, the paschal lamb, and other types and ordinances delivered to the people of the Jews, all foresignifying Christ to come; which were, for that time, sufficient and efficacious, through the operation of the Spirit, to instruct and build up the elect in faith in the promised Messiah, by whom they had full remission of sins, and eternal salvation; and is called the Old Testament.

The Old Testament economy was "differently administered in the time of the law." But the positive difference of that administration — which characterizes the oldness of the Old Testament — is defined in terms of ceremonies "all foresignifying Christ to come" which refer to the "full remission of sins, and eternal salvation." The Old Testament economy, then, is different, not in regard to its moral character or judicial makeup, but rather in its "types . . . foresignifying Christ." Nothing is said of the judicial law as an aspect of the difference in the new administration. As 19:3 says: the ceremonial law is "abrogated under the New Testament," which is precisely — and only — what we see here in chapter 7.

When the New Testament, which "abrogates" the Old Testament, finally arrives, its difference lies in its conclusive character, as opposed to the typical character of the Old. WCF 7:6 reads:

> Under the Gospel, when Christ, the substance, was exhibited, the ordinances in which this covenant is dispensed are the preaching of the Word, and the administration of the sacraments of Baptism and the Lord's Supper: which, though fewer in number, and administered with more simplicity, and less outward glory, yet, in them, it is held forth in more fullness, evidence, and spiritual efficacy, to all nations, both Jews and Gentiles; and is called the New Testament. There are not therefore two covenants of grace, differing in substance, but one and the same, under various dispensations.

Here the Confession once again fails to describe the covenantal difference of the New Testament by reference to judicial stipulations or civil ethics. In fact, this anti-ceremonial theme, along with a silence regarding judicial matters, continues in WCF 20. There in section 1 we read that "under the New Testament, the liberty of Christians is further enlarged, in their freedom from the yoke of the ceremonial law, to which the Jewish Church was subjected." Again: the focal difference is on the ceremonial, not the judicial law. Our liberty does not involve a liberty from the judicial law, but from the ceremonial. All of this will become more evident below.

Judicial expiration

Now as we move to 19:4 we note that the divines employ the milder term "expired" when dealing with the judicial laws. This implies there are elements in the judicial laws that simply fail to function any longer. They are not positively "abrogated"; they are not judicially repealed. If the same result befalls both the judicial and the ceremonial laws, as the anti-theonomic position avers, why were the judicial laws not declared "abrogated," then reference made to the New Testament for judicial principles? The Confession, after all, has a clear concern for political and judicial ethics. And why do the judicial laws appear frequently in the proof-texts for the Larger Catechism exposition of the Ten Commandments? These are inexplicable on the anti-theonomic position.

Admittedly, the Confession does note that the judicial laws "expired." That is, they expired along with the Jewish "State," the "body politic." A hermeneutically sound exegesis of WCF 19:4 must recognize that the expiring of the judicial laws in the context refers to their association with the particular "State" of Israel: the laws as literally expressed were given to a specific, historically defined "body politic." The very nature of case law is to provide sample, concrete illustrations of legally chargeable offenses for a particular culture and time. Case laws do not enumerate each and every possible conceivable criminal infraction. Consequently, were the Mosaic judicial laws to continue in toto, then we would be morally obligated to build fences around our roofs, use stoning as the method of capital punishment, provide three cities of refuge, punish certain ceremonial infractions, and so forth. Neither the Puritans, nor the Confession, nor modern Theonomists argue for such. The Israel-related, time-bound literal expression of the case laws "expired," because the specific "State" within which they derived their sense expired.

That this statement in the Confession is not functionally equivalent to a wholesale abrogation, as in the case of the ceremonial laws, is evident in the divines' choice of a conceptually different term: "expired," rather than "abrogated." We also see a difference in the proviso added: "not obliging any other now, further than the general equity thereof may require." Clearly, the "general equity" continues from the judicial law, though no such equity continues from the ceremonial law. In fact, one of the proof-texts for this section on the continuing general equity is Matthew 5:17, the theonomic proof-text: "Do not think that I came to abolish the Law or the Prophets; I did not come to abolish, but to fulfill." Obviously the divines did not equate "expired" with "abolish" (Matt. 5:17) or "abrogated" (WCF 19:3).

Elsewhere we read in WCF 6:6 that "every sin, both original and actual, being a transgression of the righteous law of God, and contrary thereunto, does in its own nature, bring guilt upon the sinner, whereby he is bound over to the wrath of God, and curse of the law, and so made subject to death, with all miseries spiritual, temporal, and eternal." In 19:6 we read: "the threatenings of [the law] serve to show what even their sins deserve; and what afflictions, in this life, they may expect for them, although freed from the curse thereof threatened in the law." Consequently, the Confession fences in and defends the moral law by allowing the continuance of "all . . . temporal" consequences of breaching it. That these "temporal" consequences include temporal sanctions imposed by the civil magistrate is obvious in that "God, the supreme Lord and King of all the world, has ordained civil magistrates, to be, under Him" and "for the punishment of evil doers" (WCF 23:1).

Thus, the divines allow revealed, temporal, judicial responses to guide the magistrate in the New Testament era. The Confession clearly declares this in the original version of WCF 23:3, where we read of one of the civil magistrates' duties that "all blasphemies and heresies be suppressed." Here the divines cited Leviticus 24:16 and Deuteronomy 13:5 as proof-texts. Obviously, an "expired" law still "requiring" a "general equity" is fundamentally different from an "abrogated" law (as per the ceremonial laws).

Furthermore, in LC 108 we read the obligation that devolves upon men "according to each one's place and calling":

> The duties required in the second commandment are, the receiving, observing, and keeping pure and entire, all such religious worship and ordinances as God has instituted in his Word; particularly prayer and thanksgiving in the name of Christ; the reading, preaching, and hearing of the Word; the administration and receiving of the sacraments; church government and discipline; the ministry and maintenance thereof; religious fasting; swearing by the name of God, and vowing unto him: as also the disapproving, detesting, opposing, all false worship; and, according to each one's place and calling, removing it, and all monuments of idolatry.

The confessional view of "calling" includes the civil magistrate in his public duty: "It is lawful for Christians to accept and execute the office of a magistrate, when called thereunto" (WCF 23:2). Thus, of the second commandment, Larger Catechism 108 directs the civil ruler to oppose and remove all monuments of idolatry — as required in various judicial laws of the Old Testament. The proof-texts cited include Deuteronomy 7:5, a judicial case law. The next question, a follow-up to LC 108, also cites Deuteronomy 13:6-8.

Larger Catechism 99, speaking on the fundamental moral law contained in the Ten Commandments, agrees:

> That what is forbidden or commanded to ourselves, we are bound, according to our places, to endeavor that it may be avoided or performed by others, according to the duty of their places. That in what is commanded to others, we are bound, according to our places and callings, to be helpful to them; and to take heed of partaking with others in what is forbidden them.

As noted previously, the unedited original of WCF 23:3 says of the magistrate that "he has authority, and it is his duty, to take order that unity and peace be preserved in the Church, that the truth of God be kept pure and entire, that all blasphemies and heresies be suppressed." Here again we find reference to Deuteronomy 13 in the proof-texts. Though the modern theonomic expression might not urge precisely this response to heresy, who can assert that the Confession has wholly removed the judicial laws from consideration? Perhaps the Confession is more theonomic than modern Theonomists! But it is certainly not less so.

Equity continuation. The exclusionary clause in 19:4 reminds us that though the judicial laws have "expired," their "general equity" has not. Indeed, their equity will "require" (not: "suggest" or "encourage" or "allow") application: "To them also, as a body politic, He gave sundry judicial laws, which expired together with the State of that people; not obliging any other now, further than the general equity thereof may require." Here we must determine the meaning of the phrase "general equity" in its historical and Confessional context.

According to the *Oxford English Dictionary* the term "equity," when applied to matters of legal jurisprudence, speaks of the "recourse to general principles of justice . . . to correct or supplement the provisions of the law." The "equity of a statute," therefore, involves "the construction of a statute according to its reason and spirit, so as to make it apply to cases for which it does not expressly provide." Obviously the divines would not assert that we need "to correct" God's law, for it is his very word (WCF 1:4). Consequently, the remaining "equity" must speak of the underlying principles, the "reason and spirit" of the law when we "make it apply to cases for which it does not expressly provide." The law's equity, then, extends to modern situations (it is still binding; it is "required"), even though the particular ancient and ceremonially-dominated features of Israel no longer exist (it "expired" because given to a specific "body politic").

Perhaps one of the best tools for understanding the Confession at this point is Scripture itself — particularly the King James Version. The Assembly wrote the Confession of Faith in Elizabethan English identical with the KJV, even employing its phraseology and using it as the text for the Scripture proof-texts. As Donald Remillard notes in his *A Contemporary Edition of the Westminster Confession of Faith*: "The initial text of the Westminster Confession of Faith was presented to the English speaking people in 1646. This occurred only thirty-five years after the publication of the King James version of the Bible in 1611. Consequently, its original grammar and vocabulary reflect a mode of communication long dated and 'foreign' to contemporary forms and styles of English usage."[99] We may reasonably conclude that the term "equity" in WCF 19:4 would have the same linguistic function as that in the KJV, which the Confession reflects.

The word "equity" appears numerous times in the KJV, several of which show that God's law is the standard of equitable righteousness and of sure justice. Psalm 98:9b reads: "with righteousness shall he judge the world, and the people with equity." Notice the parallel of "righteousness" and "equity." God's law is inherently and necessarily

---

[99] Donald Remillard, *Contemporary Edition of the Westminster Confession of Faith* (Ligonier, Penn.: Presby Press, 1988), v.

righteous, as Deuteronomy 4:8 informs us: "What great nation is there that has statutes and judgments as righteous as this whole law which I am setting before you today?" Following the Mosaic pattern here in Deuteronomy 4, God's righteousness is frequently paralleled with God's law in Scripture (Isa. 42:21; 51:7; Hab. 1:4; Rom. 3:21; 7:12). In fact, Psalm 119 frequently parallels God's law, statutes, ordinances with "righteousness" (Psa. 119:7, 40, 62, 75, 106, 121, 123, 137-138, 142, 144, 160, 164, 172)

Psalm 99:4 states that "the king's strength also loveth judgment; thou dost establish equity, thou executest judgment and righteousness in Jacob." Notice the parallel of equity with the king's judgment and righteousness. Proverbs 1:3 urges us "to receive the instruction of wisdom, justice, and judgment, and equity." Notice the inclusion of equity with wisdom, justice and judgment. Proverbs 2:9 follows suit when it observes: "Then shalt thou understand righteousness, and judgment, and equity; yea, every good path."

Isaiah 11:4a prophesies that "with righteousness shall he judge the poor, and reprove with equity for the meek of the earth." Isaiah 59:14 laments that "judgment is turned away backward, and justice standeth afar off: for truth is fallen in the street, and equity cannot enter." Micah 3:9 rebukes Israel: "Hear this, I pray you, ye heads of the house of Jacob, and princes of the house of Israel, that abhor judgment, and pervert all equity."

This concept of the continuing, obligatory equity of God's law was common among the Puritans in the era of the Westminster Assembly. According to historian Thomas Hutchinson, Thomas Cartwright "who had a chief hand in reducing puritanism to a system, held, that the magistrate was bound to adhere to the judicial law of Moses, and might not punish or pardon otherwise than they prescribed."[100] Yet in 1575 Cartwright observed, in keeping with both the theonomic principle and the Confessional equity-approach to law, observed:

And, as for the judicial law, forasmuch as there are some of them made in regard of the region where they were given,

---

[100] Thomas Hutchinson, *The History of the Colony and Province of Massachusetts Bay*, Lawrence S. Mayo ed., (New York: Kraus, rep. 1970 [1864]), 2:354.

and of the people to whom they were given, the prince and magistrate, keeping the substance and equity of them (as it were the marrow), may change the circumstance of them, as the times and places and manners of the people shall require. But to say that any magistrate can save the life of blasphemers, contemptuous and stubborn idolaters, murderers, adulterers, incestuous persons, and such like, which God by his judicial law hath commanded to be put to death, I do utterly deny, and am ready to prove, if that pertained to this question.[101]

Puritan William Perkins concurred with Cartwright's approach when he wrote circa 1600: "The witch truly convicted is to be punished with death, the highest degree of punishment, and that by the law of Moses, the equity whereof is perpetual."[102] Philip Stubbs (ca. 1555 - ca. 1610), an influential Puritan and author of *An Anatomie of Abuses* asked: "What kind of punishment would you have appointed for these notorious bloody swearers? I would wish (if it pleased God) that it were made death: For we read in the law of God, that whosoever blasphemeth the Lord, was presently stoned to death without all remorse. Which law judicial standeth in force to the world's end."[103]

According to these sample Puritans — Perkins, Cartwright, and Stubbs — the binding character of the statutes of God's law lies not in their ancient, Israel-based form (by stoning, after fleeing to cities of refuge, and upon consulting elders in the gates). Nevertheless, in the cases involving capital crimes, the underlying equity continues to require death even in the New Covenant era.

As noted earlier, the famed Puritan scholar John Owen thought along these lines:

---

[101] From Thomas Cartwright's *Second Reply, cited in Works of John Whitgift* [Parker Society ed., Cambridge: University Press, 1851], I:270.

[102] Cited in Rossell H. Robbins, *Encyclopedia of Witchcraft and Demonology* (New York: Crown, 1959), 382.

[103] Philip Stubbs, *An Anatomie of Abuses* (1583), as cited in Thomas Rogers, *Exposition of the Thirty-nine Articles* (Cambridge: Cambridge University Press, 1854), 90.

Although the institutions and examples of the Old Testament, of the duty of magistrates in the things and about the worship of God, are not, in their whole latitude and extent, to be drawn into rules that should be obligatory to all magistrates now. . . , yet, doubtless, there is something moral in those institutions, which, being unclothed of their Judaical form, is still binding to all in the like kind, as to some analogy and proportion. Subduct from those administrations what was proper to, and lies upon the account of, the church and nation of the Jews, and what remains upon the general notion of a church and nation must be everlastingly binding.[104]

Gordon is woefully mistaken when he announces in his conclusion that "it is true that Theonomy denies *WCF* 19:4" (CT, 42). The modern Theonomist agrees with the Confession when it is carefully interpreted. We believe that that which is "expired" in the judicial laws are those literal elements structuring it for Israel as a nation: the particular land arrangements which allowed for cities of refuge, blood avengers, elders in the gates, stoning, levirate marriages, and the like. Or those constructions applying to the peculiar ancient circumstances, the accidental historical and cultural factors of Israel: fences around rooftops, goring oxen, flying axheads, and so forth.

The Westminster Standards are clearly sympathetic to the theonomic viewpoint, as Gordon himself admits: "Theonomy did not appear 'out of the blue,'" for it "genuinely shares some of the distinctives embraced by others within that [Westminster] tradition. It shares the assembly's abstracting of the decalogue from the Sinai covenant" (CT, 42); it is "an extension (albeit extreme) of ideas already germinal in some dimensions of the Reformed tradition" (CT, 43). But Gordon is driven by his distinctive views to criticize the Standards. Unfortunately for him, the "others within that tradition" are the great majority who disagree with his views.

---

[104] John Owen, *The Works of John Owen*, vol.8 (London: Banner of Truth, rep. 1967), 394.

Chapter 6
Conclusion

As I draw my response to a conclusion, I will briefly summarize my reasons for dismissing Gordon's "Critique of Theonomy" as an adequate rebuttal to theonomic ethics. Before doing so, I must remind the reader of the shrill nature of Gordon's diatribe, for this has become too common among followers of Meredith G. Kline. And sadly, Gordon's vigorous assault on Theonomy seems oblivious to Bahnsen's numerous responses to his critics.

For Gordon, his critique of theonomy is not merely an academic debate in the Reformed community. It appears to be something of a consuming mission for Gordon (he deals at length with it in the *Westminster Theological Journal, Modern Reformation,* and the Kline festschrift, *Creator, Redeemer, Consummator*). He demeaningly suggests that theonomy is "a psychological phenomenon, an uprising of authoritarian personalities," though not "merely" so (CT, 42). But let us recall his emotion-laden denunciation of theonomy:

> Theonomy is not merely an error, though it has manifestly been regarded as erroneous by the Reformed tradition. It is the error du jour, the characteristic error of an unwise generation. It is the error of a generation that has abandoned the biblically mandated quest for wisdom on the assumption that the Bible *itself* contains all that we need to know about life's various enterprises. It is the proof-textual, Bible-thumping, literalist, error par excellence. It is not merely the view of the unwise, but the view of the never-to-be-wise, because it is the view of those who wrongly believe that the Scripture sufficiently governs this arena, and who, for this reason will never discover in the natural constitution of the human nature or

the particular circumstances of given peoples what must be discovered to govern well and wisely. (IS, 22)

This vitriolic response surpasses even Kline's complaining of Bahnsen's "over-heated typewriter,"[1] "the tragedy of Chalcedon" which involves "high potential wasted — worse than wasted," resulting in a "delusive and grotesque perversion of the teaching of Scripture" which is being promoted by "cult-like fanaticism."[2]

But now let me set aside Gordon's denunciations and summarize what I believe to be his academic failures.

Summary of Chapter 1

After noting the extreme invective hurled at theonomy, I pointed out that which Gordon and his Klinean kin admit: the Westminster Standards themselves have theonomic tendencies. This should serve as helpful material for Theonomists who might be brought under the scrutiny of Presbyterian church courts.

I then summarized the overall approach Gordon engages in his taxonomic critique of Theonomy, noting that he was summarizing the work of other critics and focusing on three issues in Theonomy that he deemed crucial to its success. I even commended him for his stated determination to focus on Greg L. Bahnsen, whom all Theonomists (and their critics) would recognize as the leading proponent of and apologist for Theonomic Ethics.

After laying out his method of approach, I noted general areas of failure in his critique, including failing to meet his own stated objectives. He mistakenly assumes that postmillennialism is a "leg of theonomy," confusing ethics and eschatology. In focusing on three issues within Theonomy, Gordon overlooks several of Bahnsen's own stated key arguments, despite the fact that Bahnsen very helpfully summarizes these in various places in his writings. This becomes all the more remarkable when Gordon sets forth the "argument from necessity" as a foundation stone for Theonomy, while admitting that Bahnsen himself never argues such.

---

[1] Meredith G. Kline, "Comments on an Old-New Error: A Review Article," *Westminster Theological Journal* 41:1 (Fall, 1978): 194.

[2] Kline, "Comments on an Old-New Error," 172.

Conclusion

In order to get at Gordon's underlying motives in the debate, I noted his strong resistance to "sufficiency of Scripture" for living out the Christian worldview in the "various departments of life." He criticizes Theonomists for seeking biblical directives in areas of life beyond the religious realm, whereas he would set general revelation over against special revelation in this regard. Sadly, Gordon distorts the theonomic position in complaining that we "imply that Scripture is a sufficient guide for the various departments of life, in all their specificity," which is a gross overstatement.

I finally pointed out the dangerous practical implications of his anti-theonomic, pro-general revelation views. He defended a minister in an ecclesiastical trial, which minister argued that on biblical principle Christians should not stand against same-sex marriages in the civil realm.[3]

Summary of Chapter 2

In Chapter 2 I began considering the first of Gordon's three-fold argument against Theonomy: "the argument from necessity." I once again expressed my confusion at his bringing this issue up — even as his *first* point! — because he claimed he would focus on Bahnsen, but he admits Bahnsen did not argue from this perspective. This brings dialectical tension into his critique. This is especially problematic in that Gordon claims to be dealing with the "major arguments" against Theonomy, whereas this is not an argument promoted by any published advocate of Theonomic Ethics. The matter is aggravated further by his declaring he was not intending to "advance exclusively new arguments against Theonomy," even though no one else is cited as having framed this objection previously.

Unfortunately, Gordon continues to stumble when he mischaracterizes the theonomic concern. Theonomy does *not* build its case on the philosophical issue of necessity, but rather on the theological obligation to framing in an exegetically-derived Christian worldview. Gordon attempts a *reductio* against Theonomy by claiming we should likewise expect the Bible to teach us mathematical principles so that we will know how to build suspension bridges. Here he totally overlooks

---

[3] This is not to say that either that minister or Gordon deems homosexual behavior to be a non-sinful act.

223

the categorical differences between mathematics and ethics. The field of statecraft involves intensely ethical concerns (such as who will be punished by fine or by death), whereas mathematics does not.

His error here is exacerbated by the fact that the Bible *does* speak directly to matters of statecraft, whereas it does not claim to establish mathematical principles. It finally becomes intolerable when he himself admits that "all parties agree that the only place where statecraft of any sort is comprehensively recorded in the Scriptures is in the Sinai legislation," but later asks: "where does the Bible address other matters, such as statecraft. . . ?" He even challenges the Theonomist to show "that statecraft is a different field of human endeavor, subject to special considerations"!

In Gordon's judgment "natural revelation is a sufficient guide in each of these areas" of worldview concerns. He even states that his views of the sufficiency of Scripture have changed over time as he has reflected upon the matter of general v. special revelation in the light of the theonomic debate: "Where the big change has occurred in my own thinking has been to the disastrous consequences that follow the common misunderstanding of the sufficiency of Scripture. . . . If anything has changed, then, it is that I would now argue with equal zeal for the insufficiency of Scripture in other than religious or covenantal areas."

I finally noted that Gordon commits the fallacy of hasty generalization when he argues that Theonomists believe issues of statecraft are "more pressing" than other issues facing us. Since the actual debate over Theonomy focuses on issues of criminal jurisprudence, Gordon mistakenly thinks this is the *leading* concern for Theonomists in their entire worldview. Such is patently false.

Summary of Chapter 3

In this chapter I focused on Gordon's second argument against Theonomy: the interpretation of Matthew 5:17-21. At last he comes to a key issue recognized by all parties in the debate. Sadly though, Gordon does not engage Bahnsen's own arguments sufficiently, never showing any awareness of Bahnsen's responses to the very objections he brings against Theonomy.

Gordon also wrongly argues that Bahnsen is absolutely dependent upon Matthew 5 and that he cannot make his claim from anywhere else in the New Testament, whereas Bahnsen argues his case from a number of key texts, including 2 Timothy 3:16-17 and Romans 13:1-10. And this despite the fact Bahnsen even offers two whole chapters on the matter in the one book Gordon focuses on: *Theonomy in Christian Ethics*. Chapter 12 is titled "New Testament Substantiation of the Thesis." Chapter 19: "The Civil Magistrate in the New Testament."

Though Gordon is analyzing Theonomy from within the space limits of an article, he unfortunately tends to use the shot-gun approach. He often will simply spray out a few biblical addresses that he believes are self-evidently contrary to Theonomy. In every case, though, Bahnsen has already responded to those supposed contradictions, though Gordon's reader would never know this.

Gordon attempts to rebut Theonomy by focusing on the meaning of four key phrases in Matthew 5. More often than not, his presentation involves tenuous arguments, some of which are simply one possibility among other widely-held evangelical interpretations which support Bahnsen's exegesis. Other evidences against Theonomy are greatly exaggerated, being dependent upon Gordon's peculiarly Klinean commitments (which are often complicated or counter-intuitive) or based on arguments from silence. Still others actually *allow* for Bahnsen's conclusions.

Summary of Chapters 4 and 5

In Chapters 4 and 5, I engaged Gordon's key argument against Theonomy: his understanding of covenant theology. Given the significance of this argument, I devoted two full chapters to the matter. In order to orient the reader to his presentation, I summarized the key components of his understanding of covenant theology. I pointed out that Gordon himself recognizes that Theonomy falls within the school of covenant theology, even though he dismisses it as on the "extreme" end of the spectrum.

These chapters engaged the (alleged) problems of covenant duties, covenantal discontinuity, legalistic elements in the old covenant, and decalogue abstraction. In each of these matters, I showed that the reader would have to adopt the details of Kline's own distinctive views in order to make the complaints against Theonomy stick. I pointed out, however, that on the general issues involved (even if not the distinctive details), Bahnsen falls squarely within the mainstream of Reformed orthodoxy, whereas Gordon contradicts it.

Once again I had to state methodological disappointments with Gordon's presentation. Disappointments such as: his failing to cite Bahnsen when rebutting him; his own admission that the history of covenant theology allows a Theonomy-like approach to the Mosaic covenant, despite his strong denunciations of Theonomy; and his defensive posture regarding criticisms of his mentor, Meredith Kline.

In these chapters I surveyed a good number of Reformed theologians who hold positions on the law of God that directly counter Gordon's Klinean assumptions. I cited theologians such as the early Reformers: John Calvin, Huldrych Zwingli, John Oecolampadius, Johann Bullinger and John Knox. I also quoted later Reformed theologians who disagree with Gordon, such as Warfield, Ridderbos, and Vos, as well as distinctive Reformed theological positions, including the threefold use of the law, the political use of the law, the importance of the law in the believer's life, and the law in Reformed creeds and confessions.

Regarding the matter of covenant duties found in the law of God being limited to old covenant Israel, I noted that special covenant obligations can and do involve general ethical obligations upon all men. Why would God not specifically obligate his redeemed people by the universal demands of his law, such as prohibiting them from murder, rape, and theft? Covenant obligations oftentimes *intensify* the responsibilities of the covenant people; they do not always *define* the covenant people (although the ceremonial features of the law *did* define and peculiarly obligate the covenant community). I noted that even the typological character of the people can serve as an *overlay* of universal moral obligations.

Regarding the matter of covenant continuity and discontinuity, I pointed out that Reformed theology has generally argued for a basic continuity, just as Bahnsen does. But that both Bahnsen and Reformed theology allow for certain discontinuities, when they are exegetically proven. I also argued that covenantal continuity *must* prevail in matters of morality, in that God's moral law is rooted in his eternal, unchanging character and obligates all creatures created in his image. Nor does the "unlikeness" of the New Covenant overturn this theonomic position, for the unlikeness is *not* in matters of morality but in matters of internal actualization and final redemptive conclusion.

Regarding the question of legalism inherent in the law, I pointed out that Gordon's assertions are controversial, not being held uniformly in the Reformed tradition, as he himself admits. Furthermore, his position is non-confessional (as he also admits), despite his own ordination vows committing him to the position of the Confession of Faith. To make matters worse, Gordon's position does not necessarily contradict Theonomy. He himself confesses that the law of God is multi-dimensional, which opens the door for the Theonomist to declare that if there were a legalistic element in the old covenant application of the law, it was not fundamental to the law, being only one dimension — a dimension done away with in the New Covenant.

Regarding the matter of decalogue abstraction, wherein Gordon complains that the Confession of Faith unbiblically "abstracts" the ten commandments from their covenantal setting, I had much to say. For one thing, I pointed out that not only does the historic Reformed tradition engage in the same practice, but so does even Geerhardus Vos, who is highly esteemed by Gordon and Kline. I also noted the irony that the Confession allegedly fumbles in the matter of the covenant even though it is the first Reformed creed that places covenant theology in the foreground and organizes itself around covenantal principles.

Though Gordon attempts to "defend" the Westminster Catechisms by suggesting that they were more catechetical in orientation than theological, I pointed out the error of such a statement. After all, those who draw up catechisms are summarizing their core theological convictions. How then could a catechism contradict their own theology — unless they were bunglers? Consequently, even were the Confession only "catechetical," its authors would still be presenting their underlying theology.

I then interpreted the Confession's statements on the judicial law, showing that it does *not* dismiss them for the New Covenant age.

Conclusion

Though Gordon's critique of Theonomy is widely employed against Theonomists, I believe that it is a wholesale failure. Gordon even fails from the perspective of his own stated methodology, in terms of his own theological history, and his own confessional commitments. He employs an exegetical argument regarding only Matthew 5. Elsewhere he employs a shot-gun approach to biblical passages. Gordon's critique should only be tolerable among those who are committed to the covenantal peculiarities of Gordon's mentor, Meredith G. Kline.

Appendix 1
"The Law of Christ and God's Law"

The theonomic ethic endorses the whole of God's Law for all of life. However, not all evangelicals accept the theonomic principle. And sometimes their objections (their most important ones) are based on statements of the New Testament itself. Two such Pauline statements are found in 1 Corinthians 9:20 and 21 where we read Paul's testimony regarding his Christian liberty and evangelistic mission: "To the Jews I became as a Jew, that I might win Jews; to those who are under the Law, as under the Law, though not being myself under the Law, that I might win those who are under the Law." He continues in verse 21 noting: "to those who are without law, as without law, though not being without the law of God but under the law of Christ, that I might win those who are without law." These statements are deemed a formidable objection to theonomic ethics. How shall we respond?

"Not Being Myself Under the Law"

The Theonomic Problem
In 1 Corinthians 9:20b Paul seems to disavow God's Law altogether, when he claims he himself was "to those who are under the Law, as under the Law, *though not being myself under the Law.*" If the Apostle to the Gentiles is himself *not* under "the Law," how shall we evangelical Christians today assert that we, in fact, *are* "under the Law"?

The Exegetical Solution
I will begin resolving this dilemma by stating what I believe to be Paul's point. Then I will establish that point through four exegetical observations. In this passage Paul denies he is obliged to "the Law" — and by that he means the *ceremonial* aspects of the Law, not the Law as

a system of ethical obligations. This is evident for the following reasons:

(1) The *broader contextual setting* deals with the debate Paul is engaged in regarding *Jewish* sensitivities; that is, the problem of eating meat offered to idols (1 Cor. 8—10). The *Jewish question* forms the backdrop to the whole context. The focus of the debate over foods is narrowly Jewish.

Eating such tainted meat before a Jew or Jewish Christian causes needless, harmful offense. This would pose no problem for the Gentile Christian, as is evident from the Jerusalem Council. The council merely urges Gentiles graciously (not legalistically) to forgo meat offered to idols solely for the sake of the Jewish Christians:

> Therefore it is my judgment that we do not trouble those who are turning to God from among the Gentiles, but that we write to them that they *abstain from things contaminated by idols* and from fornication and from what is strangled and from blood. For Moses from ancient generations has in every city those who preach him, since he is read in the synagogues every Sabbath. (Acts 15:19-21)

Paul concludes this whole three chapter debate declaring: "Whether, then, you eat or drink or whatever you do, do all to the glory of God. Give no offense either to Jews or to Greeks or to the church of God" (1 Cor. 10:31-32).

If the larger context has as a basic concern narrowly Jewish sensitivities and the controversy arising from that, then Paul's denying his obligation to "the Law" would surely mean only the ceremonial law. New Testament scholars recognize the "problem" of Paul's use of "the Law." Sometimes it means the whole Law; sometimes the ceremonial Law; sometimes a principle of legalism.

(2) The *immediate contextual setting* of Paul's statement suggests he is dealing with "the Law" as that which *separates the Jewish race from the Gentiles*. In the very verse in question Paul states: "to the Jews I *become* as a Jew."

This idea of "becoming a Jew" indicates *ceremonial distinctives* are in view rather than moral ones. No one "becomes a Jew" by not killing, not committing adultery, or not coveting. They *do* "become a Jew" by undergoing the ceremonial distinctives which marked the Jews off from the Gentiles (circumcision, food laws, etc.). For instance, if a non-Jew wants to partake the Passover, he must be circumcised first so that he will become a Jew: "But if a stranger sojourns with you, and celebrates the Passover to the Lord, let all his males be circumcised, and then let him come near to celebrate it; and he shall be like a native of the land" (Ex 12:48).

On one occasion Paul has Timothy circumcised so that they might associate with the ceremonially observant Jews in order to preach the gospel to them: "And he came also to Derbe and to Lystra. And behold, a certain disciple was there, named Timothy, the son of a Jewish woman who was a believer, but his father was a Greek.... Paul wanted this man to go with him; and he took him and circumcised him because of the Jews who were in those parts, for they all knew that his father was a Greek" (Acts 16:1, 3).

Paul can easily demonstrate his Jewishness by referring to his ceremonial observance: "I am a Jew, born in Tarsus of Cilicia, but brought up in this city, educated under Gamaliel, strictly according to the law of our fathers, being zealous for God, just as you all are today" (Acts 22:3). "Circumcised the eighth day, of the nation of Israel, of the tribe of Benjamin, a Hebrew of Hebrews; as to the Law, a Pharisee" (Phil 3:5).

In fact, Paul can distinguish the Law from the ceremonial aspects of the Law — and he does so in 1 Corinthians. He distinguishes "the commandments of God" from circumcision (even though that was, in fact, a commandment of God): "Circumcision is nothing, and uncircumcision is nothing, but what matters is the keeping of the commandments of God" (1 Cor. 7:19).

Thus, it seems this is further evidence for "the Law" meaning the ceremonial features of the Law.

(3) Although here in 1 Corinthians 9:20 Paul seems to *deny* the Law, elsewhere he vigorously *affirms* it. This would indicate he must have different conceptions of "the Law" in mind, which would fit the well-known distinction between *ceremonial* and the *moral* aspects of the Law.

Paul affirms the Law as an ongoing obligation among those of faith: "Do we then nullify the Law through faith? May it never be! On the contrary, we establish the Law" (Rom. 3:31). Surely "the Law" established in Romans 3 is not the Law *dis-established* in 1 Corinthians 9.

The moral elements of the Law are expressly affirmed in Romans 7:12: "The Law is holy, and the commandment is holy and righteous and good." How could he disavow his obligation to that which is "holy, righteous, and good"?

Even the judicial elements and function of the Law are endorsed by the Apostle to the Gentiles: "But we know that the Law is good, if one uses it lawfully, realizing the fact that law is not made for a righteous man, but for those who are lawless and rebellious, for the ungodly and sinners, for the unholy and profane, for those who kill their fathers or mothers, for murderers and immoral men and homosexuals and kidnappers and liars and perjurers, and whatever else is contrary to sound teaching, according to the glorious gospel of the blessed God, with which I have been entrusted" (1 Tim. 1:8-11).

(4) In the New Testament the controversy between Jew and Gentile (which forms the backdrop of the 1 Corinthians 8-10 passage) invariably revolves around the ceremonial law. Thus, the *ceremonial* law causes the conflict, not the moral or judicial law.

As whole books of testimony to this, we may consult both Galatians and Hebrews. Numerous references elsewhere distinguish the Jew and Gentile on the basis of ceremonial principles:

- Acts 10:28: "And he said to them, 'You yourselves know how unlawful it is for a man who is a Jew to associate with a foreigner or to visit him; and yet God has shown me that I should not call any man unholy or unclean.'" This passages clearly speaks to the food laws, as Peter vision of the sheet with unclean foods indicates.
- Acts 10:45: "And all the circumcised believers who had come with Peter were amazed, because the gift of the Holy Spirit had been poured out upon the Gentiles also." Note the surprise of those "circumcised" regarding God's blessing on those *uncircumcised*.
- Acts 11:2-3: "And when Peter came up to Jerusalem, those who were circumcised took issue with him, saying, "You went to uncircumcised men and ate with them." Note the angry

resistance to Peter by Jewish Christians, because Peter associated with ceremonially unclean (uncircumcised) men.

• Acts 15:1 (cp. v. 5): "And some men came down from Judea and began teaching the brethren, 'Unless you are circumcised according to the custom of Moses, you cannot be saved.'" Note the first major controversy between Jew and Gentile within developing Christianity is over the *ceremonial* matter of circumcision.

• Acts 21:21: "They have been told about you, that you are teaching all the Jews who are among the Gentiles to forsake Moses, telling them not to circumcise their children nor to walk according to the customs." Note that "forsaking Moses" (the Lawgiver) is associated with not performing ceremonial rituals (e.g., circumcision).

• Romans 2:27-3:1: "And will not he who is physically uncircumcised, if he keeps the Law, will he not judge you who though having the letter of the Law and circumcision are a transgressor of the Law? For he is not a Jew who is one outwardly; neither is circumcision that which is outward in the flesh. Then what advantage has the Jew? Or what is the benefit of circumcision?" Note that Paul *discounts* the value of ceremonial circumcision over against "keeping the Law" in its moral strictures.

Clearly, then, Paul's denying his obligation to "the Law," is a disavowal of ceremonial features of the Law. All of those have been fulfilled in Christ. For instance, Paul says we are "circumcised" when we are baptized (Col. 1:11-12).

"The Law of Christ"

In 1 Corinthians 9:21 we read the following statement by Paul:

to those who are without law, [I am] as without law, *though not being without the law of God but under the law of Christ*, that I might win those who are without law.

The italicized phrases in this statement have presented material to anti-theonomists, suggesting that Paul here declares that in Christ — and, therefore, in the Christian era — a *new law* prevails, which he denominates: "the Law of Christ." This new Law of Christ supplants the older Law of God as the ethical norm for Christian behavior.

Theonomic Issue Resolved

This statement by Paul is seriously misunderstood when raised against the theonomic system. Paul is *not* supplanting the "Law of God" with a new "Law of Christ." Note the following exegetical and literary observations:

1. Christ's Law and the internal consistency of Christ's teaching.

Any supposed "Law of Christ" must be internally consistent with Christ's own teaching. And Christ most definitely stated that he had *not* come to abolish the Law, and that if anyone denied the least of the commandments he would be least in the kingdom of heaven (Matt. 5:17-20). Consequently, any "Law of Christ" would be perfectly harmonious with and supportive of the original Law of God. Therefore, "the Law of Christ" would not be contrary to the Law of God, but actually would endorse it.

2. God's Law in Paul's ethical system.

Paul clearly states in his preceding argument (1 Cor. 9:19-20) that he does not keep the *ceremonial strictures* of the old covenant typological economy. That is, those Jewish-defining, ritual obligations demarcating Jews from the Gentiles. Then he quickly and immediately adds: "though not being without the law of God," that is, "though I am not without the law of God."

The phrase "though not being without the law of God" shows the abiding relevance of "the law of God" in Paul's *ethical* system. He most definitely is not without God's Law. He carefully adds to his previous statement that even though he is opposed to mandatory observation of *ceremonial* features of the Law, he is *not* thereby "without the law of God." This insertion is necessary to protect Paul's argument from suggesting he endorses *anomia*, "lawlessness," the word he employs in his statement *"without the law* of God."

Furthermore, this phrase harmonizes with his other observations on the continuing validity of God's Law as an *ethical* (not *ceremonial*) obligation in Paul's writings: Romans 3:31; 7:12; 8:3-4; 1 Timothy 1:8-11; and so forth.

3. Paul's point of contrast in his statement on law

Paul's statement — "though not being without the law of God, but under the law of Christ" — must be carefully interpreted *as written*. He most definitely is *not* contrasting "the Law of God"with "the Law of Christ." That is, he did *not* say: "I am not under law to God, but rather I am under law to Christ," as if two, mutually-exclusive and competing ethical systems were juxtaposed against one another.

Note carefully the *double-negative* in Paul's statement; double negatives can easily trip up the interpreter. Paul is *not* stating: "I am not under law to God"; rather he declares that he is "*not without* law to God." A world of difference separates these two assertions. That is, he claims he is "*not*"in a state of being "*without* law to God." Thus, he *denies* he is "without law to God" or that he is "apart from" the Law of God. Positively stated, therefore, he is actually *affirming* he *is*, in fact, "under law to God" by resolutely *denying* he is "without" law to God.

4. Paul's liberty is in Christ, not against Christ.

We must make several observations regarding the meaning of his tricky statement here:

First, when Paul refers to Christ's "law" he appears to mean Christ's "*authority*" (cp. Matt. 28:18; Eph. 1:21; Phil. 2:9-10; Col. 1:17-1) — not a new system of laws and obligations. Paul is under Christ's lordship; he is Christ's servant or slave (remember our exegesis of 9:16 17; note also 7:22). Paul's fuller statement, then, asserts that his being "under law to God" is *validated by* being under Christ's law or authority. Being a servant of Christ does *not* remove the obligation to God's Law. Remember, the whole debate was engaged over the matter of Christian *liberty* (8:9; 9:1a, 19; cp. Gal. 2:4); liberty in Christ. Here he is once again asserting that our liberty is not a *wholesale, unbridled* liberty, but one *constrained* by *obligations* to Christ himself.

In that Paul is highlighting the distinction between Jew and Gentile (9:19-21), he apparently assumes a distinction between being a ser-

vant of Moses (and under his ceremonial and ritual authority), as opposed to being a servant of Christ (with his superior authority, which
fulfills those ceremonial obligations in himself). That is, he is under the
new covenant in *Christ* rather than the *old covenant* administered by *Moses*.
He is no longer obligated to *Moses* who was a "servant in God's house,"
but to Christ who is a "*Son over the house*" (Heb. 3:2-6). The New Testament provides several examples of Christians being freed from *ceremonial* strictures *because* they are no longer "under Moses" but rather "under Christ." For example, in Acts 6:14 we read: "we have heard him say
that this Nazarene, Jesus, will destroy this place and *alter the customs which
Moses handed down to us*." See also: Acts 13:38-39; 15:1, 5; 21:21.

Second, consider the strong adversative *alla* (ἀλλά) in the phrase "not
being without the law of God *but* (*alla*) under the law of Christ. This is
another corrective to any misunderstanding of Paul, as well as a slap
against the abusers of liberty. Not only is he *not without* the Law of
God, *but* (strong disjunctive) he is under the authority of Christ. His
original reader cannot jump on his "without law" statement and use
the term *anomos* (ἄνομος) as if it meant "lawless," because he not only
asserts he is not without God's Law, but is, in fact, under the authoritative lordship of Christ. This agrees with his statement of liberty asserting his freedom from "all men" (1 Cor. 9:19a), while maintaining the
Christocentric obligations within truly *Christian* liberty. Paul, then, is
simultaneously under the Law of God and the authority of Christ; the
two are mutually compatible and co-extensive.

Third, Paul's using the phrase *ennomos* (ἔννομος "in lawed") to refer to Christ's "authority" rather than employing the more common
word *exousia* (ἐξουσια) is for literary reasons. Note his repetition of
"law" (using various derivations of *anomos* [ἄνομος]) :

tois hupo **nomon** *hos hupo* **nomon**	to the ones under **law** as under **law**
me hon autos hupo **nomon**	not being myself under law
hina tous hupo **nomon** *kerdeso;*	in order that the ones under **law** I might gain;
tois **anomois** *hos* **anomos**	to the ones **without law** as **without law**
me hon **anomos** *theou*	not being **without law** of God
all' **ennomos** *Christou*	but **in law** to Christ
hina kerdano tous **anomous**	in order that I might win the ones **without law**

When he refers to Christ's authority over his liberty by using a derivative of *nomos*, Paul maintains his literary cadence, driving home his point in style with this effective word-play.

Theonomic Issue Completed

Clearly then, a careful reading of this verse exposes the error of anti-theonomic exegesis. Rather than undermining God's Law as a continuing ethical obligation, Paul here *establishes* the Law as such — just as he told us he would in Romans 3:31: "Do we then nullify the Law through faith? May it never be! On the contrary, we establish the Law."

Appendix 2
Apostasy Legislation

A brief comment on capital sanctions against apostasy is in order, due to the ease with which this matter is misunderstood. How does the theonomic ethic understand the capital sanctions regarding apostasy, as recorded, for instance in Deuteronomy 13 and 17:2-7? Do we call for civil governmental enforcement of all excommunication decrees by capital punishment? These are important questions. Let us set forth some critical observations regarding the application of these laws "when properly interpreted." (TCE, xvi).

First, it should be noted at the outset that the framing of the law in Deuteronomy 13 has in view solicitation and seduction to idolatry (Deut. 13:2, 6, 13). It does not have in mind personal unbelief or even personal rejection of faith in Jehovah God. Those who mistakenly assume that this law would inevitably draw the State sword into church discipline for unbelief are mistaken. In point of fact, unbelief in Israel was not punishable by death. For one to refuse to be circumcised (an expression of unbelief, cf. Lev. 26:41; Deut. 30:6; Jer. 9:25-26; Eze. 44:7) meant that he was "cut off" from the religious community (Gen. 17:14). He was excluded from the worship in Israel (Exo. 12:48; Eze. 44:7, 9); he was not capitally punished.

Second, in Deuteronomy 13, we have what in essence is the framing of a law against treason. This is evident on the basis of the following three-staged consideration: (1) By the very nature of the case, the god of a society is that society's source of law.[1] It has been thus in the fallen world since the temptation of Eve to be as "God" by "knowing" (determining, legislating) good and evil (Gen. 3:5). Hence, the pagan tendency for political rulers to be deified, as illustrated in the Babylonian

---

[1] See R. J. Rushdoony, *The One and the Many: Studies in the Philosophy of Order and Ultimacy* (Fairfax, Vir.: Thoburn, 1971).

king (Isa. 14:4, 13-14) and the Roman emperor (Matt. 22:15-22;[2] 2 Thess. 2:4; Rev. 13:4ff). Hegel clothed this pagan conception in modern dress: "The State is the Divine Idea as it exists on Earth."[3] To seek another god, therefore, is to turn from the Law of the present God, Jehovah, which Law was the constitutional basis of the nation of Israel.

(2) The context preceding Deuteronomy 13 speaks of the gods of the nations around Israel. It speaks of nations serving their gods: "When the LORD your God cuts off from before you the nations which you go to dispossess, and you displace them and dwell in their land, take heed to yourself that you are not ensnared to follow them, after they are destroyed from before you, and that you do not inquire after their gods, saying, How did these nations serve their gods? I also will do likewise'" (Deut. 12:29-30). This leads me to note that:

(3) The Deuteronomic law is developed in such a way as to indicate the ultimate outcome of such apostasy. It is wholesale, treasonous rebellion against the lawful authority and integrity of the nation: "If you hear someone in one of your cities, which the LORD your God gives you to dwell in, saying, 'Certain corrupt men have gone out from among you and enticed the inhabitants of their city, saying, "Let us go and serve other gods," gods whom you have not known'" (Deut. 13:12-13). As Craigie puts it: "In its implications, the crime would be equivalent to treason or espionage in time of war."[4] Thus, in a certain respect such a law was a right to "self-defense" for the nation, as was the right to wage defensive warfare.

Third, any perception of idolatry as a quietistic unbelief is wholly mistaken. The very nature of idolatry involved the ancient worshiper in a number of capital crimes.[5] Thus, the punishment for idolatry is a punishment for those particular crimes. As Mayes notes, Deuteronomy 12:29-32 is the "general introduction" to chapter 13.[6] This "general introduction" clearly speaks of certain "abominable acts" of idol worshipers:

---

[2]For helpful insights see: Will S. Barker and W. Robert Godfrey, *Theonomy: An Informed Critique* (Grand Rapids: Zondervan, 1990), 234ff.

[3]Georg Wilhelm Friedrich Hegel, *Philosophy of History*, trans. by J. Sibree (New York: P. F. Collier & Son, 1901), p. 87.

[4]Craigie, *Deuteronomy*, p. 222.

[5]In fact, it is only in modern times that worship and faith could be separated from life and practice.

[6]A. D. H. Mayes, *Deuteronomy* (*New Century Bible*) (Grand Rapids: Eerdmans, 1979), p. 230.

When the LORD your God cuts off from before you the nations which you go to dispossess, and you displace them and dwell in their land, take heed to yourself that you are not ensnared to follow them, after they are destroyed from before you, and that you do not inquire after their gods, saying, 'How did these nations serve their gods? I also will do likewise.' You shall not worship the LORD your God in that way; for every abomination to the LORD which He hates they have done to their gods; for they burn even their sons and daughters in the fire to their gods. (Deut. 12:30-31)

Idolatry involved wide-scale criminal conduct and was a dangerous cancer.[7] The Canaanites were not thrust out of the land for unbelief, but for wholesale moral and criminal perversion.[8] That idolatry was a real danger is evident in the days of Israel's apostasy, when abominable acts were committed (2 Kgs. 16:3; 21:6; 23:10). All nations served idols in those days (2 Kgs. 17:29). Israel fell right in with them and with their grossly immoral crimes (2 Kgs. 17:7ff, 17-19), thus corrupting and subverting the moral fiber of their culture by legalizing child sacrifice, bestiality, homosexual conduct, cult prostitution, and the like.

Thus, as we have seen, the apostasy laws of God's Laws are not laws against mere unbelief or against misguided worship. Those laws were designed to protect the legal integrity of the nation (criminalizing such actions as treason, conspiracy, seditious revolt, and espionage) and to bring judgment against wicked idolatry (criminalizing such actions as cultural subversion and public mayhem).[9]

---

[7] See Lev. 18:21-30; Rom. 1:21-32. 1 Cor. 10:20 shows the connection with Satan worship.

[8] Lev. 18:3, 24ff; 20:23; Deut. 9:5; 18:9-12.

[9] The false prophet in Deuteronomy 13:5 is not just a foolish mouther of error, but is a focus point for agitating the masses to rebellion. The prophets of Israel "demanded that same obedience to their words as was due to the Law of God." E. J. Young, *Introduction to the Old Testament* (Grand Rapids: Eerdmans, 1964), p. 34. The false prophets would tend to mirror the cultural function of the true prophets, and were, thus, dangerous as conspirators.

www.ingramcontent.com/pod-product-compliance
Lightning Source LLC
Chambersburg PA
CBHW022014090426
42739CB00006BA/134